WITHDRAWN

REDUCING INTERGROUP BIAS

Essays in Social Psychology

General Editors: MAHZARIN BANAJI, Yale University, and
                MILES HEWSTONE, University of Cardiff

Essays in Social Psychology is designed to meet the need for rapid publication of brief volumes in social psychology. Primary topics will include social cognition, interpersonal relationships, group processes, and intergroup relations, as well as applied issues. Furthermore, the series seeks to define social psychology in its broadest sense, encompassing all topics either informed by, or informing, the study of individual behavior and thought in social situations. Each volume in the series will make a conceptual contribution to the topic by reviewing and synthesizing the existing research literature, by advancing theory in the area, or by some combination of these missions. The principle aim is that authors will provide an overview of their own highly successful research program in an area. It is also expected that volumes will, to some extent, include an assessment of current knowledge and identification of possible future trends in research. Each book will be a self-contained unit supplying the advanced reader with a well-structured review of the work described and evaluated.

Published titles

Dweck: *Self-Theories*
Sorrentino and Roney: *The Uncertain Mind*
Tyler and Blader: *Cooperation in Groups*
Van der Vliert: *Complex Interpersonal Conflict Behaviour*

Titles in preparation

Bodenhausen and Macrae: *Person Perception and Executive Function*
Carnevale: *The Psychology of Agreement*
Kruglanski: *The Psychology of Closed-Mindedness*
Mackie: *Emotional Aspects of Intergroup Perception*
Semin and Fiedler: *The Linguistic Category Model*
Turner: *Self-Categorization and Social Identity*

REDUCING INTERGROUP BIAS

The Common Ingroup Identity Model

Samuel L. Gaertner
University of Delaware

John F. Dovidio
Colgate University

Essays in Social Psychology

PSYCHOLOGY PRESS
ALERE FLAMMAM
Taylor & Francis Group

USA	Publishing Office:	PSYCHOLOGY PRESS
		A member of the Taylor & Francis Group
		325 Chestnut Street
		Philadelphia, PA 19106
		Tel: (215) 625-8900
		Fax: (215) 625-2940
	Distribution Center:	PSYCHOLOGY PRESS
		A member of the Taylor & Francis Group
		7625 Empire Drive
		Florence, KY 41042
		Tel: 1-800-624-7064
		Fax: 1-800-248-4724
UK		PSYCHOLOGY PRESS
		A member of the Taylor & Francis Group
		27 Church Road
		Hove
		E. Sussex, BN3 2FA
		Tel: +44 (0)1273 207411
		Fax: +44 (0)1273 205612

REDUCING INTERGROUP BIAS: The Common Ingroup Identity Model

1 2 3 4 5 6 7 8 9 0

Printed by Sheridan Books, Ann Arbor, MI, 2000.
Cover design by Rob Williams.

A CIP catalog record for this book is available from the British Library.
∞ The paper in this publication meets the requirements of the ANSI Standard Z39.48-1984 (Permanence of Paper).

Library of Congress Cataloging-in-Publication Data
Gaertner, Samuel L.
    Reducing intergroup bias : the common ingroup identity model / Samuel L. Gaertner, John F. Dovidio.
        p. cm.— (Essays in social psychology)
    Includes bibliographical references and indexes.
    ISBN 0-86377-571-3 (alk. paper)
    1. Intergroup relations.   2. Discrimination—Prevention.   3. Racism—Prevention.
I. Dovidio, John F.   II. Title.   III. Series.

HM1111.G34 20000
302.4—dc21   00-036606

ISBN 0-86377-571-3
ISSN 1367-5826

To our parents:

Henrietta, Abraham, Florence, and John

CONTENTS

ABOUT THE AUTHORS

Professor Samuel L. Gaertner received his B.A. from Brooklyn College in 1963 and his Ph.D. in Psychology from the City University of New York: Graduate Center in 1970. Since then, he has been on the Psychology faculty at the University of Delaware. His research interests focus primarily on subtle forms of racism (e.g., aversive racism) and on identifying strategies (e.g., the Common Ingroup Identity Model) for producing more harmonious intergroup attitudes. Dr. Gaertner's research on aversive racism (together with Jack Dovidio) won the Gordon Allport Intergroup Relations Prize in 1985, and his work on the Common Ingroup Identity Model (together with Jack Dovidio, Jason Nier, Christine Ward, and Brenda Banker) won the Gordon Allport Intergroup Relations Prize in 1998. He has served on the editorial boards of the *Journal of Personality and Social Psychology, Personality and Social Psychology Bulletin,* and *Group Processes and Intergroup Relations.* Also, he has been a member of the Council of the Society for the Psychological Study of Social Issues.

Professor John F. Dovidio (M.A., Ph.D. in social psychology from the University of Delaware) is Charles A. Dana Professor and Chair of the Department of Psychology at Colgate University. At Colgate, he has also served as the Director of the Division of University Studies and Director of the Division of Natural Sciences and Mathematics. Dr. Dovidio has been Editor of *Personality and Social Psychology Bulletin* and is currently Associate Editor of *Group Processes and Intergroup Relations.* He is a Fellow of the American Psychological Association and of the American Psychological Society, and is currently President of the Society for the Psychological Study of Social Issues (SPSSI; Division 9 of APA) and Secretary-Treasurer of the Society for Experimental Social Psychology (SESP). Dr. Dovidio's research interests are in stereotyping, prejudice, and discrimination; social power and nonverbal communication; and altruism and helping. He has published over 100 books, articles, and chapters on these topics. He has shared the 1985 and 1998 Gordon Allport Intergroup Relations Prize with Samuel L. Gaertner for their work on aversive racism and ways to reduce bias.

IX

ACKNOWLEDGMENT

Brief excerpts from *The Robbers Cave Experiment: Intergroup Conflict and Cooperation.* Copyright © 1988 by Muzafer Sherif, Wesleyan University Press, University Press of New England. Reprinted with permission of the publisher.

PREFACE

We are grateful to Miles Hewstone, one of the Series Editor for Essays in Social Psychology, for inviting and encouraging us to write this volume, for his advice and guidance on the project, and for his valuable comments on an earlier version of the manuscript. He asked us to write a book about our research on reducing intergroup bias and to use this perspective as an organizing framework for assessing current knowledge on intergroup relations, making links to the broader literature on intergroup attitudes, and identifying future empirical and conceptual trends. We were intrigued by the challenge and opportunity. The book we have written is thus about our personal journey toward understanding intergroup bias and developing ways to combat it. It was *not* our goal to write a comprehensive text on intergroup relations. We consider, of course, the broad context of research on intergroup relations. However, rather than trying to summarize the vast literature on intergroup relations generally, we describe a more singular program of research. This book presents a recategorization approach to reducing bias and uses the Common Ingroup Identity Model (Gaertner, Dovidio, Anastasio, Bachman, & Rust, 1993) as an organizing framework.

Our focus is not meant to imply that we believe that our approach is superior to other approaches. In fact, we see different approaches, such as those de-emphasizing group membership, encouraging personalized interactions, or engineering other forms of group differentiation and categorization, as complementary rather than competing strategies. Different strategies may be most effective under different circumstances and constraints or for different stages of intergroup relations. Furthermore, we believe that these strategies may facilitate processes associated with one another over time. That is, personalized interactions can encourage recategorized impressions of the memberships of both groups as belonging to a more inclusive superordinate entity, and recategorization can induce outgroup members to have more personalized, self-disclosing interactions with one another. Our approach is therefore intended to contribute to a broad repertoire of theoretical and practical approaches to combating intergroup bias.

This book examines how intergroup biases, including subtle, contemporary forms of racism, can be combated. Specifically, the book begins by tracing how the challenges of addressing aversive racism, an indirect and typically unconscious type of racial bias, led to the development of the Common Ingroup Identity Model. This model outlines strategies for reducing biases that are rooted, in part, in fundamental, normal psychological processes, such as the categorization of people into ingroups ("we's" who are favored) and outgroups ("They's" who are not). Thus, changing the nature of categorization from ingroups and outgroups (e.g., on the basis of race) to one more common inclusive identity (e.g., university affiliation or nationality) can harness the cognitive and motivational forces of ingroup favoritism and redirect them to reduce bias. This process, described by the Common Ingroup Identity Model, not only produces more positive intergroup attitudes and more inclusive and generous standards of justice and fairness but also increases positive and trusting intergroup behaviors, such as helping and personal disclosure. This book considers situations and interventions that can foster more inclusive representations and ways, both theoretically and practically, that a common ingroup identity can facilitate more positive and productive relations between groups.

This book represents a synthesis and extension of our previous work in this area. As a consequence, although each chapter was prepared specifically for this book, many of the chapters build upon ideas and findings reported in earlier works. We acknowledge these foundational works for Chapter 2 (Gaertner, Dovidio, Banker et al., 1997), Chapter 3 (Gaertner et al., 1993; Gaertner, Dovidio, Nier, Ward, & Banker, 1999), Chapter 5 (Gaertner, Dovidio, & Bachman, 1996; Gaertner, Dovidio, Rust et al., 1999; Gaertner, Rust, Dovidio, Bachman, & Anastasio, 1996), Chapter 6 (Dovidio & Gaertner, 1993; Dovidio, Gaertner, Isen, Rust, & Guerra, 1998; Dovidio, Gaertner, & Loux, 2000), Chapter 7 (Dovidio, Gaertner, Isen et al., 1998), and Chapter 8 (Gaertner, Dovidio, Banker et al., 2000). We express our appreciation to all of the co-authors and editors who contributed to those works.

The present book is intended both for people who are interested theoretically in understanding and reducing intergroup bias and those who have dedicated themselves to addressing bias and prejudice in "real-world" educational, organizational, and residential settings. Theoretically, the book should be of interest to scholars in this area of sociology, education, and political science, as well as in psychology. Beyond collegial communication, the primary use for this volume is in graduate and advanced undergraduate courses where the issues raised in the book will give students an appreciation of the complexity of the practical and conceptual issues, the perspective and methods of behavioral science, and the formidable challenges that must be faced to reduce a range of intergroup biases and achieve more harmonious intergroup relations.

We gratefully acknowledge the significant support and contributions offered by a number of organizations and people. We are deeply indebted to the National Institute of Mental Health Public Health Services for its generous support for our work on the Common Ingroup Identity Model. The Office of Naval Research, the Colgate University Research Council, The University of Delaware Research Foundation, and the Dana Foundation also provided essential financial assistance. We are grateful for the patience, support, and encouragement of our wives, Shelley and Linda, not only for this book but for our collaborative endeavors over the past 30 years.

We also acknowledge the important contributions, both empirical and conceptual, of our students who worked collaboratively on the research: Phyllis Anastasio, Betty Bachman, Brenda Banker, Kelly Beach, Cheryl Drout, Stacy Frazier, Paula Guerra, Missy Houlette, Adaiah Howard, Brenda Johnson, Kelly Johnson, Gladys Kafati, Stephenie Loux, Rob Lowrance, Elizabeth McGlynn, Jeffrey Mann, Kim Matoka, Gary Mottola, Audrey Murrell, Jason Nier, Sheila Rioux, Abby Russin, Mary Rust, Jen Smith, Marnie Tobriner, Ana Validzic, and Christine Ward. In addition, we recognize our colleagues who have taught us so much about the research described in this book: Jack Brigham, Marilynn Brewer, Rupert Brown, Russ Clark, Bob Eisenberger, Russ Fazio, Michael Gurtman, Alice Isen, Blair Johnson, James Jones, Kerry Kawakami, Mike Kuhlman, Norman Miller, Brian Mullen, Yolanda Flores Niemann, Jane Allyn Piliavin, Charlie Perdue, Eun Rhee, Bo Sanitioso, Kevin Snider, and Rich Tyler. We are also indebted to the scholars whose seminal works have influenced the field of intergroup relations: Gordon Allport, Muzifer and Carolyn Sherif, and Henri Tajfel. We thank Debbie Burkhart for her assistance in obtaining permissions to reprint figures from other publications and acknowledge Ron Crans for his technical support for the research and for the preparation of the volume. We are indebted to Marilynn Brewer, Rupert Brown, and Norman Miller for the constructive and insightful comments on an earlier version of the manuscript. We feel privileged to have such helpful colleagues. And last, but certainly not least, we express our gratitude to Alison Mudditt, the staff at Psychology Press, and Miles Hewstone for their confidence in us and for their patience and support.

Introduction and Overview

This book is about reducing intergroup bias. Over the past century, psychologists have made substantial strides in identifying the causes and consequences of fundamental biases, such as racism. The field has been less successful, however, in developing theories and pragmatic interventions to reduce these biases. In a sense, this book is an autobiographical account of our attempts to delineate the nature of contemporary racial attitudes and then to pursue a theoretically-grounded strategy we have been developing for combating their destructive consequences. We have *not* tried to write an encyclopedic text on intergroup relations, one that documents all of the literature in intergroup relations but without structure. Instead, we were asked to produce a more focused monograph, organized around our own research. We greeted the invitation to prepare such a volume with great excitement and sense of challenge. This book extends far beyond our own work, however. We use the Common Ingroup Identity Model, the model we developed through our research, as an integrating framework for understanding the connections among a range of other relevant theories and studies in the literature more broadly. In addition, although this is not a "how to" book, the principles outlined in the volume have direct relevance to practical interventions.

You might say that this book took almost 30 years to write. The research on which it is based developed out of a collaboration that began that long ago. The first author, a professor at the University of Delaware, had been working for several years on the topic of aversive racism, a contemporary and subtle manifestation of racial bias. His work on this

1

topic began with a serendipitous finding in what otherwise would have been an interesting but theoretically unexciting field experiment (Gaertner, 1973).

The study involved the willingness of registered Liberal and Conservative Party members in New York City to help a Black or White motorist (identifiable on the basis of their dialects) whose car has broken down on a local highway, who further claimed to have been dialing their mechanic's telephone number from a public telephone. Our Black or White callers explained that they now needed the respondent's help to call the mechanic because they used their last coin for this wrong number call. Consistent with the classical research literature on political ideology and prejudice (e.g., Adorno, Frenkel-Brunswik, Levinson, & Sanford, 1950), Conservative Party members discriminated by helping Black callers less frequently than White callers, whereas liberals did not discriminate in terms of helping. Surprisingly, however, Liberal Party members discriminated in a different way. Although Liberals helped without regard to race when they knew their assistance was needed, they terminated this encounter more readily for Black than for White callers *prior to* learning fully of the caller's need for their help. That is, they hung-up prematurely. The results were puzzling, and we began by applying the notion of aversive racism (Kovel, 1970) to explain why supposedly non-prejudiced Liberals discriminated against Blacks, but only when they were not sure their help was needed.

In 1973, the second author came to Delaware as a graduate student. He came with a range of interests, including altruism and nonverbal behavior, but with a primary personal interest in intergroup relations and prejudice. Together, the two of us collaborated on many articles, chapters, and books on a variety of topics. But the work on aversive racism was the start and is at the heart of it all.

In this chapter, we next consider the nature of contemporary racism, and aversive racism in particular. We then explore the relationship between this specific type of prejudice and the development and nature of intergroup biases, illustrated more generally almost 50 years ago by the compelling field research at Robbers Cave by Muzafer Sherif and his colleagues. Drawing on this classic work and the pioneering research of Henri Tajfel, Gordon Allport, and others, we outline basic principles of intergroup processes that form the foundation of the Common Ingroup Identity Model. We present the model briefly and provide overviews of the chapters that review the relevant research and theory associated with its key elements.

☐ Aversive Racism

What specifically is aversive racism? In contrast to "old-fashioned" racism, which is blatant, aversive racism (Dovidio & Gaertner, 1998; Gaertner & Dovidio, 1986a; Kovel, 1970) represents a subtle, often unintentional, form of bias that characterizes many well-intentioned White Americans who possess strong egalitarian values and who believe that they are nonprejudiced. Aversive racists also possess negative racial feelings and beliefs (which develop through normal cognitive biases and socialization) of which they are unaware or which they try to dissociate from their nonprejudiced self-images. Because aversive racists consciously endorse egalitarian values, they will not discriminate directly and openly in ways that can be attributed to racism; however, because of their negative feelings they will discriminate, often unintentionally, when their behavior can be justified on the basis of some factor other than race (e.g., attributions to a perceived lack of effort of the other person; see Frey & Gaertner, 1986). Thus, aversive racists may regularly engage in discrimination while they maintain a nonprejudiced self-image. The negative feelings that aversive racists have for Blacks do not reflect open hostility or hate. Instead, their reactions involve discomfort, uneasiness, disgust, and sometimes fear. That is, they find Blacks "aversive," while at the same time find any suggestion that they might be prejudiced "aversive" as well.

Other current theories of racism also propose that racism is now more subtle, indirect, and less conscious than in the past. According to symbolic racism theory (Sears, 1988) and its related variant modern racism theory (McConahay, 1986), negative feelings toward Blacks, which Whites acquire early in life, are relatively stable across the life span and thus persist into adulthood. When primed, these predispositions influence responses to racially-associated attitudinal objects, such as race-related policies (Sears, van Laar, Carillo, & Kosterman, 1997). However, because explicit beliefs change more fully and rapidly than these racial feelings and are likely to be more egalitarian to conform to prevailing norms, these negative attitudes are expressed indirectly and symbolically, in terms of opposition to busing or resistance to preferential treatment, rather than directly or overtly, as in support for segregation. McConahay (1986) further proposed that because modern racism involves the rejection of traditional racist beliefs and the displacement of anti-Black feelings onto more abstract social and political issues, modern racists, like aversive racists, are relatively unaware of their racist feelings. However, whereas symbolic and modern racism are subtle forms of contemporary racism that seem to exist among political conservatives, aversive racism seems to be more strongly associated with liberals. Nevertheless, like aversive racism,

the negative effects of modern and symbolic racism are observed primarily when discrimination can be justified on the basis of factors other than
race.

In summary, aversive racism, modern racism, and symbolic racism theories all hypothesize that discrimination is currently expressed more subtly than in the past, but they differ in their assumptions about the underlying causes and general motivations associated with this discrimination.
Whereas modern and symbolic racism perspectives emphasize the central
role of particular political and social ideologies (e.g., meritocracy and the
Protestant Ethic), aversive racism theory focuses on the conflict between
an individual's negative feelings and his or her personal self-image of
being fair and nonprejudiced.

When we described our findings formally, in papers and presentations,
and informally, a common question arose: What can we do about subtle
biases, particularly when we don't know for sure whether we have them?
Like a virus that has mutated, racism may have evolved into different
forms that are more difficult not only to recognize but also to combat. The
subtle processes underlying discrimination can be identified and isolated
under the controlled conditions of the laboratory. However, in organizational decision making, in which the controlled conditions of an experiment are rarely possible, this process presents a substantial challenge to
the equitable treatment of members of disadvantaged groups. Krieger
(1995), in the *Stanford Law Review*, notes that this aspect of contemporary
bias poses a particular problem for society and the legal system: "Herein
lies the practical problem. . . . Validating subjective decision making systems is neither empirically nor economically feasible, especially for jobs
where intangible qualities, such as interpersonal skills, creativity, and
ability to make sound judgments under conditions of uncertainty are critical" (p. 1232).

In addition, to the extent that legal proof of discrimination requires the
demonstration that race is *the* determining factor and that the actions
were intentional, the biases of aversive racists are immune to legal prosecution. Aversive, modern, and symbolic racists discriminate only when
other, non-race-related factors can justify their negative treatment of
Blacks, and their biases are normally unconscious and unintentional—
factors that may disqualify many employment discrimination suits from
successful outcomes (Krieger, 1995). Krieger (1998) concludes, "These
more subtle, incremental forms of discrimination are difficult to recognize, and neither our cultural understanding nor our jurisprudential models illuminate or provide ways to reckon with them" (pp. 1332–1333).

Because of its pervasiveness, subtlety, and complexity, the traditional
techniques for eliminating bias that emphasize the immorality of prejudice and illegality of discrimination are not effective for combating aver-

sive racism. Aversive racists recognize that prejudice is bad, but they do not recognize that they are prejudiced. Modern and symbolic racists believe that discrimination "is a thing of the past." Thus, contemporary, subtle forms of racism must be addressed at multiple levels—at the societal and intergroup level, as well as the personal level.

Although we continue to pursue research on aversive racism, much of our earlier work was summarized in our edited book, (Dovidio & Gaertner, 1986) *Prejudice, Discrimination, and Racism*. We had three chapters in that book. The first reviewed historical trends and contemporary approaches in the study of prejudice and racism. Another summarized our research on aversive racism. The last chapter of the book, "Problems, Progress, and Promise," considered new ways of fighting racism and introduced the basic ideas and initial research on the Common Ingroup Identity Model. Where that book left off, this book begins. This book is about the Common Ingroup Identity Model: past research, current challenges, and promise as a theoretical framework and a potentially practical strategy for fighting bias, including subtle types such as aversive racism.

One basic argument we have made in our research on aversive racism is that the negative feelings that develop toward other groups may be rooted, in part, in fundamental, normal psychological processes. One such process, identified in the classic work of Tajfel, Allport and others, is the categorization of people into ingroups and outgroups—"we's" and "they's." People respond systematically more favorably to others whom they perceive to belong to their group than to different groups. Thus, if bias is linked to fundamental, normal psychological processes, then attempts to ameliorate bias should be directed not at eliminating the process but rather at redirecting the forces to produce more harmonious intergroup relations. By shifting the basis of categorization from race to an alternative dimension, we can potentially alter who is a "we" and who is a "they," undermining a contributing force to aversive racism.

As these ideas were developing, we also began to consider the possibility that the discrimination we were observing in our studies of aversive racism may have reflected discrimination not only *against* Blacks but also discrimination *in favor of* Whites. That is, we began to view aversive racism as a problem that, in part, involved Whites having a more generous and forgiving orientation toward Whites than toward Blacks. Even though this form of racism can be very pernicious, it does not assume an underlying motivation to be hurtful—either consciously or unconsciously. Rather, for aversive racists, part of the problem may be that they do not regard Blacks and other minorities as part of their circle of sharing and caring as readily as they accept Whites. Racially dissimilar others, then, do not ordinarily have the same capacity as fellow Whites to elicit empathic, prosocial reactions. But, what if Whites perceived Blacks and other minorities, even temporarily, as members of their own group—as ingroup members—rather than as members of different groups? Would behavior toward them become more favorable? And how specifically can intergroup contact be structured to reduce bias and conflict?

☐ Conflict, Categorization, and Recategorization

In 1954, Muzafer Sherif and his colleagues (Sherif, Harvey, White, Hood, & Sherif, 1961, reprinted in 1988) conducted the third of a series of field studies about the creation and reduction of intergroup bias and conflict. This particular study was conducted at Robbers Cave State Park in Oklahoma. In the Robbers Cave study, Sherif and his colleagues engaged psychologically healthy 12-year-old boys from Oklahoma City, Oklahoma, in what turned out to be a clever (some might say diabolical), carefully orchestrated social psychology experiment about intergroup relations. These boys, who had signed up for three weeks of summer camp, were assigned (without their knowledge) to two groups that arrived at camp on different days. To permit time for group formation (e.g., the development of norms, and a leadership structure), these groups were kept almost completely apart for one week during which they were not given information about each other's existence. The two groups named themselves the Eagles and the Rattlers.

During the second week, the investigators introduced competitive relations between the groups in the form of repeated competitive athletic activities centering around tug-of-war, baseball, and touch football. As expected, the introduction of competitive activities generated derogatory stereotypes and conflict between the Eagles and the Rattlers. These boys, however, did not simply show ingroup favoritism. Rather, there was genuine hostility between these groups. Each group conducted raids on the other's cabins that resulted in the destruction and theft of property. The boys carried sticks, baseball bats, and socks filled with rocks as potential weapons. Fistfights broke out between members of the groups, and food and garbage fights erupted in the dining hall. In addition, group members regularly exchanged verbal insults (e.g., "ladies first") and name calling (e.g., "sissies," "stinkers," "pigs," "bums," "cheaters," and "communists").

During the third week, Sherif and his colleagues arranged intergroup contact under neutral, noncompetitive conditions. These interventions did not calm the ferocity of the exchanges, however. Mere intergroup contact was not sufficient to change the nature of the relations between the groups. Only after the investigators altered the functional relationship between the groups by introducing a series of superordinate goals—

ones that could not be achieved without the full cooperation of both groups and which were successfully achieved—did the relations between the two groups become more harmonious. But specifically how, psychologically, did cooperation toward superordinate goals change intergroup attitudes?

In our work on the Common Ingroup Identity Model, we have proposed that social categorization—specifically how people conceive of group boundaries—is a key factor. We have attempted to reduce intergroup bias by changing group members' cognitive representations from different groups to one group (Gaertner et al., 1993; Gaertner, Rust, Dovidio, Bachman, & Anastasio, 1994). This framework is what this book is about. Rather than trying to summarize the vast literature on intergroup relations generally, consistent with the theme of this book series, we describe a more singular program of research. This book presents a recategorization approach to reducing bias and uses the Common Ingroup Identity Model as an organizing framework.

In application, recategorization from different, potentially competing groups to one group can be achieved by inducing intergroup cooperation, calling attention to existing common superordinate group memberships (e.g., their common university identity) or by introducing new factors (e.g., common goals or fate) that are perceived to be shared by members. We have found that evaluations of former outgroup members significantly improve as these individuals become identified with the superordinate, more inclusive ingroup (Gaertner et al., 1993).

We view the recategorization of different groups into one group as a particularly powerful and pragmatic strategy for combating subtle forms of bias. Creating the perception of a common ingroup identity not only reduces the likelihood of discrimination based on race but also increases the likelihood of positive interracial behaviors. People are more helpful toward ingroup members (Kramer & Brewer, 1984; Piliavin, Dovidio, Gaertner, & Clark, 1981; Schroeder, Penner, Dovidio, & Piliavin, 1995) and apply different and more generous standards of morality, justice, and fairness to ingroup members than to outgroup members (Opotow, 1990). It is important to note however, that recategorization does not necessarily require members to forsake their earlier group identities because it is possible to maintain a "dual" representation in which both superordinate and original group identities are salient simultaneously (e.g., a football team composed of both offensive and defensive units).

We describe the model and its theoretical and empirical underpinnings more fully in Chapter 3. In general, we propose that factors that affect *intergroup differentiation*, that influence the nature of *intergroup contact* (as outlined by the Contact Hypothesis), and that *cognitively or affectively prime* interactants can shape how people conceive of the memberships. These factors can emphasize intergroup differences and reinforce *different group* categorizations. Alternatively, they can emphasize the individuality of group members and produce *decategorized* representations. It is also possible that these factors can engineer *recategorization* by leading people to represent ingroup and outgroup members as now members of a common, superordinate ingroup or as two subgroups working as a team as part of a larger group. Whereas a different-groups representation maintains or exacerbates intergroup bias, recategorization and decategorization can reduce bias—but in different ways. Decategorization reduces bias primarily by reducing attractiveness to former ingroup members; once they are seen primarily as separate individuals, they no longer benefit from the forces of ingroup favoritism. Recategorization reduces intergroup bias primarily by increasing the attractiveness of former outgroup members. It harnesses the forces of ingroup favoritism and redirects them to apply now to the newly incorporated member.

Clearly, our research builds upon classic work by Sherif on superordinate goals, by Williams, Allport and others on the Contact Hypothesis, and by Tajfel and his colleagues on Social Identity Theory. We are indebted to them for their pioneering work and acknowledge the importance of their ideas. The Common Ingroup Identity Model extends these earlier contributions by focusing on how the diverse factors that have been identified as critical for reducing bias may operate through common mediating cognitive mechanisms. By understanding the psychological processes that influence intergroup bias, we can design multiple interventions that target those processes. Then, for practical applications, when one strategy is not possible (e.g., equal status contact), alternative and more realistic strategies (e.g., creating common goals) may be substituted. To paraphrase Lewin, there's nothing so practical as a good theory. In the next section we present an overview of each of the chapters in the remainder of this book.

☐ Chapter Overviews

Chapter 2 introduces the theoretical and empirical basis for the aversive racism framework and describes selected empirical support for the position. In addition, in this chapter we examine the possibility that whereas traditional racism is characterized by anti-Black attitudes and behavior, aversive racism may primarily reflect pro-White feelings and actions. Brewer (1979) proposed that much of intergroup bias, particularly when interactants do not perceive themselves in direct conflict, is characterized by ingroup favoritism rather than outgroup derogation. To the extent that intergroup processes initiated by social categorization represent a foundation for aversive racism to develop, aversive racism may be characterized by similar effects. We do not intend to argue that all of racism can be attributed simply to ingroup–outgroup, we–they distinctions. Racism is also deeply embedded in a historical, social, political, and economic context that sculpts its characteristics. However, we do want to suggest that if aversive racism is rooted at least in part on social categorization, then strategies to eliminate aversive racism may be productively directed at this underlying process.

The Common Ingroup Identity Model, which is designed to capitalize on the psychological forces of ingroup favoritism, is introduced formally in Chapter 3. Intergroup differentiation, the nature of intergroup contact, and cognitive and affective priming are hypothesized to influence the extent to which people conceive of the memberships as one group, two groups within one, two different groups, or separate individuals. These representations, in turn, influence attitudes toward the outgroup, bias, and discrimination. By facilitating a recategorization of original outgroup members as now members of the ingroup, the forces of ingroup favoritism will now apply to these representatives. Consequently, attitudes will improve and bias will be reduced. We survey other related perspectives on intergroup relations in this chapter, and then we review the theoretical underpinnings and rationale of our model.

Chapter 4 explores the psychological concomitants of social categorization. It focuses on how the salience of group boundaries can influence intergroup representations and consequent attitudes. Moreover, we argue that although the social categorization process is typically spontaneous, it is not completely unalterable. Interventions can systematically influence whether people develop individuated impressions of others or group-based impressions, and if so, what types of group-based impressions occur. Here we provide empirical evidence of laboratory interventions that directly produce recategorization and decategorization and consequently successfully reduce intergroup bias. Among other supporting evidence, we illustrate how recategorization can reduce bias between racial groups.

The Contact Hypothesis has been a guiding framework for reducing bias over the past 50 years. It identifies a number of conditions (e.g., personalized interaction, equal status relations) that are needed for intergroup contact to improve attitudes and relations. In Chapter 5 we examine these factors and propose that these diverse features may operate—at least in part—through the common mechanism of group representations. We also demonstrate that some factors, such as equal status contact, under some conditions can produce feelings of threat to collective identity and thereby exacerbate, not reduce, levels of intergroup bias. With respect to group representations, the interpretation of and reaction to a two-groups-within-one representation may thus vary as a function of the intergroup context.

Chapter 6 considers how cognitive priming, which people may not even be aware of, and affective priming, from incidental sources unrelated to intergroup interaction, can have profound consequences on the nature of group representations and intergroup attitudes. In terms of cognitive priming, we present evidence that people have automatic positive reactions to the category "We." The response to the category "They" is relatively less positive, but not necessarily negative in an absolute sense. Furthermore, application of the term "we" rather than "they" when referring to others may produce, perhaps without awareness, more favorable attitudes toward them. These effects are mediated by more inclusive representations. With regard to affective priming, we report the results of a series of studies on the influence of incidental positive affect on intergroup attitudes. The effect is moderated by the nature of immediate and historical intergroup relations (e.g., cooperative or competitive). In addition, over and above the mediating effects of group representations, positive affect can influence how people weigh information about others (e.g., involving potential threat), their reliance on category-based impressions (e.g., stereotypes), and their likelihood of developing detailed, elaborative, and personalized impressions of others. Taken together, the experiments in this chapter reveal the importance of events in intergroup contact situations that are seemingly irrelevant to the nature of the interaction but that affect relations in significant ways.

In the previous chapters reporting empirical support for the Common Ingroup Identity Model, the vast majority of studies used group evaluative biases concerning members present in the contact setting as the dependent variable. Chapter 7 examines how the benefits of recategorization extend to other, behavioral measures and how attitudes toward members present may generalize to the groups as a whole. Although the connection between positive group attitudes and behaviors appears straightforward, the empirical demonstration of this effect is far from trivial. Intergroup attitudes and intergroup aggression are only weakly related and appear to have different causes (Struch & Schwartz, 1989); in addition, prejudice is only modestly related to actual discrimination (Dovidio, Brigham, Johnson, & Gaertner, 1996). Nevertheless, we find that a common ingroup identity can facilitate not only more positive attitudes but also encourage self-disclosing and prosocial behaviors that can initiate complementary, individuating processes, which can further reduce bias. We also explore how increasing the salience of the different group identities within an inclusive common group representation can increase the generalizability of the benefits of intergroup contact. The common group membership improves attitudes toward members present, whereas the salience of the subgroup identities provides an associative link for these more positive attitudes to generalize to group members not present and to the groups as a whole.

As with our volume on prejudice (see Chapter 11, Gaertner & Dovidio, 1986b), we conclude this book with a chapter on Problems, Progress, and Promise. In Chapter 8 we first briefly summarize evidence for the Common Ingroup Identity Model and critically examine empirical, theoretical, and practical problems that challenge our search for a strategy that effectively reduces intergroup bias. Then—despite these challenges—we discuss progress in theoretically understanding and combating intergroup bias. In doing so, we consider the potentially complementary and reciprocal relationships among the three category-based strategies for changing intergroup bias and conflict: decategorization, recategorization, and mutual differentiation. To illustrate these relationships, we turn to the richly detailed descriptions of how cooperation reduced intergroup bias and conflict among Sherif et al.'s (1961) groups of summer campers and its relevance to recent research of our own that also demonstrates the potential for reciprocal relations between these category-based processes. We conclude by discussing promising avenues for further theoretical development and practical applications to reduce intergroup bias and conflict.

2
CHAPTER

神族议

Aversive Racism and Intergroup Biases

As we described in the previous chapter, over the past thirty years, we, with a number of our colleagues, have investigated a prevalent type of modern racial bias, called aversive racism (Dovidio & Gaertner, 1996, 1998; Dovidio, Gaertner, & Bachman, in press; Gaertner & Dovidio, 1986a; Gaertner, Dovidio, Banker et al., 1997; Kovel, 1970). In contrast to "old-fashioned" racism, which is expressed directly and openly, aversive racism represents a subtle, often unintentional, form of bias that characterizes many White Americans who possess strong egalitarian values and who believe that they are nonprejudiced.

Like other approaches to attitudes in general (see Eagly & Chaiken, 1998, pp. 279–281) and to contemporary forms of prejudice (i.e., attitudes toward social groups) more specifically (e.g., Devine, Plant, & Blair, in press; MacDonald & Zanna, 1998), we propose that aversive racists experience *ambivalence* in their reactions to Blacks and other people of color. In this respect our position is very much aligned with that of Katz and his colleagues (see Katz & Hass, 1988; Katz, Wackenhut, & Hass, 1986). However, whereas Katz and his associates proposed that ambivalence is the result of tension between negative and genuinely positive (e.g., sympathetic) feelings toward Blacks, the ambivalence associated with aversive racism is rooted in the conflict between feelings and values. Specifically, according to the aversive racism perspective, many people who explicitly support egalitarian principles and believe themselves to be nonprejudiced also unconsciously harbor negative feelings and beliefs about Blacks and other historically disadvantaged groups. A more cognitive perspective of ambivalence (Operario & Fiske, in press) proposes that stereotypes toward most groups involve ambivalent belief systems (e.g., they are competent but not nice) that vary in potency depending upon the situation.

Moreover, in contrast to the traditional emphasis on the *psychopathological* aspects of prejudice (e.g., Adorno et al., 1950), the aversive racism framework suggests that biases related to *normal* cognitive, motivational, and sociocultural processes may predispose a person to develop negative racial feelings (see Gaertner & Dovidio, 1986a). These negative feelings do not reflect open hostility or hate; instead, the feelings involve discomfort, uneasiness, disgust, and sometimes fear. Furthermore, as a function of pervasive cultural influences and repeated racial associations (Devine, 1989), aversive racists may not be fully aware that they harbor negative racial feelings (Dovidio, Kawakami, Johnson, Johnson, & Howard, 1997; Greenwald & Banaji, 1995). Thus, for aversive racists there is a disassociation between their self-reported egalitarian attitudes and implicit measures of their automatically activated (and uncontrollable) feelings and beliefs about Blacks (see Dovidio, Kawakami, & Beach, in press; Fazio, Jackson, Dunton, & Williams, 1995; Vanman, Paul, Ito, & Miller, 1997). As mentioned earlier, at the root of aversive racism are two types of aversions: Aversive racists find Blacks "aversive," while at the same time find any suggestion that they might be prejudiced "aversive" as well.

As a consequence of these widespread influences promoting both negative feelings and egalitarian beliefs, aversive racism is presumed to characterize the racial attitudes of a substantial portion of well-educated and liberal Whites in the United States (Gaertner & Dovidio, 1986a) and its principles and processes extend to other groups for whom strong norms for egalitarian treatment and social sensitivity exist (e.g., Hispanics and women; see Dovidio & Gaertner, 1983; Dovidio & Fazio, 1992; Dovidio, Gaertner, Anastasio, & Sanitioso, 1992) as well as to other nations that value principles of egalitarianism (e.g., the Netherlands, see Kleinpenning & Hagendoorn, 1993).

The type of subtle, unintentional bias that is reflected in aversive racism is particularly resistant to change. Whereas expressed racial prejudice has declined over the past decade, the pattern of subtle bias associated with aversive racism has persisted (Dovidio & Gaertner, 2000). Aversive racism is rooted, in part, in fundamental, normal psychological processes, such as the categorization of people into ingroups and outgroups, "we's" and "they's" (see Brewer, 1979; Tajfel, 1969). Moreover, because of its pervasiveness, subtlety, and complexity, the traditional techniques for eliminating bias that emphasized the immorality of prejudice and illegality of discrimination are not effective for combating aversive racism. Aversive racists recognize prejudice is bad, but they do not recognize that they are prejudiced.

Our work on aversive racism stimulated our interest in the processes of intergroup relations more generally. The Common Ingroup Identity Model, the focus of this book, evolved out of those interests. Within the Common Ingroup Identity Model, pro-ingroup biases (as well as anti-outgroup biases) are hypothesized to play a critical role in shaping intergroup relations. People respond systematically more favorably to others whom they perceive to belong to their group than to different groups. Thus, changing the basis of categorization from race to an alternative dimension can alter who is a "we" and who is a "they," undermining a contributing force to aversive racism. This chapter provides an overview of our work on aversive racism with a reinterpretation of the findings in terms of pro-ingroup biases rather than as primarily anti-outgroup biases.

☐ Prejudice and Bias

Prejudice has traditionally been considered an unfavorable attitude toward another group, involving both negative feelings and beliefs. For example, Allport (1954, 1958) defined prejudice as "an antipathy based on faulty and inflexible generalization. It may be felt or expressed. It may be directed toward a group as a whole, or toward an individual because he [sic] is a member of that group" (p. 9); Ashmore (1970, p. 253) described it as "a negative attitude toward a socially defined group and any person perceived to be a member of that group." Perhaps as a consequence of this perspective, the prejudice of Whites toward Blacks has typically been measured using scales reflecting Whites' degree of endorsement of a range of statements about negative attributes of Blacks (e.g., such as inferiority), negative feelings toward the group (e.g., hostility or fear), and support for policies that restrict opportunities for Blacks (e.g., in housing or in intimate relations) (Brigham, 1993; McConahay, 1986; Sears, 1988; Woodmansee & Cook, 1967). Lower levels of endorsement of these negative statements about Blacks has generally been assumed to indicate lower levels of racial bias and racism.

In our earlier work on aversive racism, however, we challenged the assumption that Whites who appear nonprejudiced on these types of instruments, and who may truly believe that they possess egalitarian principles, are nonracist. Specifically, our research on aversive racism (see Dovidio, Mann, & Gaertner, 1989; Gaertner & Dovidio, 1986a; see also Kovel, 1970) revealed that many of these well-intentioned Whites have not entirely escaped cultural and cognitive forces that promote racial bias. Rather, aversive racists, who appear nonracist on these measures, dis-

criminate in subtle, rationalizable ways that insulate them from awareness of their prejudice (see Crosby, Bromley, & Saxe, 1980).

In this chapter, we examine an additional aspect of the nature of contemporary racial attitudes and how racial bias may be expressed by aversive racists. Specifically, we explore the "flip side" of the conventional
assumption that the racial bias of Whites primarily reflects anti-Black attitudes. We consider the possibility that modern, subtle forms of bias—
such as aversive racism—may be characterized by a significant component of pro-White attitudes (Brewer, 1999). An asymmetry in which
intergroup bias is expressed more as ingroup favoritism than outgroup
derogation (Brewer, 1979) and more on positive than negative dimensions (e.g., Wenzel & Mummendey, 1996; see also Mummendey & Otten,
in press) has been found for other groups. We propose, however, that the
particular motivations of aversive racists help to account for this pattern
of bias of Whites toward Blacks.

This distinction between anti-Black and pro-White attitudes is important for at least two reasons. One reason is that it may provide a more
comprehensive and accurate understanding of contemporary racism. The
conclusions drawn from considering only the anti-outgroup portion of
these attitudes in isolation of pro-ingroup attitudes might misrepresent
the overall phenomenon. For example, researchers have commonly concluded on the basis of evidence that people with low self-esteem rate
outgroups more negatively than do those with high self-esteem and, that
people with low self-esteem are more biased (see Wills, 1981). Consistent
with this evidence, Crocker and Schwartz (1985) demonstrated that when
examining only outgroup ratings, people with low self-esteem offered
less positive evaluations than did those with high self-esteem. However,
considering *both* ingroup and outgroup ratings yielded a different conclusion. Reflecting a general tendency for those low self-esteem to evaluate
people and objects relatively unfavorably, low self-esteem participants
also rated their own group less positively than did high self-esteem people.
As a consequence, Crocker and Schwartz found that they were not more
biased than high self-esteem people. Thus, examination of ingroup favoritism as well as outgroup derogation produces a different perspective on
the phenomenon.

Another reason that the distinction between pro-White and anti-Black
attitudes is important involves the implications that these different motivational orientations have for understanding the problem of racism specifically among people with egalitarian values (i.e., aversive racists). To
the extent that pro-White rather than anti-Black biases reflect the motivational dynamics of aversive racism, we would have some explanation
of why many Whites who do discriminate claim that they genuinely do
not experience negative racial feelings.

Thus, this chapter is about White Americans who possess genuinely egalitarian values, who identify with a politically liberal agenda, who believe that they are not prejudiced and that they do not discriminate against Blacks or other minorities. These people, in many ways, represent the "Great White Hope" in the quest for interracial harmony; they are genuinely motivated to treat Blacks fairly. In this chapter, we re-evaluate the motivation underlying aversive racism and briefly review evidence about how and when this form of racism operates. As we review the evidence we will reconsider whether aversive racism is driven primarily by anti-Black feelings as we originally proposed, or whether this form of racism may plausibly be interpreted as reflecting pro-White biases.

☐ Aversive Racism

Whereas traditional forms of prejudice are direct and overt, contemporary forms may be indirect and subtle. Aversive racism (see Gaertner & Dovidio, 1986a; Kovel, 1970; Murrell, Dietz-Uhler, Dovidio, Gaertner, & Drout, 1994) has been identified as a form of modern prejudice that characterizes the racial attitudes of many Whites with egalitarian values, who regard themselves as nonprejudiced, but who discriminate in subtle, rationalizable ways. We propose that aversive racism represents a particular type of ambivalence (see Katz & Hass, 1988; Katz, Wakenhut, & Hass, 1986) in which an egalitarian value system is brought into conflict with unacknowledged negative racial beliefs and feelings that resulted from (a) historical and contemporary culturally racist contexts and, (b) the informational processing biases that result when people are categorized into ingroups and outgroups (see Hamilton & Trolier, 1986; Rothbart, 1996; Rothbart & John, 1985). Relative to symbolic (see Sears, 1988) or modern racism (see McConahay, 1986) that are forms of contemporary racism that seem to exist among political conservatives, the aversive racist is more strongly liberal and egalitarian. Also, while symbolic and modern racists do not regard themselves to be motivated by racial malevolence, the aversive racist is more strongly motivated by the desire to avoid the self-attribution of bigoted intent.

Relative to the more overt, red-necked, dominative racists (see Kovel, 1970), aversive racists do not represent the open flame of racial hatred nor do they usually intend to act out of bigoted beliefs or feelings. To the contrary, awareness of such beliefs and feelings would seriously threaten their nonprejudiced, nondiscriminatory self-images. Without being hypocritical, aversive racists actively avoid behaving in ways that could be attributable, by themselves or by others, to bigoted intent. Thus we propose that their major motive in interracial contexts may be to avoid acting inappropriately, that is, in ways that could be attributed to racial prejudice. We hypothesized in terms of our research across a variety of different studies that in situations rich in social norms that help to clearly distinguish appropriate from inappropriate behavior, aversive racists would not discriminate. Rather, they may overcompensate in these contexts and respond more favorably to Blacks than to Whites. We proposed, therefore, that aversive racists can successfully suppress negative beliefs, feelings, and behavior toward Blacks and other minorities when it is clear that expressing such attitudes would be attributable to prejudice. This motivation to avoid wrong-doing, however, has two important potential costs for interracial interactions. First, this concern with avoiding wrong-doing increases anxiety and could motivate premature withdrawal from the situation that would preclude the opportunity for meaningful, self-revealing interaction. Second, in view of recent work on stereotype suppression and rebound (e.g., Bodenhausen & Macrae, 1996), it is possible that once the self imposed suppression is relaxed, the negative beliefs, feelings, and behaviors would be even more likely to occur than if they were not suppressed initially.

We further hypothesized that when the situational context was normatively impoverished, making the distinction between appropriate and inappropriate behavior more ambiguous, or when the situational context permits unfavorable behavior to be attributed to nonrace-related factors, aversive racists would reveal intergroup biases (see also McConahay, 1986; Rogers & Prentice-Dunn, 1981). In the absence of normative standards or when unfavorable treatment could be attributable to factors other than race, aversive racists could treat Blacks and Whites differently yet not experience awareness that they are racially biased.

In terms of motivation, we proposed that the interracial behavior of aversive racists was driven by mildly negative feelings such as fear, disgust, and uneasiness that tend to motivate avoidance rather than intentionally destructive behavior. Thus, aversive racists, unlike dominative racists, were not believed to be motivated primarily by strongly anti-Black feelings such as anger or hostility. But why should people with egalitarian values discriminate and have even mildly negative feelings for Blacks or have more favorable feelings for Whites than for Blacks?

Among the several factors involved in the etiology of aversive racism, we considered the cognitive and motivational processes associated with social categorization of people into "us" and "them" (Tajfel, 1969; Turner, 1981). Without even a history of conflict between groups, people behave more positively toward ingroup than toward outgroup members (Billig & Tajfel, 1973). Also, people evaluate ingroup members more favorably and attribute more positive personal characteristics to ingroup than to outgroup members. Needs for personal self-esteem and superior status coupled with drives for social comparison have been proposed (Tajfel & Turner, 1979; Turner, Hogg, Oakes, Reicher, & Wetherell, 1987) to motivate the more favorable treatment and evaluations of ingroup relative to outgroup members. In laboratory contexts, even when people know that they were divided randomly into two groups, ingroup members are favored over outgroup members (Rabbie & Horwitz, 1969). This is revealing because it suggests that even in relatively unimportant situations and when group membership is, at best only weakly linked to personal identity, people positively differentiate their ingroup from other groups. In these situations stripped of cultural significance without a history of intergroup conflict, it is difficult to believe that the differential evaluations and treatment of ingroup and outgroup members are driven primarily by negative feelings toward outgroup members.

Rather, it seems more likely that these biases result from pro-ingroup rather than anti-outgroup orientations. Brewer's (1979) analysis of the intergroup literature supports the idea that bias due primarily to social categorization largely reflects ingroup favoritism rather than outgroup rejection. This bias, which can occur when people are arbitrarily assigned to categories or groups, is even more pronounced when the groups have meaning and function (Mullen, Brown, & Smith, 1992). Consequently, bias derived from social categorization *per se*, while fundamental, is not necessarily characterized by disparagement or hostility. Because of social categorization, however, the balance scale for the even-handed treatment of other people begins off center; ingroup status, *per se*, is sufficient to elicit favored treatment. From this perspective, the racial biases of aversive racists rests partially on a failure to expand their circle of inclusion beyond Whiteness when considering the ingroup and outgroup status for people of color.

Our earlier research revealed that people who scored from very high to very low on prejudice inventories, or who were politically liberal or conservative discriminated against Blacks, but usually in different ways (see Gaertner & Dovidio, 1986a). Thus, racism as reflected by the patterns of discrimination we observed was quite widespread throughout the population. Regardless of political values and expressed racial attitudes the behavior of many Whites was not consistently reflective of their low prejudiced self-images. As the sequence of studies was being completed, the social categorization approach became more appealing to us because it proposed that people quite generally favor ingroup relative to outgroup members. Indeed, this position offers partial explanation for the discrimination we observed among our liberal, very low prejudice scorers as well as the more strongly authoritarian types. Although other factors beyond mere social categorization are important in shaping racial attitudes, initial levels of ingroup favoritism may chart the course for the more ready acceptance of negative feelings and beliefs that result from realistic competition between groups over political and economic issues. Thus, feelings of ingroup favoritism would not be irrelevant to either those Whites who acknowledge that they are prejudiced or to those who discriminate but who do not have awareness of anti-Black feeling. It is this latter group that represents the focus of our analysis.

The consequences of bias due to pro-ingroup intentions are not necessarily more benign than bias driven by anti-outgroup intentions. For example, in terms of ultimate consequences, the failure of minority applicants to obtain employment because someone else enjoyed ingroup ties to a personnel director is not that different from the personnel director refusing to hire minority applicants outright. In the case of pro-ingroup bias, attitudes toward the minority applicants were irrelevant to the decision, however, and no harm was intended. Many Whites seem willing to endorse color blind programs in which hiring and promotions are based exclusively on the candidates' qualifications. These same people, however, often object to affirmative action programs that are not color blind and that seem to show preferential treatment to Blacks over Whites. From the perspective we are considering in this chapter, this resistance by Whites to preferential treatment toward Blacks may indeed reflect pro-White rather than anti-Black feelings.

☐ An Attributional Analysis of Anti-Black versus Pro-White Attitudes

In many circumstances, behavior that favors members of one's own group or family is regarded as appropriate but does not necessarily denote negative feelings toward others. Inviting only members of one's immediate family to a holiday dinner, for example, would not be interpreted as expressing ill will toward people outside of family. Given the normative appropriateness of inviting only family to such an event, the failure to invite others, at best, may only inform us about attitudes toward family. Of course, if invitations were issued to some nonfamily members, or if invitations were withheld from some family members, the attitudinal implications would be clear. These events would inform us about the positive feelings toward invited nonfamily members and the likely negative feelings toward the uninvited family members.

As we review our earlier experiments, which usually involved the delivery of prosocial behavior to Blacks or to Whites, we use a similar attributional strategy that considers the normative structure and social forces within the situation to determine whether the racial discrimination that we observed among our White participants most likely resulted from either anti-Black or pro-White feelings. We argue that when the social forces to take action are very weak or strongly inhibiting, the failure to intervene would not be particularly revealing of a bystander's feelings toward the victim. In contrast, helping when situational forces inhibit action can inform us about a bystander's likely positive attitude toward the recipient. Only when social forces strongly promote intervention, however, would the failure to help be attributable to possible negative feelings toward the victim.

In general, the pattern we observed in our research is that Whites treated Blacks and Whites differently only when the forces to act were weak — when action, but not inaction, would more likely reveal something about the bystanders' regard for the victim. In the next section, we describe some of our earlier studies in view of their potential to possibly reflect pro-White sentiments among people with more liberal, egalitarian values but who do discriminate on the basis of race.

The Wrong-Number Study

The first study which initiated our interest in aversive racism was a field experiment that examined the likelihood of Black and White persons obtaining nonemergency assistance from caucasian Liberal Party and Conservative Party members residing in Brooklyn, New York (Gaertner, 1973). Members of these political parties received apparent wrong-number telephone calls from Black and White members of the research staff whose race was clearly identifiable from their dialects. Each caller explained that his or her car was disabled and that he or she was trying to reach a service station from a parkway telephone. Just about all participants explained that our caller had reached the wrong number. Then our "motorist" explained that he or she did not have more coins to make another call and asked if the participant would telephone the garage to report the problem.

Supportive of the authoritarian personality framework (Adorno et al., 1950), Conservative Party members who learned of the motorist's entire dilemma discriminated on the basis of race. Conservatives telephoned the garage significantly less frequently for Black than for White motorists (65% vs 92%). Liberal Party members, however, helped Black and White motorists equivalently (75% vs. 85%). Not every participant, though, stayed on the line long enough to learn of the full dilemma; indeed, many participants hung-up "prematurely" immediately after the opening greeting, "Hello, Ralph's Garage this is George Williams. I'm stuck out here on the highway. . . . " Hanging-up prematurely was particularly characteristic of Liberal Party members—and we soon discovered that they did not ignore the "motorist's" race in this regard. Rather, Liberal Party members hung-up prematurely more frequently on Blacks (19% of the time) than on Whites (3% of the time). The premature hang-up rate for Conservative Party members was very low (about 5%), and they did not discriminate in this way.

Initially, we assumed that both Liberal and Conservative Party members discriminated against Blacks, but in different ways. We believed that learning of the motorist's full dilemma would arouse the salience of the social responsibility norm (Berkowitz & Daniels, 1963)—a standard that suggests that a person usually should help other people who are dependent upon their assistance. In the presence of this standard, Conservatives, but not Liberals, more frequently refused help to Blacks than Whites. We assumed that refusing to help Blacks in the presence of this standard could be self-attributed to bigoted intent; thus, it would be particularly costly to the self-images of Liberals to discriminate in this way.

But why did Liberals discriminate by hanging-up prematurely more frequently on Blacks than on Whites, and does this reflect pro-White or anti-Black feelings? Initially, we believed that Liberals unwittingly expressed anti-Black affect in this way. At the stage of the encounter when premature hang-ups occurred there was no clear standard to direct behavior. Indeed, the appropriateness of staying on the line or hanging-up quickly has no clearly prescribed answer. Thus, Liberals could hang-up prematurely on Blacks because it would be difficult to self-attribute this decision to negative racial attitudes. It would not be clear that they did anything wrong. We believed that hanging-up prematurely permitted Liberals to express anti-Black feelings and also protected their non-prejudiced self-images.

The attributional re-analysis of this behavior that we are proposing, however, suggests that because the normative structure to stay on the phone beyond this point was so weak, hanging-up would not necessarily be informative about a person's attitude toward the caller. Instead, staying in the interaction and not hanging-up prematurely can be regarded as behavior beyond the call of duty or normative obligation. It is this type of behavior that our analysis suggests would be informative about the person's attitude toward the caller. From this perspective, Liberals remaining in the encounter more frequently with Whites than with Blacks could be reflective of their positive attitudes toward Whites rather than reflective of anti-Black attitudes. Just as the failure to invite nonfamily members to holiday dinner does not inform us of the host's attitude toward them, Liberals hanging-up prematurely more frequently on Blacks than on Whites may not indicate their attitudes toward Blacks. Liberals just did not treat Blacks as *positively* as they treated family.

If the responses of aversive racists reflect primarily ingroup favoritism, and not necessarily negative behavior towards the outgroup, these actions should be most apparent when they have the opportunity to benefit the person even when there is ample reason *not* to help. The premature hang-ups in the telephone study suggested that in the absence of clear norms for helping, Liberals were more responsive to the need of Whites than of Blacks. In the next study that we present, we extend this attributional analysis to consider how much attitudinal information is revealed by decisions to help or withhold assistance from ingroup and outgroup members when they are clearly undeserving of assistance.

Helping the Undeserving

Frey and Gaertner (1986) conducted a laboratory experiment in which they varied the race of a participant's partner as well as the reason why this partner needed assistance. In one condition, the White participants' Black or White partner needed help because the partner was assigned a very difficult anagram task. This task was described as more difficult than the participant's own and although this partner was described as working exceptionally hard on the task, the partner did not yet form enough words to qualify for the bonus points that were valuable in the context of this experiment. Participants then received a note in which the Black or White partner asked if the participants could give them some of their own scrabble letters to help them form enough words to earn the bonus points. In the second condition, everything was the same except that participants learned their Black or White partner's anagram task was very much easier than theirs and that the partner was playing around rather than working hard, and of course, did not form enough words yet to earn bonus points. These participants also received the note from the partner asking for help. Pilot testing established that helping in the first condition was seen as more appropriate and that the recipient was more deserving of assistance than in the second condition, as we had anticipated.

Consistent with the aversive racism theoretical framework, when the partner was deserving and, hence, it was clearly appropriate to help, participants helped Black and White partners equally (95% vs 100%). However, when the partner was undeserving and when the appropriateness of helping was less clear, participants helped Black partners reliably less frequently than they helped White partners (30% vs 93%). We assumed, of course, that when the partner was undeserving of assistance, failure to help Blacks as readily as Whites was indicative of anti-Black prejudice. Whites only discriminated against Blacks when the failure to help would not likely be regarded as inappropriate (given that the recipient was undeserving) and thus not easily self-attributed to bigoted intent.

Our current attributional analysis, however, suggests that failure to help someone who is undeserving does not necessarily inform us of the potential donor's attitude toward this recipient's racial or ethnic group identity. Here the normative pressures to help are weak, such that only by helping someone who is undeserving are we informed of the donor's possibly very positive attitudes toward this recipient. That is, help was delivered even when the recipient did not deserve it. Paralleling the results of this study, we sometimes help our children even when they are undeserving, although we would not likely help others under similar circumstances. Thus, from this perspective, it seems more plausible that helping undeserving Whites reveals pro-White feelings, whereas the failure to help undeserving Blacks does not necessarily reflect ill-will toward them. We will next apply this attributional analysis to the failure to help during an emergency situation when the consequences of not helping are particularly severe.

Diffusion of Responsibility

Gaertner and Dovidio (1977) engaged White students in a laboratory experiment in which a simulated emergency involving a Black or a White was overheard. The emergency was created by a stack of heavy chairs ostensibly falling on another participant of the experiment who was located in a different room than the participant. This experiment systematically varied the victim's race and also the presence or absence of two other bystanders, each located in separate rooms. In their classic study, Darley and Latané (1968) discovered that the mere belief that other bystanders are aware of an emergency decreases the likelihood that any one bystander will intervene. Darley and Latané explained that when a person is alone at the time of an emergency, all of the responsibility for helping is focused on this one bystander. Therefore, the forces propelling action by this single bystander are very strong. As the number of additional bystanders is increased, however, the responsibility for helping becomes diffused and consequently, the forces propelling intervention on any one of them becomes weaker.

Gaertner and Dovidio (1977) introduced the presence of other bystanders in their study to provide participants with a nonrace-related justification that would allow them to rationalize their failure to intervene. It was predicted that the belief that other bystanders are present would have a greater inhibiting effect on participants' helping when the emergency involved a Black victim than a White victim. The belief that one of the other bystanders could intervene was expected to be particularly influential when the victim was Black. We suspected at that time, that participants' negative affect for Blacks would sharply increase their susceptibility to diffuse responsibility for helping Black victims. The presence of other bystanders, not bigoted intent, could be used by participants to explain their failure to help. Thus, there should be hardly any awareness that the victim's race influenced the participants' behavior. With the potential for such rationalization, participants could fail to help Black victims while their nonprejudiced self-images would remain unscathed. When participants were the only bystander however, the situation was quite different and they were expected to help readily, regardless of the victim's race. In view of the clarity of the emergency, failure of the single bystander to help a Black victim could very easily be self-attributed to bigoted intent. Therefore, the forces propelling action were expected to be especially strong and effective on behalf of Black victims when the bystander was alone.

The results were supportive of these predictions. Participants believing themselves to be the only bystander helped Black victims somewhat more than White victims (94% vs 81%) as we expected. Bystanders who believed that two other bystanders could also intervene, however, helped White victims more frequently than they helped Black victims (75% vs 38%). As we expected, participants with other bystanders succumbed to the opportunity to diffuse responsibility more readily for Black than for White victims. But, does this reflect participants' anti-Black sentiment as we initially believed?

Imagine yourself about to cross a busy intersection in the company of your 6-year-old nephew and other pedestrians. As you are waiting for the light to change, your nephew steps off the curb just as a huge, fast-moving truck enters the intersection. Without a moment's hesitation you reach out and pull your nephew out of harm's way. You were the only bystander to respond; the other pedestrians remained inactive. From our current perspective, the failure of these other pedestrians to intervene would not inform us about their feelings for your nephew. In the presence of other bystanders, the forces propelling action on any one of them became weaker. Only you helped when situational forces inhibited the action of others. On the basis of our attributional analysis, your intervention informs us about your sense of responsibility or your positive feelings for your nephew. We should not infer that the inaction of the others was motivated by malevolent intent toward your nephew. Similarly, the tendency to diffuse responsibility more readily for Black victims than for White victims in the Gaertner and Dovidio (1977) experiment, most likely informs us only about participants' positive attitudes toward fellow Whites and does not necessarily suggest that participants were anti-Black. Only if White bystanders who were alone helped Black victims less readily than White victims would this analysis suggest that participants' behavior was motivated by anti-Black attitudes. The results of the experiment simply do not warrant this conclusion. Rather, the findings of this study, as well as the others we have discussed, suggest that the attitudes of many Whites, particularly those who claim to be nonprejudiced but who discriminate on the basis of race nonetheless may plausibly be the result of pro-White rather than anti-Black biases.

In summary, the empirical studies reviewed in this section of the chapter illustrate that evidence originally interpreted as indicating subtle anti-Black prejudice may instead represent pro-White bias. This attributional analysis may similarly account for the results of other studies, examined in the next section, that have revealed asymmetries in the attributions and associations of positive and negative characteristics to Blacks and Whites.

Positive and Negative Attributions, Associations, and Actions

The assumption that the expression of aversive racism may be more subtle than traditional forms led us to explore alternatives to the conventional ways of assessing prejudice. Evidence has demonstrated that aversive racists do not express their bias openly on self-report scales in which the assessment of negative racial attitudes is obvious. For example, when we asked college students to evaluate Black and White people on *bipolar* scales (e.g., from "good" to "bad") we found no differences in the evaluative ratings of Blacks and Whites (Dovidio & Gaertner, 1991). We explained that, because a biased response ("bad") was obvious, aversive racists would avoid the negative end of the scales and evaluate Blacks as favorably as Whites. Thus, we explored more indirect measures of assessing bias in an attempt to capture the more subtle manifestations of contemporary forms of racism. These measures involved new types of self-report instruments and response latency techniques.

Self-Reported Biases

We pursued our rating scale studies of bias by modifying the measurement instrument slightly, placing positive and negative characteristics in separate scales (e.g., one scale for the dimension "good," another for "bad"; see Dovidio & Gaertner, 1991). Here we found that bias did exist—but in a subtle form. When the ratings of Blacks and Whites on the negative scales were examined, no racial bias appeared: Blacks were *not* rated more negatively than Whites. The ratings on the positive scales, however, did reveal a significant difference. Whereas Blacks were not rated more negatively than Whites, Whites *were* evaluated more positively than Blacks.

Similarly, Gaertner and McLaughlin (1983, Study 3) replaced conventional positive to negative scales (e.g., Ambitious–Unambitious) with negative–negative scales (e.g., Unambitious–Lazy) and positive–positive scales (e.g., Ambitious–Not Lazy). Discrimination did not appear on the negative-negative scales but did appear on the positive–positive scales. For example, Blacks were not rated as being lazier than Whites, but Whites were evaluated as being more ambitious than Blacks.

We interpreted these convergent self-report data as support for the aversive racism framework. Aversive racists would not characterize Blacks more negatively than Whites because that response could readily be interpreted, by others or oneself, to reflect racial prejudice. Bias on the positive scales is, however, more subtle and less overtly prejudiced. Thus, this pattern does not represent the phenomenon of old-fashioned racism, reflecting open and unqualified negative feelings and beliefs about Black inferiority. Nevertheless, although less overtly negative, it is still racial bias. Furthermore, this pattern of subtle bias obtained in these studies is entirely consistent with the thesis of this chapter—that contemporary bias may primarily reflect pro-White attitudes rather than anti-Black sentiments. In these studies, respondents did not indicate that Blacks were worse than Whites (outgroup derogation), only that Whites were better than Blacks (ingroup favoritism). Clearly, self-reports such as these are susceptible to evaluative concerns and impression management motivations. Consequently, we followed up these self-report studies with a series of response latency experiments (see Dovidio & Gaertner, 1993). Response latency techniques can limit the influence of consciously controlled processes and provide more social-desirability free measures of racial bias (Dovidio & Fazio, 1992).

Response Latency Measures of Bias

Response latency techniques reflect a range of different paradigms. We have used two in our investigations of racial bias. In one study (Gaertner & McLaughlin, 1983), a lexical decision task was used. Participants were presented simultaneously with two strings of letters and were asked to decide (yes or no) if both strings were words. Meyer and Schvaneveldt (1971) reported that highly associated words (e.g., doctor–nurse) produce faster response times than do unassociated words (e.g., nurse–apple). Gaertner and McLaughlin paired the words "Blacks" and "Whites" with positive and negative attributes. In a second response latency experiment (Dovidio & Gaertner, 1993), a priming paradigm was used. Rosch (1975) found that "priming" by first presenting the name of a category, such as "fruit," facilitates decisions about typical instances (e.g., "orange") more than atypical instances (e.g., "prune"). In our study, participants were first presented with the category primes "Black" and "White," representing racial groups. These primes were then followed by positive and negative characteristics. The participant's task was to decide if the characteristic could ever describe a member of the primed social category. Faster response time are assumed to reflect greater association.

The results of our two response latency studies were consistent, and they converged with the findings of the self-report studies. As indicated by response latencies, negative characteristics were not more associated with Blacks than with Whites; in both experiments, positive characteristics were more associated with Whites than with Blacks. As in our previous studies, bias exists but is expressed in an indirect and less overtly anti-Black form.

These self-report and response latency findings, using completely different paradigms than the bystander intervention studies, suggest that the biases of Whites may involve both pro-White and anti-Black components. Overall, the evidence suggests that we should consider the possibility that motives driving interracial behavior may be multi-dimensional and that pro-ingroup and anti-outgroup components may each, independently or singly, influence interracial interactions and behavior. Furthermore, as the original Gaertner (1973) telephone study suggested, the relative influence of pro-White and anti-Black components may vary systematically between aversive racists and people who express more traditional forms of racial prejudice. A study by Faranda and Gaertner (1979; see Gaertner & Dovidio, 1986a) examined this hypothesis in the context of simulated jury decisions.

Jury Decisions

This experiment by Faranda and Gaertner (1979) investigated the hypothesis that, whereas the racial biases of those who are likely to have traditionally racist attitudes (high authoritarians) will reflect primarily anti-Black biases, the racial biases of those who are likely to exhibit aversive racism (low authoritarianism) will mainly represent pro-White biases. Specifically, the experiment examined the extent to which high- and low-authoritarian scoring White college students playing the role of jurors would follow a judge's instruction to ignore inadmissible prosecution testimony that was damaging to a Black or White defendant.

Participants in this study were presented with a court transcript of a fictitious criminal case in which the defendant was accused of murdering a storekeeper and the storekeeper's child while committing a robbery. Participants receiving a description of the trial in one condition were presented with the prosecution's evidence that was weak. Participants in a second condition were presented with the same weak prosecution case plus an extremely damaging statement introduced by the prosecution that indicated that the defendant confessed about the crimes to a third party. The defense attorney objected to this statement as hearsay because the prosecution was not able to produce the third party in court. Sustaining the motion by the defense, the judge instructed the jurors to ignore this inadmissible evidence.

Both high- and low-authoritarian participants showed racial biases in their reactions to the inadmissible evidence, but they did so in different ways. In their ratings of certainty of guilt, high authoritarians did *not* ignore the inadmissible testimony when the victim was Black: They were more certain of the Black defendant's guilt when they were exposed to the inadmissible evidence than when they were not presented with this testimony. For the White defendant, however, high-authoritarian participants followed the judge's instructions perfectly: Ratings of certainty of the White defendant's guilt were equal across the two conditions. High-authoritarian participants thus showed an anti-outgroup bias. Low-authoritarian participants, in contrast, followed the judge's instructions about ignoring the inadmissible testimony when the defendant was Black. However, they were biased *in favor* of the White defendant when the inadmissible evidence was presented. That is, low-authoritarian participants were *less* certain of the White defendant's guilt when the inadmissible evidence was presented than when it was omitted. These participants later reported that they were angry with the prosecution for trying unfairly to introduce hearsay testimony. They did not express this anger, however, when the defendant was Black. Thus low-authoritarian participants demonstrated a pro-ingroup bias. It is important to note that the anti-outgroup bias of high-authoritarian participants and the pro-ingroup bias of low-authoritarian participants disadvantage Blacks relative to Whites—but in fundamentally different ways.

☐ Conclusion

This chapter has examined the possibility that racial bias, particularly in its contemporary manifestations, may reflect a pro-White, not simply anti-Black, sentiment that many traditional theories and measures have implied. Specifically, the studies reviewed pertaining to aversive racism seem amenable to this pro-White rather than anti-Black interpretation. Pro-Whiteness does not necessarily imply anti-Blackness. This does not mean, however, that anti-Black intentions do not drive interracial behavior among many Whites. Not all racists are aversive types.

Considering pro-Whiteness as an important element in intergroup relations has both theoretical and applied value for understanding, assessing, and addressing issues of racism in our society. With respect to enhancing an understanding of contemporary racism, this perspective helps to identify when and how Whites' bias will be expressed. By and large, within the studies reviewed here, Blacks were treated differently than Whites only when the forces to act favorably were weak. With regard to assessing prejudice, our analysis suggests that traditional prejudice scales that measure primarily anti-Black attitudes, either directly or indirectly, are limited in the extent to which they can capture Whites' racial attitudes. They may provide relatively accurate assessments of the intergroup attitudes of traditional racists, whose attitudes are composed mainly of anti-Black sentiments, but they offer relatively poor estimates of the attitudes of aversive racists, whose interracial attitudes apparently have a significant pro-White emphasis. Indeed, we have found across a range of studies that responses on traditional prejudice scales do not predict behavioral expressions of aversive racism (Gaertner & Dovidio, 1986a). For aversive racists, the development of self-report and response latency measures that independently assess pro-White and anti-Black sentiments (see Dovidio & Fazio, 1992) may provide more valid representations of their racial attitudes.

Appreciating the impact of pro-White attitudes in contemporary racism also offers important insight into legal, social, and personal actions that can eliminate racial bias. Current anti-discrimination laws are based largely on the premise that racial discrimination by Whites is primarily the result of anti-Black attitudes and actions. For example, the second author of this book served as an expert witness for the plaintiff in an employment discrimination case. The plaintiff, a Black man, was placed on probationary status by his employer because of some deficiencies in his performance. After review of his performance during the probationary period, the employer terminated his appointment with the company and had him physically escorted off the premises by security. The plaintiff's claim was not that his treatment violated the company's procedure but that another person—a White man—who was also on probation and whose performance during this time was comparable to that of the plaintiff's was retained and given reassignment with the company. The argument was that this represents different and unfair treatment for equivalent performance. The defense argued successfully that although the plaintiff was indeed treated differently for equivalent performance, he was not treated unfairly. His case was handled in accordance with the procedures of the company. It was acknowledged that, perhaps because of a closer personal relationship between the other worker and the supervisor, that the White employee was given an *extra* opportunity within the company. However, this special and favorable treatment toward the White (ingroup) worker, the defense claimed, is not valid *legal* grounds for demonstrating unfair and discriminatory treatment toward the Black (outgroup) employee. The defense's arguments were persuasive, and the plaintiff's case was dismissed. Thus, laws designed to protect disadvantaged individuals and groups from one type of discrimination based on anti-outgroup actions may be ineffective for addressing biased treatment based on ingroup favoritism. Awareness of the changing nature of contemporary racism may thus lead to the recognition of the need for new policies and types of laws to ameliorate the consequences of racism.

Ironically, however, motivations toward ingroup favoritism may also provide a mechanism for combating this subtle form of intergroup bias. If mere social categorization results largely in pro-ingroup biases and if aversive racism reflects primarily pro-White rather than anti-Black orientations, then the process of social categorization may play a central role in contemporary forms of racism and perhaps should be the process that is targeted for change. Factors that induce an ingroup social identity that is inclusive of both Blacks and Whites should prime more positive feelings, beliefs and behaviors toward people who would otherwise be regarded as outgroup members. This, essentially, is our objective as we review in the remainder of this book the potential of the Common Ingroup Identity Model to change intergroup behavior and then consider its potential to modify the patterns of interracial behavior like those in our research on aversive racism. Thus, although pro-Whiteness can form a basis for contemporary forms of racism, understanding its dynamics, re-structuring the definition of the ingroup, and redirecting the forces of ingroup favoritism offers a powerful strategy for addressing, socially and personally, the unintentional but insidious racial biases of aversive racists. The next chapter presents the Common Ingroup Identity Model and its theoretical foundation.

CHAPTER

Theoretical Background and the Common Ingroup Identity Model

Our purpose here is to introduce the Common Ingroup Identity Model and to describe its theoretical underpinnings. We begin by discussing some basic cognitive and motivational consequences of categorizing people into different groups and how this awareness contributes to intergroup bias. Then we discuss the importance of the social categorization perspective for reducing these biases. In this regard, we consider three categorization-based strategies for reducing bias: decategorization, mutual differentiation, and recategorization. Each of these strategies targets the social categorization process as the place to begin to understand and to combat intergroup biases. *Decategorization* encourages members to de-emphasize the original group boundary and to conceive of themselves as *separate individuals* rather than as members of different groups. *Mutual differentiation* maintains the original group boundaries, maintaining perceptions as *different groups,* but in the context of intergroup cooperation during which similarities and differences between the memberships are recognized and valued. *Recategorization* encourages the members of both groups to regard themselves as belonging to a common, superordinate group—*one group* that is inclusive of both memberships. Rather than viewing these as competing positions and arguing *which* one is correct, we suggest that these are complementary approaches and propose that it is more productive to consider *when* each strategy is most effective.

33

☐ Etiology of Intergroup Bias: The Role of Categorization

A universal facet of human thinking essential for efficient functioning is the ability to sort the many different objects, events and people encountered into a smaller number of meaningful categories (Hamilton & Trolier, 1986; Hamilton & Sherman, 1996). Categorization enables decisions to be made swiftly about incoming information because the instant an object is categorized, it is assigned the properties shared by other category members. Time consuming consideration of each new experience is forfeited because it is usually wasteful and unnecessary. Categorization often occurs spontaneously on the basis of physical similarity, proximity, or shared fate (Campbell, 1958). In this respect, people may be characterized as "cognitive misers," who compromise total accuracy for efficiency when confronted with the often overwhelming complexity of their social world (Fiske & Taylor, 1991; Macrae, Milne, & Bodenhausen, 1994).

The process of social categorization, however, is not completely uncontrollable and unalterable. Which category becomes activated is a function of the characteristics of the target person, the readiness of the perceiver (e.g., on the basis of goals or motivations), and the appropriateness of the category to the social context (Oakes, 1987; Oakes & Turner, 1990; Oakes, in press). This perspective views categorization "as a socially meaningful and appropriate activity, structured by the social realities of group life" (Spears & Haslam, 1997, p. 174). Moreover, categories may be hierarchically organized, and higher level categories (e.g., animals) are more inclusive of lower level ones (e.g., cats and dogs). By modifying a perceiver's goals, motives, past experiences, expectations, as well as factors within the perceptual field and the situational context more broadly, there is opportunity to alter the level of category inclusiveness that will be primary in a given situation. Allport's (1954, 1958) "circles of inclusion" diagram (see Figure 3.1) nicely depicts the idea that a person's potential ingroups can vary hierarchically in inclusiveness, for example from one's family to one's neighborhood, to one's city, to one's nation, to one's race, to all of humankind. Recognizing that racial group identity had become the dominant allegiance among many White racists. Allport, with hopeful intentions, questioned the common belief that ingroup loyalties need always to grow weaker and weaker the larger their circle of inclusion. In this regard Allport recognized the potential value of shifting the level of category inclusiveness from race to humankind. He recognized that "The clash between the idea of race and of One World (the two outermost circles) is shaping into an issue that may well be the most decisive in human history. The important question is, Can a loyalty to mankind be fashioned before interracial warfare breaks out?" (pp. 43–44).

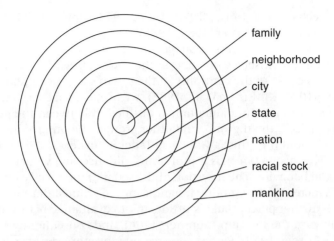

family
neighborhood
city
state
nation
racial stock
mankind

FIGURE 3.1. Rings of inclusion. From *The nature of prejudice* by G. W. Allport. Copyright 1988 by Perseus Book Publishers. Reprinted with permission.

Although perceiving people in terms of these social categories is easiest and most common in forming impressions, appropriate goals, motivation, and effort can produce more individuated impressions of others (Brewer, 1988; Fiske & Neuberg, 1990). This flexibility of the level at which impressions are formed—from broad to more specific categories to individuated responses—is important because of its implications for altering the way people think about members of other groups, and consequently about the nature of intergroup relations.

When people or objects are categorized into groups, actual differences between members of the same category tend to be perceptually minimized (Tajfel, 1969) and often ignored in making decisions or forming impressions. Members of the same category seem to be more similar than they actually are, and more similar than they were before they were categorized together. In addition, although members of a social category may be different in some ways from members of other categories, these differences tend to become exaggerated and overgeneralized. Thus, categorization enhances perceptions of similarities within groups and differences between groups—emphasizing social difference and group distinctiveness. For social categorization, this process becomes more ominous because these within- and between-group distortions have a tendency to generalize to additional dimensions (e.g., character traits) beyond those that differentiated the categories originally (Allport, 1954, 1958). Furthermore, as the salience of the categorization increases, the magnitude of these distortions also increase (Abrams, 1985; Brewer, 1979; Brewer & Miller,

1996; Dechamps & Doise, 1978; Dion, 1974; Doise, 1978; Skinner & Stephenson, 1981; Turner, 1981, 1985).

Moreover, in the process of categorizing people into groups, people typically classify themselves *into* one of the social categories (and *out of* the others). Because of the centrality of the self in social perception (Higgins & Bargh, 1987; Kihlstrom et al., 1988), we propose that social categorization involves most fundamentally a distinction between the group containing the self, the ingroup, and other groups, the outgroups—between the "we's" and the "they's" (see also Tajfel & Turner, 1979; Turner et al., 1987). This distinction has a profound influence on evaluations, cognitions, and behavior. The insertion of the self into the social categorization process increases the emotional significance of group differences and thus leads to further perceptual distortion and to evaluative biases that reflect favorably on the ingroup (Sumner, 1906), and consequently on the self (Tajfel & Turner, 1979). Perhaps one reason why ethnocentrism is so prevalent is because these biases operate even when the basis for the categorization is quite trivial, as when group identity is assigned randomly (Billig & Tajfel, 1973).

Tajfel and Turner's (1979) Social Identity Theory proposes that a person's need for positive self-identity may be satisfied by membership in prestigious social groups. Thus, this need motivates social comparisons that favorably differentiate ingroup from outgroup members. This perspective also proposes that a person defines or categorizes the self along a continuum that ranges at one extreme from the self as the embodiment of a social collective or group to the self as a separate individual with personal motives, goals, and achievements. At the individual level, one's personal welfare and goals are most salient and important. At the group level, the goals and achievements of the group are merged with one's own (see Brown & Turner, 1981), and the group's welfare is paramount. At each extreme, self interest fully is represented by the pronouns "I" and "we," respectively. Intergroup relations begin when people in different groups think about themselves as group members rather than as distinct individuals.

Self-Categorization Theory (Turner et al., 1987) is similar to Social Identity Theory but is a more general theory of inter- and intra-group processes and places greater emphasis on the cognitive processes involved. Self-Categorization Theory also makes a fundamental distinction between personal and collective identity, but these are seen more as different levels on a continuum rather than as qualitatively distinct and mutually exclusive states. When personal identity is salient, an individual's needs, standards, beliefs, and motives primarily determine behavior. In contrast, when people's social identity is activated, "people come to perceive themselves more as interchangeable exemplars of a social category than as unique personalities defined by their individual differences from others"

(Turner et al., 1987, p. 50). Under these conditions, collective needs, goals, and standards are primary. For example, Verkuyten and Hagendoorn (1998) found that when individual identity was made salient, individual differences in authoritarianism were the major predictor of prejudice of Dutch students toward Turkish migrants. In contrast, when social identity (i.e., national identity) was primed, ingroup stereotypes and standards primarily predicted attitudes toward Turkish migrants. Thus, whether a person's personal or collective identity is more salient critically shapes how a person perceives, interprets, evaluates, and responds to situations and to others.

Although the categorization process may place the person at either extreme end of the continuum from social identity to personal identity, Brewer's (1991) Theory of Optimal Distinctiveness suggests that there is a point along this continuum that optimally satisfies a person's needs for identity. At some intermediate point, an individual's need to be different from others and need to belong and share a sense of similarity to others are balanced. Optimally, perceiving one's group as especially positive and distinctive relative to other groups satisfies both needs for belonging and distinctiveness simultaneously. Unfortunately, one consequence of this process can be intergroup bias. Thus, social categorization into ingroups and outgroups may lay a foundation for intergroup bias or ethnocentrism to develop.

Sherif et al. (1961), however, proposed that the functional relation between groups is the critical factor determining intergroup attitudes. According to this position, which is also known as realistic conflict theory (see Bobo, 1999; Campbell, 1965; LeVine & Campbell, 1972), competition between groups for scarce tangible resources bodes poorly for harmonious intergroup relations. When groups are competitively interdependent, the interplay between the actions of each group results in positive outcomes for one group and negative outcomes for the other. Thus, in the attempt to obtain favorable outcomes for themselves, the actions of the members of each group are also realistically perceived to be calculated to frustrate the goals of the other group. Thus, a win–lose, zero-sum competitive relationship between groups can initiate mutually negative feelings and stereotypes toward the members of the other group (cf. L. Gaertner & Schopler, 1998).

To test these ideas, Sherif et al. (1961, reprinted in 1988) engaged 22 twelve-year-old boys in a social psychology experiment about the creation and reduction of intergroup bias and conflict. This was the third study (actually conducted in 1954) in a series of studies, the others of which were performed in 1949 and 1953. In this particular study (see also Chapter 1), the boys were initially assigned to two groups that arrived separately at the campsite. Over a three-week period, they became aware of the other group's existence, engaged in a series of competitive activities that generated overt intergroup conflict, and ultimately participated in a series of cooperative activities that successfully ameliorated conflict and bias. To permit time for group formation (e.g., norms, and a leadership structure), these groups were kept completely apart for the first week.

Sherif et al.'s (1961) detailed account of the first few days at Robbers Cave reveals that intergroup bias actually *preceded* the introduction of functionally competitive relations between the groups. Even before the groups met face-to-face or engaged one another in competitive activities, the groups had developed separate identities (self-identified as the Rattlers and Eagles), and intergroup tension and conflict were already brewing. Knowledge of the mere existence of the other group appeared to initiate bias. Sherif et al. observed:

> When the in-group began to be clearly delineated, there was a tendency to consider all others as out-group. . . . The Rattlers didn't know another group existed in camp until they heard the Eagles on the ball diamond; but from that time on the out-group figured prominently in their lives. . . . Simpson [a Rattler] was convinced that "those guys" were down at our diamond again. . . . When the Eagles were playing on the ball diamond and heard the Rattlers, Wilson [an Eagle] referred to those "nigger campers." (pp. 94–95)

Although Sherif et al. (1961) interpreted the events at Robbers Cave primarily within a functional perspective, this early observation suggests that the mere delineation of an ingroup and an outgroup, independent of and prior to win–lose, zero-sum competition, was sufficient to instigate intergroup biases (see also Billig, 1988). Consistent with a social categorization perspective (Doise, 1978; Doise & Sinclair, 1973; Tajfel, 1969), the recognition of the existence of two distinct groups may be all that was needed to foster intergroup bias, although we may not want to discount entirely the role of a perceived territorial invasion in this episode.

Additional research reveals that upon social categorization, people favor ingroup members in reward allocations (Tajfel, Billig, Bundy, & Flament, 1971; cf. L. Gaertner & Insko, in press), in esteem (Rabbie, 1982), and in the evaluation of the products of their labor (Ferguson & Kelley, 1964). People also tend to see members of the ingroup as more unique and distinct from one another than are members of the outgroup (Mullen & Hu, 1989; Ryan, Park, & Judd, 1996). Also, ingroup membership decreases psychological distance and facilitates the arousal of promotive tension or empathy (Hornstein, 1976); as a consequence, prosocial behavior is offered more readily to ingroup than to outgroup members, (Piliavin et al., 1981; Schroeder et al., 1995). Moreover, people are more likely to be cooperative and exercise more personal restraint when using endangered common resources when these are shared with ingroup members than with others (Kramer & Brewer, 1984). In terms of information processing, people retain more information in a more detailed fashion for ingroup members than for outgroup members (Park & Rothbart, 1982), have better memory for information about ways ingroup members are similar and outgroup members are dissimilar to the self (Wilder, 1981), and remember less positive information about outgroup members (Howard & Rothbart, 1980).

In addition, people are more generous and forgiving in their explanations for the behaviors of ingroup relative to outgroup members, an effect that has been called the "ultimate attributional error" (Pettigrew, 1979). Positive behaviors and successful outcomes are more likely to be attributed to internal, stable characteristics (the personality) of ingroup than outgroup, whereas members' negative outcomes are more likely to be ascribed to the personalities of outgroup members than of ingroup members (Hewstone, 1990; Pettigrew, 1979). Relatedly, observed behaviors of ingroup and outgroup members are encoded in memory at different levels of abstraction (Maass, Ceccarelli, & Rudin, 1996; Maass, Salvi, Arcuri, & Semin, 1989). Undesirable actions of outgroup members are encoded at more abstract levels that presume intentionality and dispositional origin (e.g., she is hostile) than identical behaviors of ingroup members (e.g., she slapped the girl). Desirable actions of outgroup members, however, are encoded at more concrete levels (e.g., she walked across the street holding the old man's hand) relative to the same behaviors of ingroup members (e.g., she is helpful).

These cognitive biases help to perpetuate social biases and stereotypes even in the face of countervailing evidence. For example, because positive behaviors of outgroup members are encoded at relatively concrete levels, it becomes less likely that counter-stereotypic positive behaviors would generalize across situations or other outgroup members (see also Karpinski & von Hippel, 1996). People do not remember that an outgroup member was "helpful," but only the very concrete descriptive actions. Thus, outgroup stereotypes containing information pertaining to traits, dispositions or intentions are not likely to be influenced by observing counter-stereotypic outgroup behaviors.

Language plays another role in intergroup bias through associations with collective pronouns as well as through other subtle but powerful ways (Fiedler & Schmid, in press). Collective pronouns such as "we" or "they" that are used to define people's ingroup or outgroup status are frequently paired with stimuli having strong affective connotations. As a consequence, these pronouns may acquire powerful evaluative properties of their own. These words (we, they) can potentially increase the availability of positive or negative associations and thereby influence beliefs about, evaluations of and behaviors toward other people, often automatically and unconsciously (Perdue, Dovidio, Gurtman, & Tyler, 1990).

Whereas social categorization can initiate intergroup biases, the type of bias due largely to categorization primarily represents a pro-ingroup orientation (i.e., preference for ingroup members) rather than an anti-outgroup orientation usually associated with hostility or aggression (Brewer, 1979). Nevertheless, disadvantaged status due to preferential treatment of one group over another can be as pernicious as discrimination based on anti-outgroup orientations (Murrell et al., 1994). Pro-ingroup biases can also provide a foundation for generating hostility and conflict that can result from intergroup competition for economic resources and political power.

Because categorization is a basic process that is also fundamental to intergroup bias, social psychologists have targeted this process as a place to begin to improve intergroup relations. In the next section we explore how the forces of categorization can be harnessed and redirected toward the elimination of intergroup bias.

☐ Reducing Intergroup Bias: The Role of Categorization

While it may be impossible to short-circuit the categorization process altogether, it may be possible to change the tone of the original categorical scheme as proposed by the mutual intergroup differentiation approach (e.g., from mutually threatening to trustful), proposed by Hewstone and Brown (1986), in ways that reduce the original intergroup biases. Alternatively, it may be possible to affect the level(s) of category inclusiveness people use when categorizing other people, including themselves, by altering whether people identify themselves as distinct individuals or as group members on the continuum proposed by Tajfel and Turner (1979, see also Brewer, 1988; Brewer & Miller, 1984; Fiske & Neuberg, 1990; Wilder, 1978). From these perspectives, it is possible to initiate a *decategorization* or *recategorization* of perceived group boundaries. We explore the potential roles of group differentiation, decategorization, and recategorization for reducing bias (see also, Brewer & Gaertner, in press).

Mutual Intergroup Differentiation

The Mutual Intergroup Differentiation Model (Hewstone & Brown, 1986) encourages groups to emphasize their mutual distinctiveness, but in the context of cooperative interdependence. Also, by dividing the labor in a complementary way to capitalize maximally on each group's relative superiorities and inferiorities, the members of each group can recognize and appreciate the indispensable contribution of the other. In the attempt to obtain favorable outcomes for both memberships, the actions of each group would now be realistically perceived to be calculated to satisfy their mutual goals. Thus, win–win cooperative relationships can initiate mutually favorable feelings and stereotypes toward the members of the other group while emphasizing each group's positive distinctiveness.

Evidence in support of this approach comes from the results of an experiment by Brown and Wade (1987, see also Deschamps & Brown, 1983) in which teams composed of students worked to produce a two-page magazine article. When the members of the two groups worked apart but were assigned separate roles on the joint task (one group working on figures and layout, the other working on text), the contact experience had a more positive effect on intergroup attitudes than when the groups worked apart but were assigned similar roles (both did the layout and the text for a single page), or when the groups worked together face-to-face during which no distinctive role was assigned to either group.

Similarly, the Deschamps and Brown (1983) study indicated that more favorable attitudes toward out-group members' contributions were achieved when groups worked separately but maintained different, noncomparable roles while working cooperatively on a joint product than when these roles were identical. Importantly, in the Deschamps and Brown (1983) study when the roles were noncomparable, the groups were assigned parts of the project that capitalized on their unique strengths. Science students were assigned the mathematical portion of the task, and the Arts students were assigned the verbal portion of the task. Thus, these roles were not only noncomparable, but were assigned in a complementary and functionally advantageous way. Both groups could capitalize on the special talents of the other. This very nicely exemplifies the circumstances proposed by Hewstone and Brown (1986) of how group differentiation can foster the development of mutual respect for members of each group. Cooperation can lead to more positive intergroup attitudes when the division of labor maximizes the likelihood of achieving the groups' mutual goals.

Hewstone and Brown (1986) further proposed that interactions that maintain the salience of the separate group identities are more likely to generalize to outgroup members beyond the immediate contact situational than when the distinctiveness of these group identities is degraded. Thus, generalization should be more likely with mutual differentiation than with decategorization or complete recategorization (i.e., when the dual identity representation is not primary). That is, when the associative links to initial category identities are weakened, information that is gleaned from these interactions will not likely be stored at the level of these category labels and thus preclude generalization (see Rothbart, 1996; Rothbart

& John, 1985). Supportive of these assertions, positive outgroup attitudes are more likely to generalize when interactions involve highly typical rather than atypical outgroup members (Brown, Vivian, & Hewstone, 1999; Johnston & Hewstone, 1992; van Oudenhoven, Groenwoud, & Hewstone, 1996; Vivian, Hewstone, & Brown, 1997; Wilder, 1984). In general then, there is also evidence that cooperative interactions that maintain the salience of an *us and them* representation can reduce intergroup biases. In the next section we examine the roles of these different, possibly competing but also potentially complementary, categorization approaches to improving intergroup relations.

Decategorization and Recategorization

Rather than maintaining the salience of social categories, as proposed by the Mutual Intergroup Differentiation Model, decategorization and recategorization approaches posit that intergroup bias can be decreased by reducing the salience of original group boundaries. In terms of decategorization, if group members are induced to conceive of themselves or others as separate individuals (Wilder, 1981) or to have more personalized interactions with outgroup members, intergroup bias should also be reduced (Brewer & Miller, 1984), but in ways that possibly degrade these pro-ingroup biases or by undermining the validity of outgroup stereotypes (Miller, Brewer, & Edwards, 1985). With recategorization as proposed by the Common Ingroup Identity Model (Gaertner et al., 1993), if members of different groups are induced to conceive of themselves as a single more inclusive, superordinate group, rather than just as two completely separate groups, attitudes toward former outgroup members should become more positive through processes involving pro-ingroup bias.

Theoretically, the rationale for these changes in intergroup bias rests on two related conclusions from Brewer's (1979) analysis that fit nicely with Social Identity Theory (Tajfel & Turner, 1979; Turner, 1975) and Self-Categorization Theory (Turner, 1985). First, intergroup bias often takes the form of ingroup enhancement rather than outgroup devaluation. Second, the formation of a group brings ingroup members closer to the self (Cadinu & Rothbart, 1996), whereas the distance between the self and non-ingroup members remains relatively unchanged. Thus, upon ingroup formation or when an individual assumes a group level identification, the egocentric biases that favor the self are transferred to other ingroup members. Thus, increasing the inclusiveness of group boundaries enables some of those cognitive and motivational processes that contributed initially to intergroup bias to be redirected or transferred to former outgroup members. Whereas, if ingroup and outgroup members are induced to conceive of themselves as separate individuals rather than as group members, former ingroup members would no longer benefit from the egocentric biases transferred to the group upon self-identification as a group member.

These ideas about recategorization and decategorization have also provided explanations for how the apparently loosely connected diverse features specified by the Contact Hypothesis may operate psychologically to reduce bias. Allport's (1954, 1958) revised Contact Hypothesis proposed that for contact between groups to be successful, certain prerequisite features must be present. These include equal status between the groups, cooperative (rather than competitive) intergroup interaction, opportunities for self-revealing personal acquaintance between the members, especially with those whose personal characteristics do not support stereotypic expectations, and supportive norms by authorities within and outside of the contact situation. Whereas this prescription for successful intergroup contact has been easier to write than to implement, there is evidence to support this formula when those conditions are present particularly for changing attitudes toward outgroup members who are present in the contact setting (Cook, 1984; Johnson, Johnson, & Maruyama, 1983).

Decategorization and Personalization

Brewer and Miller (1984) offered an integrative theoretical framework that proposed that the features specified by the Contact Hypothesis (e.g., equal status, cooperative interaction, self-revealing interaction, and supportive norms) share the capacity to *decategorize* group boundaries and to promote more differentiated and personalized conceptions, particularly of outgroup members. With a more differentiated representation of outgroup members, there is the recognition that there are different types of outgroup members (e.g., sensitive as well as tough professional hockey players) thereby weakening the effects of categorization and the tendency to perceptually minimize and ignore differences between category members. When personalized interactions occur, ingroup and outgroup members slide even further toward the individual side of the self as individual–group member continuum. Members "attend to information that replaces category identity as the most useful basis for classifying each other" (Brewer & Miller, 1984, p. 288) as they engage in personalized interactions.

During personalization, members focus on information about an outgroup member that is relevant to the self (as an individual rather than self as a group member). Repeated personalized interactions with a variety of outgroup members should over time undermine the value of the category stereotype as a source of information about members of that group. Thus, the effects of personalization should generalize to new situations as well as to heretofore unfamiliar outgroup members. For the benefits of personalization to generalize, however, it is of course necessary for outgroup members' group identity to be salient—at least some-what—during the interaction to enable the group stereotype to be weakened.

A number of experimental studies provide evidence supporting this theoretical perspective (Bettencourt, Brewer, Croak, & Miller, 1992; Marcus-Newhall, Miller, Holtz, & Brewer, 1993; Miller et al., 1985). In Miller et al. (1985), for example, contact that permitted more personal-ized interactions (i.e., interaction that was person-focused rather than task-focused) resulted not only in more positive attitudes toward those outgroup members who were present, but also to other outgroup mem-bers who were viewed on videotape. Thus, these conditions of intergroup contact reduced bias in both an immediate and generalizable fashion. Furthermore, personalized interaction between members of different groups can moderate the effects of task assignments to groups for reduc-ing bias, perhaps by reducing intergroup anxiety (see Stephan & Stephan, 1984), facilitating communication and encouraging more positive con-nections and sense of commonality between group members. As we dis-cussed earlier in this chapter, assigning groups to different, noncomparable tasks is more effective than assigning the groups to the same task when personalized interaction is not possible (Brown & Wade, 1987; Deschamps & Brown, 1983). When personalized interaction is possible and potential effectiveness is not threatened by the specific task assignments, however, intergroup bias is reduced more when the groups are assigned the same task than the different, noncomparable tasks (Marcus-Newhall et al., 1993). Thus, personalizing interaction can improve intergroup attitudes directly or indirectly by altering responses to different structural factors of intergroup contact.

Although there are similarities between perceiving ingroup and outgroup members as "separate individuals" and having "personalized interactions" with outgroup members, these are related but theoretically distinct con-cepts. Personalization involves receiving self-relevant, more intimate in-formation about members of the outgroup such that each can be differ-entiated from the others in relation to comparisons with the self. In contrast, perceiving either outgroup members (see Wilder, 1986) or both memberships structurally as "separate individuals" denotes perceiving them as individuals, not as groups. It does not necessarily imply that this perception is based on the exchange of personally relevant information. For example, strangers waiting for a bus may regard themselves as sepa-rate individuals, as opposed to a group, even though there may be no personal interaction between people. Increasing the perception that outgroup members are "separate individuals" by revealing variability in their opinions or having out-group members respond as individuals rather than as a group may also render each member more distinctive, and thus potentially blur the prior categorization scheme (Wilder, 1978), without the occurrence of personalized interaction.

Another decategorization strategy of repeatedly criss-crossing category memberships by forming new subgroups each composed of members from former subgroups changes the pattern of who's "in" and who's "out" (Brewer, Ho, Lee, & Miller, 1987; Deschamps & Doise, 1978; Vanbeselaere, 1987). However, the effectiveness of crossed-categorization approaches depends on the salience and dominance of the categories involved (see Crisp & Hewstone, 1999; Migdal, Hewstone, & Mullen, 1998; Urban & Miller, 1998 for reviews). Moreover, different processes may account for the reduction in bias. Consistent with a decategorization approach, crossed-categorization can decrease the salience of earlier group categories (Brown & Turner, 1981), and thereby reduce bias. Alternatively, it may shift the primary basis of categorization to a new category, a form of recategorization. Under some conditions, crossed-categorization may threaten the positive distinctiveness of important group identities and thereby exacerbate bias (see Crisp & Hewstone, 1999). Thus, decategorization is just one potential effect of crossed-categorization.

Evidence of the value of personalized interactions for reducing intergroup bias comes from data on the effects of intergroup friendships (Hamberger & Hewstone, 1997; Pettigrew, 1997; Pettigrew & Meertens, 1995). For example, across samples in France, Great Britain, the Netherlands, and Germany, Europeans with outgroup friends were lower on measures of prejudice, particularly affective prejudice (Pettigrew, 1998a). This positive relationship did not hold for other types of acquaintance relationships in work or residential settings that did not involve formation of close interpersonal relationships with members of the outgroup. In terms of the direction of causality, although having more positive intergroup attitudes can increase the willingness to have cross-group friendships, path analyses indicate that the path *from* friendship *to* reduction in prejudice is stronger than the other way around (Pettigrew, 1998a).

Other research reveals three valuable extensions of the personalized contact effect. One is evidence that personal friendships with members of one outgroup may lead to tolerance toward outgroups in general and reduced nationalistic pride, a process that Pettigrew (1997) refers to as "deprovincialization." Thus, decategorization based on developing cross-group friendships that decrease the relative attractiveness of a person's ingroup, provides increased appreciation of the relative attractiveness of other outgroups more generally. A second extension is represented by evidence that contact effects may operate indirectly or vicariously. Although interpersonal friendship across group lines leads to reduced prejudice, even knowledge that an ingroup member has befriended an outgroup member has potential to reduce bias while the salience of group identities remains high for the observer (Wright, Aron, McLaughlin-Volpe, & Ropp, 1997). A third extension relates to interpersonal processes involving the arousal of empathic feelings for an outgroup member, which can increase positive attitudes toward members of that group more widely (Batson et al., 1997). Thus, personalized interaction and interpersonal processes more generally can directly and indirectly reduce bias through a variety of processes.

In addition to *decategorization*, we propose that the features specified by the Contact Hypothesis also reduce bias through *recategorization* that increases rather than decreases the level of category inclusiveness (Gaertner et al., 1993, 1994). That is, these contact conditions facilitate a reduction in bias, in part, because they share the capacity to transform members' representations of the memberships from separate groups to a more inclusive social entity. We do not necessarily, however, regard the *decategorization* and *recategorization* frameworks to be completely mutually exclusive theoretically; we believe them to be capable of working in parallel and complementary ways as we describe in Chapter 7. Given the complexity of intergroup attitudes, it is plausible that these features of contact operate through several related as well as different pathways.

In the next section, we will present The Common Ingroup Identity Model and the potential effects of *recategorization*. Recategorization approaches are designed to alter the salient dimension of categorization, thereby changing who is considered an ingroup member. The Common Ingroup Identity Model considers factors that facilitate recategorization and the importance of the mediating role of cognitive representations of the memberships on a range of cognitive, affective, and behavioral outcomes. This model represents the organizing theme of this book.

☐ The Common Ingroup Identity Model

In contrast to the decategorization approaches described earlier, recategorization is not designed to reduce or eliminate categorization but rather to structure a definition of group categorization at a higher level of category inclusiveness in ways that reduce intergroup bias and conflict. Specifically, we hypothesize that if members of different groups are induced to conceive of themselves within a single group rather than as completely separate groups, attitudes toward former outgroup members will become more positive through the cognitive and motivational processes involving pro-ingroup bias (Gaertner et al., 1993; see also Gaertner, Dovidio, Nier et al., in press; Gaertner, Dovidio, Nier et al., 2000). Thus, for example, the newly recategorized ingroup (formerly regarded as outgroup) members will become the beneficiaries of more generous reward allocations, more positive personal evaluations, more empathic help-ful, cooperative and generally more prosocial behaviors, more forgiving situational attributions to explain failure and more dispositional attribu-tions to explain success, and information about them will be processed, stored and recovered differently than when they were regarded only as outgroup members.

This model identifies potential antecedents and outcomes of

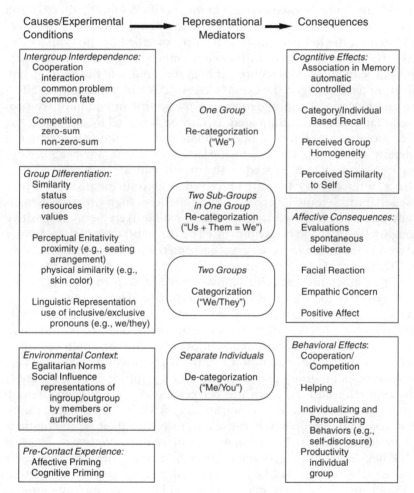

FIGURE 3.2. The Common Ingroup Identity Model. From "Across Cultural Divides: The Value of a Superordinate Identity" by S. L. Gaertner, J. F. Dovidio, J. A. Nier, C. M. Ward, & B. S. Banker, 1999. In D. A. Prentice & D. T. Miller (Eds.), *Cultural divides: Understanding and overcoming group conflict*, pp. 173–212. Copyright by the Russell Sage Foundation, New York, NY.

recategorization, as well as mediating processes. Figure 3.2 summarizes the general framework and specifies the causes and consequences of a common ingroup identity. Specifically, it is hypothesized that the different types of intergroup interdependence and cognitive, perceptual, linguistic, affective, and environmental factors can either independently or in concert alter individuals' cognitive representations of the aggregate. These resulting cognitive representations (i.e., one group, two subgroups within one group (i.e., a "dual identity"), two groups, or separate individuals) are then proposed to result in the specific cognitive, affective and overt behavioral consequences (listed on the right). Thus, the causal factors listed on the left (that include features specified by the Contact Hypothesis) are proposed to influence members' cognitive representations of the memberships (center) that in turn, mediate the relationship, at least in part, between the causal factors (left) and the cognitive, affective and behavioral consequences (on the right). In addition, we proposed that common ingroup identity may be achieved by increasing the salience of existing common superordinate memberships (e.g., a school, a company, a nation) or by introducing factors (e.g., common goals or fate) that are perceived to be shared by the memberships.

Once outgroup members are perceived as ingroup members, it is proposed that they would be accorded the benefits of ingroup status heuristically and in stereotyped fashion. There would likely be more positive thoughts, feelings, and behaviors (listed on the right) toward these former outgroup members by virtue of categorizing them now as ingroup members. These more favorable impressions of outgroup members are not likely to be finely differentiated, at least initially (see Mullen & Hu, 1989). Rather, we propose that these more elaborated, personalized impressions can soon develop within the context of a common identity because the newly formed positivity bias is likely to encourage more open communication and greater self-disclosing interaction between former outgroup members. Thus, over time, a common identity is proposed to encourage personalization of outgroup members and thereby initiate a second route to achieving reduced bias. From the perspective of the Common Ingroup Identity Model, cooperation among Sherif et al.'s groups of summer campers reduced intergroup bias because it transformed their representations of themselves from "us" and "them" to a more inclusive "we."

The development of a common ingroup identity does not necessarily require each group to forsake its less inclusive group identity completely. As Ferdman (1995) notes, every individual belongs to multiple groups. For example, Rodriguez-Scheel (1980) found that Chicanos in Detroit chose nonethnic categories, such as religion, occupation, and family, as often as ethnic labels to describe themselves. Furthermore, with regard to the "circles of inclusion" diagram (see Figure 3.1), Allport (1954, 1958) proposed, "Concentric loyalties need not clash. To be devoted to a large circle does not imply the destruction of one's attachment to a smaller circle" (p. 44). As depicted by the "subgroups within one group" (i.e., a dual identity) representation, we believe that it is possible for members to conceive of two groups as distinct units within the context of a superordinate identity (for example, parents and children within a family, or salespeople and accountants within a company). When group identities and the associated cultural values are central to members' functioning or when they are associated with high status or highly visible cues to group membership, it would be undesirable or impossible for people to relinquish these group identities or, as perceivers, to be colorblind. Indeed, demands to forsake these group identities or to adopt a color-blind ideology would likely arouse strong reactance and result in especially poor intergroup relations (see Schofield, 1986). If, however, people continued to regard themselves as members of different groups but all playing on the same team or as part of the same superordinate entity, intergroup relations between these "subgroups" would be more positive than if members only considered themselves as "separate groups" (see Brewer & Schneider, 1990). Under conditions in which subgroup identities are recognized and valued and linked positively to the superordinate group identity, a dual identity may be more effective for reducing intergroup bias and maintaining harmonious relations between groups. In the next section, we address the issue of how theoretically the benefits of intergroup contact can generalize to other group members who are not present.

☐ Generalization

Although research on the effects of intergroup contact has found support for the Contact Hypothesis for group members directly involved, these beneficial effects typically do not reliably generalize to the outgroup as a whole or to intergroup attitudes more generally (Stephan & Stephan, 1996). Nevertheless, success in promoting harmony among the members of different groups present in the contact situation is not a trivial accomplishment. In many intergroup contexts, this is precisely the major goal to be achieved.

One major reason why generalization fails is that the now positively evaluated outgroup members are regarded as exceptions and not necessarily typical of outgroup members more generally (Allport, 1954, 1958; Wilder, 1984). In this respect, the dual identity (e.g., African-American) may be a particularly promising mechanism for generalization to occur (see also Turner, 1981). A dual identity involves the recognition of both connection (superordinate group identity) and difference (original subgroup identity). The superordinate identity activates and redirects pro-ingroup biases to improve attitudes toward original outgroup members present, whereas the simultaneous salience of original identities provide the associative links for these attitudes to generalize to other members of these groups. Thus, in contrast to a separate individuals or purely one group representation, the dual identity maintains the associative link (see Rothbart, 1996; Rothbart & John, 1985) to additional outgroup members.

A dual identity, however, may be a double-edged sword. Although it may have beneficial consequences for reducing intergroup bias under many circumstances, as Social Identity Theory (Tajfel & Turner, 1979) posits, the tension created between the two identities may trigger greater intergroup conflict under other conditions. As recent national crises in Ireland and the former Yugoslavia suggest, in times of unusual competition or threat within a country or political instability, the existence of a dual identity may intensify the salience of the separate group identities and thus may refuel intergroup conflict compared to a purely one group or separate individuals representation.

Theoretically, a dual identity representation is compatible with a "Mutual Intergroup Differentiation Model" (Hewstone & Brown, 1986; Hewstone, 1996) that proposes that introducing a cooperative relationship between groups without degrading the original ingroup-outgroup categorization scheme is an effective way to change intergroup attitudes and to have these attitudes generalize to additional outgroup members. The "Trade-Off Hypothesis" (Gaertner et al., 1993), however, proposes that while attitudes toward outgroup members present during contact would be less favorable with a dual than with a purely one group identity, the modest change in attitude could more easily generalize to additional outgroup members because the associative link to their group identity remains intact.

☐ Conclusion

Social categorization is a powerful force in the development and maintenance of intergroup biases, both blatant and subtle. As suggested by the Contact Hypothesis, intergroup contact has proven to represent an effective strategy for combating bias. But, both theoretically and practically, it is important to understand *how* intergroup contact reduces bias. The benefits of this contact can occur through many routes, such as producing more individuated perceptions of outgroup members and more personalized relationships. As we propose in the Common Ingroup Identity Model, intergroup contact can also produce more inclusive, superordinate representations of the groups, which can harness and the psychological forces that contribute to intergroup bias and redirect them to improve attitudes toward people who would otherwise be recognized only as outgroup members. Understanding the processes involved in the nature and development of prejudice can thus guide, both theoretically and pragmatically, interventions that can effectively reduce both traditional and contemporary forms of prejudice. In the next chapters we offer evidence in support of the Common Ingroup Identity Model and consider its implications.

CHAPTER

Altering the Perception of Group Boundaries

The series of studies summarized in this chapter examines how a range of factors, including experimental interventions and race, can influence perceptions of group boundaries; their effects on categorical representations of the members as one group, two groups, or separate individuals; and their influence on intergroup attitudes and bias. Within the context of the Common Ingroup Identity Model and the processes outlined in Chapter 3, we hypothesized that factors that increase salience of different group boundaries in the absence of a larger connection will produce stronger two-group and weaker one-group representations which, in turn, will mediate higher levels of intergroup bias. Conversely, interventions that emphasize common group identity, even while separate group identities remain salient, are hypothesized to facilitate the development of a one, common group representation and thereby reduce intergroup bias. The next section presents studies of experimentally manipulated differentiation (e.g., on the basis of proximity); the section that follows it considers more enduring and naturalistic forms of differentiation (e.g., on the basis of race).

☐ Studies of Ad Hoc Laboratory Groups

In this section, we explore how experimental manipulations designed to increase or decrease differentiation between groups of randomly assigned participants can influence cognitive representations of the groups and intergroup attitudes. The first and third studies, drawing on principles of groupness in Gestalt psychology (see Campbell, 1958), manipulated differentiation in terms of proximity and similarity, respectively. The second study varied a range of contextual factors designed to produce representations primarily as one group, two groups, or separate individuals. The fourth and last study in this section manipulated the nature of intergroup differentiation (e.g., a blending of the groups or a take-over) in a simulated corporate merger. These studies were designed to demonstrate not only how intergroup differentiation can affect intergroup attitudes, but also how group representations play a role in this process.

Proximity

An early test of our model (Gaertner & Dovidio, 1986b) examined the way physical arrangements of the memberships in space (in terms of the seating patterns) affect the degree to which two groups perceive themselves as one unit rather than two. The idea that the arrangements of people or objects in space can influence the manner in which elements are perceptually organized is derived from some basic postulates of Gestalt psychology (i.e., laws of similarity, proximity, and common fate; see Campbell, 1958). Perhaps, in addition to other strategies, approaches that engage the visual system to induce the perception of one entity would be particularly effective with groups that are physically differentiated. Thus, if Campbell's (1958) assumption that visual processes analyze groupness rapidly and vividly compared to other perceptual and inferential processes is valid, then these forces too may be used productively toward the elimination of a problem that they may have helped to perpetuate. It was expected that the manner in which people from different subgroups are dispersed in space (e.g., around a conference table, classroom, or city) would influence their conceptual representation of the aggregate as either one group, two groups, or separate individuals and consequently their degree of intergroup bias.

In this study, two groups of four students (two males and two females) met in separate rooms to reach consensus on the best solution to the Winter Survival Problem (Johnson & Johnson, 1975). This problem is engaging and requires participants to imagine that their plane has crash-landed in the woods of northern Minnesota in mid-January and to rank-order items salvaged from the plane (e.g., a gun, newspaper, can of shortening) in terms of their importance for survival. Following the group discussion and consensus, the two groups (AAAA and BBBB) were merged together in a single room around a octagonal table. Using color-coded identifications that matched color-coded positions around a table, participants were arranged in one of three seating patterns: Segregated (AAAABBBB), Partially Integrated (AABABBAB), and Fully Integrated (ABABABAB). The participants were then asked to reach consensus again on the Winter Survival Problem. Next, questionnaires were administered to assess each participant's impression of his or her group experience. For example, participants were asked whether the merged group felt like one unit, two units or separate individuals, and whom they would vote for to be leader if the survival problem were real rather than hypothetical. It was predicted that as the seating pattern varied from Segregated (a pattern which physically emphasized subgroup boundaries) to Partially Integrated to Fully Integrated (a pattern which physically degraded subgroup boundaries) there would be decreased salience of the premerger group boundaries resulting in a greater sense of unity and decreased intergroup bias.

The results indicated that with greater integration in seating, participants more frequently experienced the merged aggregate as one unit rather than two and showed less ingroup bias in their choice for leader (see Table 4.1). Similarly, this pattern of reduced ingroup favoritism as a function of seating integration characterized participants' perceptions of the relative value of members' contributions to the solution and their ratings of friendliness between and within subgroups. When the group was used as the unit of analysis, the results also revealed that the Fully Integrated, relative to the Segregated, seating pattern increased feelings that the merged entity was one unit and reduced ingroup bias in leader selection. Furthermore, participants' individual solutions to the Winter Survival Problem at the end of the experiment suggested that participants in the

TABLE 4.1. The Effects of Seating Arrangement during the Merger.

	Segregated (15 groups)	Partially integrated (15 groups)	Fully integrated (16 groups)
Do you feel that this group acted more like:			
One unit	51.7%	63.5%	65.6%
Two units	37.9%	27.8%	21.9%
Separate individuals	10.3%	8.7%	12.5%
Voting for leadership of merged group:			
Voted for previous ingroup member	62.2%	59.5%	48.3%

From "Prejudice, Discrimination, and Racism: Problems, Progress and Promise" by S. L. Gaertner & J. F. Dovidio, 1986. In J. F. Dovidio & S. L. Gaertner (Eds.), *Prejudice, Discrimination, and Racism*, pp. 315–332. Copyright 1986 by Academic Press, Orlando, FL.

Fully Integrated condition tended to internalize the merged group's solution more than did participants in the Segregated condition.

Further evidence of the positive effects of seating arrangement is revealed in an internal analysis that examined the consequences of members conceiving the merged unit as one entity rather than as two groups. In this analysis, the impression of one unit or two was treated as an independent variable. The results revealed that participants who conceived of the aggregate as one unit perceived the merged group as more cooperative, democratic, pleasant, close, and successful than did participants who saw the group as two units. In addition, participants who perceived the merged group as one unit were more satisfied with the group atmosphere, believed that members worked better together, and had greater confidence in the group's solution. Although it is not a statistically significant effect, participants who perceived the merged group as two units tended to show an ingroup favoritism effect: They liked people who were formerly from their subgroup more than people formerly from the other subgroup. This bias did not exist among participants who saw the merged group as one unit.

These analyses suggest that the manipulation of seating arrangement influenced reductions in group bias through its effect on changing group representations. It is also possible that the effects could occur through other routes, such as personalization through greater communication (see Gaertner, Dovidio, Rust et al., 1999), or indirectly with inclusive representations leading to more intimate and personalizing exchanges (Dovidio, Gaertner et al., 1997). As we noted in Chapter 3, we view decategorization, mutual intergroup differentiation, and recategorization approaches as complementary, rather than competing strategies, that can have their effects in parallel, in concert, or sequentially.

Emphasizing Identities

This study directly investigated how categorization and cognitive representations, which are central mediating factors in our model, influence intergroup bias (Gaertner, Mann, Murrell, & Dovidio, 1989). In particular, several aspects of the intergroup interaction conditions were manipulated in ways to maintain the original categorization of members as two groups or to facilitate recategorizations as one group or as separate individuals. On the basis of the social categorization approach (Brewer, 1979; Hogg & Abrams, 1988; Tajfel & Turner, 1979; Turner, 1985; see also Chapter 3), we expected that changing members' categorized representations from two groups to either recategorized representation would reduce intergroup bias. Consequently, we expected that when members of two groups were induced to conceive of themselves as either one group or as separate individuals (i.e., no groups), they would have lower degrees of bias than those encouraged to maintain the earlier two-groups representation.

Although there was no *a priori* reason to expect different degrees of bias between one-group and separate-individuals conditions, there is a reason to expect that they would reduce bias through different processes. If the consequences of imposing a common ingroup categorization involve moving ingroup members closer to the self (Brewer, 1979; Turner, 1985; Turner et al., 1987), then bias in the one-group condition should be reduced primarily by increasing the attractiveness of former outgroup members because of their revised group status. Alternatively, decategorization to separate individuals should move ingroup members further away from the self; therefore, bias should be reduced primarily by decreasing the attractiveness of former ingroup members.

First as two three-person laboratory groups and then as a six-person aggregate, participants in this study discussed the Winter Survival Problem. The major focus of this study involved inducing the members of the original three-person groups to recategorize the six participants as one group, to continue to categorize the participants as two groups, or to decategorize the participants and conceive of them as separate individuals (i.e., no groups) by systematically varying factors within the contact situation. We manipulated aspects of the situation such as the spatial arrangement of the members (i.e., integrated, segregated, or separated seating pattern), the nature of the interdependence among the participants, and the assignment of names (i.e., assigning a group name to represent all six participants, maintaining the two earlier three-person group names, or using six different nicknames to represent the six participants). In this research, our objective was to maximally affect group representations; other research, however, was designed to examine more specifically the potentially separable influence of different components of the manipulation (e.g., seating pattern, cooperative interdependence).

Participants' subsequent ratings of the extent to which the aggregate felt like one group, two groups, or separate individuals indicated that the experimental manipulations influenced participants' conceptual representations of the aggregate as intended. For example, when asked to select which representation best characterized their view of the aggregate, 71% of the participants in the one-group condition reported "one group," 80% of the two-group condition indicated "two groups," and 68% in the separate individuals condition selected "separate individuals."

The measures of intergroup bias in this study involved evaluative ratings of each participant (e.g., How much did you like each participant? How cooperative, honest, and valuable was each person during the interaction?). An index, composed of the average of these four evaluative ratings for each participant, was calculated for ingroup and outgroup members separately. In addition, participants were asked which participant they would vote to be leader of the six participants if the survival problem were real rather than hypothetical. Because of the possible interdependence of ratings within each six-person group, the group was used as the unit of analysis.

In terms of reducing intergroup bias, the one group and the separate individuals conditions each had lower levels of bias compared to the two groups control condition, which maintained the salience of the intergroup boundary (Table 4.2). Furthermore, as expected, the recategorized (one group) condition and the decategorized (separate individuals) condition reduced bias in different ways (see Table 4.3). Specifically, in the one group condition bias was reduced (compared to the two groups control condition) primarily by increasing the attractiveness of former outgroup members, whereas in the separate individuals condition bias was reduced primarily by decreasing the attractiveness of former ingroup members. The voting measure concerning preference for an overall group leader revealed, as predicted, that a lower percentage of participants voted for an original ingroup member in the one group condition than in the two groups condition (44% vs. 62%). Voting for an ingroup member was

TABLE 4.2. Recategorization, Representations, and the Reduction of Intergroup Bias.

Members' Representations of the Aggregate

	Treatment condition		
	One group (20 groups)	Two groups (20 groups)	Separate individuals (20 groups)
Mean percentage of members selecting			
One group	71.67%	18.88%	15.83%
Two groups	21.67%	80.00%	16.67%
Separate individuals	6.67%	1.67%	67.50%
The extent to which it felt like (1–7)			
One group	5.37	3.72	2.95
Two groups	2.21	4.35	2.92
Separate individuals	1.94	1.77	4.94

From "Reducing Intergroup Bias: The Benefits of Recategorization" by S. L. Gaertner, J. Mann, A. Murrell, & J. F. Dovidio, 1989, *Journal of Personality and Social Psychology, 57*, 239–249.

Table 4.3. Evaluative Ratings of In-Group and Out-Group Members.

Rating and group member	Treatment conditions		
	One group (20 groups)	Two groups (20 groups)	Separate individuals (20 groups)
Like			
In-group	5.56	5.59	5.03
Out-group	5.31	4.90	4.59
Honest			
In-group	6.04	6.13	5.78
Out-group	5.98	5.76	5.71
Cooperative			
In-group	5.80	6.00	5.51
Out-group	5.68	5.61	5.28
Valuable			
In-group	5.45	5.46	5.24
Out-group	5.20	4.99	4.91
Average[a]			
In-group	5.71	5.80	5.39
Out-group	5.54	5.31	5.12

[a]Average of like, honest, cooperative, and valuable.
From "Reducing Intergroup Bias: The Benefits of Recategorization" by S. L. Gaertner, J. Mann, A. Murrell, & J. F. Dovidio, 1989, *Journal of Personality and Social Psychology, 57,* 239–249.

equivalent for the separate individuals condition (65%) and the two groups condition, but, consistent with the intended manipulation, this was due in part to the fact that a higher percentage of participants voted for themselves in the separate individuals condition (27%) compared to the one group (9%) and two groups (17%) conditions.

In general, the pattern of findings supports the Common Ingroup Identity Model and, in particular, the proposed processes by which reduced bias would be achieved within the one group and separate individuals conditions. Specifically, these strategies reduced bias in different ways. Recategorizing ingroup and outgroup members as members of a more inclusive group reduced bias by increasing the attractiveness of the former outgroup members. Decategorizing members of the two groups by inducing conceptions of themselves as separate individuals, decreased bias by diminishing the attractiveness of former ingroup members, an effect similar to deprovincialization (Pettigrew, 1997) involving the reduction of nationalistic pride as a mechanism for alleviating intergroup bias. Considering both decategorization and recategorization, the findings are consistent with Turner's (1985) theory of self-categorization: "the attractiveness of an individual is not constant, but varies with the ingroup membership" (p. 60; see also Turner & Reynolds, in press).

Similarity

Another principle of Gestalt psychology that is proposed to influence perceptions of entitativity is perceptual similarity. Thus in another study (Dovidio, Gaertner, Isen, & Lowrance, 1995) designed to test the Common Ingroup Identity Model we varied as a perceptual cue of similarity the distinctiveness of dress (as well as group size and affect, which will be discussed in detail in Chapter 6). Previous research has demonstrated that similarity of dress can influence intergroup bias (Worchel, Axsom, Ferris, Samaha, & Schweitzer, 1978); our primary focus was on the intervening role of cognitive representations of the groups, and thus the direct *and* indirect paths from this manipulation to bias.

Participants in the present study first participated in groups in a problem-solving task, as in our previous studies. Then, in preparation for a combined-group interaction, they saw a videotape, ostensibly of the other group. The videotape portrayed three confederates, always wearing regular clothing, performing a similar problem-solving task. The perceptual cue that was varied in the present study related to whether participants wore laboratory coats or not during the session. It was hypothesized that wearing laboratory coats would provide a visual cue that would accentuate both intragroup similarity and intergroup differentiation (see Campbell, 1958; Worchel et al., 1978) and increase the likelihood of a two-group representation (relative to a one-group representation) compared to the condition in which participants did not wear laboratory coats. Stronger two-group representations relative to the one, superordinate group representation was expected, in turn, to predict less positive outgroup evaluations and higher levels of bias.

As predicted, participants in dissimilarly dressed groups expected the memberships to feel more like two groups and less like one group. Consistent with the Common Ingroup Identity Model, stronger two-group representations predicted less favorable outgroup attitudes and higher levels of bias. Stated another way, stronger superordinate group representations are related to lower levels of intergroup bias. In addition, similarity of participants' dress reduced bias, although this effect was indirect, occurring primarily because it created stronger superordinate group representations. In a path analysis (see Chapter 6 for more details), the direct path from dress to evaluations was not significant. Overall, these findings are consistent with the model and highlight the importance of considering the potential mediating role of group representations.

Mergers

The nature of intergroup relations and identities can be profoundly important in corporate mergers. Nearly 6,000 mergers and acquisitions occurred in 1995 with a total value of over 388 billion dollars (M & A Almanac, 1996). However, it is estimated that between 50% and 80% of all mergers end in financial failure (Marks & Mirvis, 1985). Although strategic, financial, and operational issues are important (Jemison & Sitkin, 1986), interpersonal and intergroup processes are also critical (Buono & Bowditch, 1989). Merging two previously separate organizations often results in low levels of commitment to the merged organization (Schweiger & Walsh, 1990). To examine how the processes we hypothesize in the Common Ingroup Identity Model apply to intergroup contact within the context of a corporate merger, we executed a laboratory experiment (Mottola, Bachman, Gaertner, & Dovidio, 1997) that varied participants' perceptions of the contact conditions for the merger.

In this study we manipulated group differentiation in terms of the merger integration pattern. Specifically, undergraduates role-played employees of a merging organization, and written scenarios manipulated the integration pattern and membership in the acquired or acquiring organization. The culture (policies and norms) of the merged organization reflected either just one of the premerger company's culture (an *absorb* pattern), aspects of both companies (a *blend* pattern), or an entirely new culture (a *combine* pattern). Measures included expectations of the favorability of contact between the company memberships, perceptions of organizational support (Eisenberger, Huntington, Hutchinson, & Sowa, 1986), ratings of organizational unity, feelings of threat, and organizational commitment. The measure of organizational unity corresponded to a superordinate group representation, and the primary dependent measure was organizational commitment. It was hypothesized that merger conditions would significantly influence the favorability of anticipated group relations and personal support, with responses being most positive for the *combine* condition, intermediate for the *blend* conditions, and least positive in the *acquire* condition. Higher ratings of organizational unity, in turn, were expected to predict lower levels of employee threat and ultimately higher levels of organizational commitment.

The results supported the predictions. As expected, perceptions of the conditions of contact, organizational support, and organizational unity were most favorable with the *combine* pattern followed in turn by the *blend* and the *absorb* patterns. Also, more central to the Common Ingroup Identity Model, the effects of more favorable conditions of contact and greater organizational support on increased organizational commitment was mediated by participants' perceptions of organizational unity (i.e., one group).

The support for the Common Ingroup Identity Model provided by the laboratory studies reported in the previous section highlights the importance of both cognitive and motivational processes for reducing biases and potentially for changing stereotypes. As Turner's (1981) analysis of the literature indicates, it is "difficult to explain discrimination on the basis of ingroup-outgroup divisions solely in terms of cognitive processes; motivational factors need to be superimposed" (p. 82). The Common Ingroup Identity Model assumes that viewing former outgroup members as part of a larger ingroup provides the motivation to evaluate these members in a more positive light while relying on (rather than undermining) the tendency for people to categorize. These studies are also important because they help to establish experimentally the direction of causality proposed by the model. Thus, we can be more confident about the plausibility of the direction of causality suggested in subsequent correlational studies.

But this does not necessarily mean that a one-group identity is necessary or even desirable in every situation. For instance, a one-group identity under more naturalistic conditions might require participants to forsake their former group identity, an approach which does not promote the multicultural environment many groups desire. Furthermore, it is possible that even if a common ingroup identity improved relations among members present, the benefits might not generalize to attitudes toward the groups as a whole. A common, one-group identity (or even seeing people only as individuals) may sever cognitive associations with one's former ingroup identity to some extent; should that occur, then it is also possible that the resulting positive evaluations of former outgroup members have few if any links to the original outgroup (see Rothbart, 1996, in press; Rothbart & John, 1985; Hewstone & Brown, 1986). A one-group representation therefore may not be desirable for purposes of generalization. However, if members of different groups maintained their ethnic identities but conceived of themselves as having a dual identity (as though they were members of different groups but all playing on the same team or two subgroups within one larger group), the intergroup consequences may be more favorable than if they only regarded themselves as separate groups. The set of studies reported in the next section, conducted by us and by other researchers, helps to extend the principles outlined by the Common Ingroup Identity Model to situations involving racial and ethnic identities in both naturalistic and laboratory settings.

☐ Studies of Naturalistic Groups

In this section, we first consider the results of two of our own experiments involving race, one conducted in the field and the other in the laboratory. Then we review related findings from other researchers that investigate how the different salience of ethnic group and superordinate group identities relates to intergroup behavior, attitudes, orientations, and relations.

Race

The potential of a common ingroup identity to facilitate helping may extend to naturalistic groups having histories of past and contemporary conflict. A field experiment (Nier, Gaertner, Dovidio, Banker, & Ward, 1999, Study 2) conducted at the University of Delaware football stadium prior to a game between the University of Delaware and Westchester State University demonstrates how salient superordinate and subgroup identities can increase behavioral compliance with a request for assistance from a person of a different race. In this experiment, Black and White, male and female students approached fans of the same sex as themselves from both universities just before the fans entered the stadium. These fans were asked if they would be willing to be interviewed about their food preferences. Our student interviewers systematically varied whether they were wearing a University of Delaware or Westchester State University hat. By selecting fans who similarly wore clothing that identified their university affiliation, we systematically varied whether fans and our interviewers had a common or different university identity in a context in which we expected university identities to be particularly salient. Although we planned to over-sample Black fans, the sample was still too small to yield any informative findings.

Among White fans, however, sharing common university identity with the Black interviewers reliably increased their compliance (50%) relative to when they did not share a common identity with the Black interviewer (38%). When the interviewers were White, however, they gained similar levels of compliance when they shared common university identity with the fan (43%) than when they appeared to be affiliated with the rival university (40%). These fans were not color-blind—only Black interviewers who shared a common university affiliation with the fans were accorded especially high levels of compliance. Although there are a number of different plausible explanations for this particular pattern of compliance (which we soon discuss), we note that these findings offer support for the idea that outgroup members can be treated especially favorably when they are perceived to also share a more inclusive, common ingroup identity.

The especially positive reaction to racial outgroup members who share common superordinate identity was also revealed in a laboratory experiment (Nier et al., 1999, Study 1). In this study, White students participating with a Black or White confederate were induced to perceive themselves as individuals participating simply at the same time or as members of the same laboratory team. The results demonstrated a significant interaction involving the other participant's race and the team manipulation. Whereas the evaluations of the White partner were virtually equivalent in the Team and Individual conditions, the evaluations of the Black partner were significantly more positive when they were teammates than when they were just individuals without common group connection. In fact, for members of the same team, Black partners were evaluated *more* favorably than were White partners. Thus, in field and laboratory settings, racial outgroup members were accorded especially positive reactions when they shared common group identity with White participants relative to when the context did not emphasize their common group membership.

The differences in behavior toward Blacks with and without common team affiliations across both studies suggest that a common team affiliation *increased* positive reactions to Blacks, rather than that different team affiliations decreased these behaviors. In both studies, the reactions of the respondents to Blacks in the different group (team or university) conditions were roughly equivalent to their reactions to Whites. That is, relative to the other conditions, Blacks who were portrayed as sharing common identity with our participants were treated particularly positively relative to each of the other three conditions.

Ironically for us, given our current focus on the Common Ingroup Identity Model, one alternative explanation for the especially positive reaction to racial outgroup members in the common group conditions of these last two studies involves aversive racism. The aversive racism perspective suggests that bias by Whites against Blacks occurs primarily when it can be rationalized on the basis of some factor other than race (see Chapter 2). Identification with an opposing team may serve as one such factor. For example, a White fan who was approached by a Black interviewer affiliated with the opposing team's university could refuse the request on the basis of the person's university affiliation rather than on his or her race. That is, the respondent may reason, "I refuse to be interviewed by someone from the opposing team's school; it has nothing to do with that person's race." In the Common University condition, in which the interviewer is from the respondent's own institution, this nonracial rationalization for refusing to participate is unavailable. Moreover, in the absence of this nonrace-related justification, respondents in the Common University condition may be especially likely to comply with a Black interviewer's request to avoid acting in a way that could be attributed to racial prejudice. Nevertheless, although an aversive racism interpretation is possible, not all of the data are consistent with it. In particular, if different university affiliations provided a sufficient nonracial justification for refusing the interviewer's request, Black interviewers would be expected to receive less assistance than White interviewers in the Different University condition. This was not the case, however: White fans complied equally often with these requests.

Another possible explanation, which is more consistent with the Common Ingroup Identity framework, for the very positive treatment of Blacks who share common identity with White respondents is that "newly regarded" ingroup members are often accorded special treatment by group members (Moreland & Levine, 1982). In our field study, respondents may not have previously shared a sense of common group membership or closeness with a Black person. The salience of a common university identification in this context may have thus produced recategorization in which Blacks were now conceived as "new" ingroup members, thus producing an amplified positive response to Black interviewers. Clearly, additional research that teases apart these alternative explanations would be very useful. In general, however, we are encouraged by the results of these last two field and laboratory studies for the value of emphasizing common group membership for addressing traditional racial biases.

Ethnicity

We are also encouraged by some independent evidence demonstrating the capacity of increasing the salience of a common, superordinate identity on reducing subtle linguistic biases that serve to perpetuate stereotypes (Maass, Ceccarelli, & Rudin, 1996; Study 2). Semin and Fiedler (1992) observed that reports of others' behaviors can vary systematically from concrete and specific (e.g., A hits B) to abstract and generally dispositional (e.g., A is aggressive). Although these descriptions may be equally accurate, the meaning and implications differ significantly. More abstract descriptions imply greater consistency over time, stability, and typicality. Their effects are also more perseverant because they are more difficult to refute or undermine with counterexamples. Maass and her colleagues have extended this analysis to linguistic intergroup bias. Specifically, Maass and Arcuri (1996) stated:

> Because abstract terms such as "state" verbs and adjectives imply great temporal and cross-situational stability, as well as a high likelihood of repetition in the future, this differential language use may indeed bolster existing stereotypic beliefs. Behaviors that confirm negative expectations about the out-group are communicated in an abstract way, suggesting that the observed act reflects a stable characteristic or psychological state of the

actor. In contrast, an unexpectedly positive behavior from an out-group member is described in concrete terms, without generalizing beyond the specific context, thereby leaving the stereotype intact. (p. 210)

In the Maass et al. (1996) laboratory experiment, northern and southern Italians living in Switzerland received messages that emphasized the differentiation between northern and southern Italians (in a two groups condition), or between Italians and the Swiss (in a superordinate "Italian" condition). These participants were then shown cartoons depicting northern and southern Italians performing positive and negative behaviors. Participants were then asked to choose one of four response alternatives corresponding to the four levels of abstraction (see Semin & Fiedler, 1988).

When the distinction between northern and southern Italians was emphasized, the results replicated the linguistic bias effect. Higher levels of abstraction were used to describe positive behaviors of ingroup members (e.g., she is helpful) than for outgroup members (e.g., she walked with the old lady). Also, higher levels of abstraction were used to describe undesirable behavior of outgroup members than for ingroup members. This linguistic bias was not evident in the superordinate identity condition. While this is quite supportive of the value of emphasizing a common, superordinate identity, the exact pattern of change was a bit different than what we would expect. Bias decreased, but not because participants decreased the level of abstraction used to describe the negative behaviors of outgroup members. Rather, participants increased the level of abstraction to describe the negative behaviors of ingroup members. Also, a superordinate identity decreased the bias participants used to encode positive behaviors of ingroup and outgroup members. Specifically, participants decreased the level of abstraction used to describe desirable ingroup behaviors and also, as expected, they increased the level of abstraction used to encode the positive behaviors of outgroup members. While this pattern of results is reasonably complicated, it is clear that a superordinate identity fundamentally changed the way behavioral information about ingroup and outgroup members was processed and importantly, in a way that reduced this subtle bias in information processing.

Social Justice and Social Categorization

In general, people consider the fairness of both outcomes (distributive justice) and procedures (procedural justice) when evaluating their satisfaction with decisions and their consequences (Tyler, in press). The weights given to outcomes and procedures vary, however, as a function of context. For example, van den Bos, Wilke, Lind, and Vermunt (1998) found that the effects of procedural fairness were stronger when outcomes were better or worse than expected than when they corresponded to expectations. Tyler and Lind (1992) demonstrate that the *social context*, specifically identification with groups, is also important. Cross-culturally, people consider procedural fairness (relational concerns) more strongly than personal outcomes (instrumental concerns) in exchanges with ingroup relative to outgroup members (Tyler, Lind, Ohbuchi, Sugawara, & Huo, 1998).

Other research involving social justice supports the value of a dual racial or ethnic identity for reducing bias and improving intergroup relations. With respect to the importance of group identities, two studies further suggest that the intergroup benefits of a strong superordinate identity remain relatively stable even when the strength of the subordinate identity becomes equivalently high (Huo, Smith, Tyler, & Lind, 1996; Smith & Tyler, 1996). This suggests that social cohesion does not require individuals to deny or forsake their ethnic identity.

One of these studies, a survey study of White adults by Smith and Tyler (1996, Study 1), measured the strength of respondents' superordinate identity as "American" and also the strength of their identification as "White." Following Berry's (1984) strategy of creating four groups on the basis of a median split on each measure, the investigators identified four groups of respondents that varied in terms of the relative strength of their superordinate and subgroup identities. The results revealed that regardless of whether they strongly identified with being White, those respondents with a strong American identity were more likely to base their support for affirmative action policies that would benefit Blacks and other minorities on relational concerns regarding the fairness of congressional representatives than on whether these policies would increase or decrease their own well being. However, for the group members who identified themselves more strongly with being White than being American, their position on affirmative action was determined more strongly by concerns regarding the instrumental value of these policies for themselves.

In a subsequent survey study by Huo et al. (1996) of people of color, strong identification with one's ethnic group in the absence of identification with a superordinate entity (work organization) was related to a focus on concrete outcomes, which adversely affects cohesion in a multicultural setting. In contrast, strong identification with the superordinate group—even in combination with strong ethnic group identification—was related to greater consideration of relational justice, which involves perceptions that others are fair, unbiased, and trustworthy.

The pattern of findings across these two survey studies suggests that a strong superordinate identity allows individuals to support policies and actions that would benefit members of other racial subgroups without giving primary consideration to their own instrumental needs. Furthermore, once people identify with the superordinate entity, the relative strength of their subgroup identities does not strongly change the basis for determining their support for policies that will benefit other groups within the superordinate collective. This also provides evidence that superordinate identities influence attitudes toward members of other subgroups more broadly rather than being limited to only those specific subgroup members encountered during intergroup contact.

☐ Conclusion

Taken together, the studies reported in this chapter provide convergent evidence for not only predictions derived from the Common Ingroup Identity Model about intergroup attitudes and bias but also about the key mediating role of group representations. The laboratory studies permit direct manipulation of factors that facilitate *one group, two groups,* or *separate individuals* representations. As expected, recategorization from two groups to one group or separate individuals reduces intergroup bias—but in different ways. With the one-group representation, bias is reduced by increasing the attractiveness of former outgroup members; with the separate individuals representation, bias is reduced by decreasing the attractiveness of former ingroup members. Because of the experimental control involved, these studies help to establish the order of causality proposed in our model.

One question raised about the Common Ingroup Identity approach involves the robustness of the effects. Hewstone (1996), for example, wrote: "The first and most obvious criticism of this approach is that it may not be realistic. Can the recategorization process and the creation of a superordinate identity overcome powerful ethnic and racial categorizations on more than a temporary basis?" (p. 351). The results of our football fans study indicate that interventions designed to increase the salience of a common ingroup identity are sufficient to produce, *at least temporarily*, more positive interracial behavior. Thus, returning to the issues we raised in Chapter 2, the Common Ingroup Identity Model has the potential to address contemporary and subtle forms of racism, such as aversive racism. Moreover, the research by Maass and her colleagues and by Tyler and his colleagues suggests that the effects may be more enduring. The experiment by Maass et al. (1996) demonstrated that emphasizing common nationality significantly reduced the linguistic intergroup bias effect, an effect that helps to perpetuate stereotyping and intergroup bias. The work of Smith and Tyler (1996) and Huo et al. (1996) indicates that identification with a superordinate entity (a nation or a work organization) influences the extent to which people focus on concerns of fairness and justice rather than their own personal outcomes and benefits. Whites who identified themselves primarily as Americans (rather than as Whites) were more supportive of policies designed to ameliorate the consequences of past injustices for people of color. People of color who showed strong identification with their work organization, regardless of the strength of their ethnic or racial group identification, exhibited greater trust and confidence in their supervisors and also focused more on fairness than personal outcomes in their interactions within the organization. These findings suggest that the benefits of recategorization may extend, directly and indirectly, beyond a temporary basis. We return to this issue in Chapters 6 and 7 of the book. It is also possible that the development of a common ingroup identity in combination with functional aspects of intergroup contact may promote more enduring effects. Whereas the present chapter examined factors that primarily relate to variations in the salience of a common group or different group identities, the next chapter explores the roles of other factors traditionally identified as critical within the Contact Hypothesis (Allport, 1954; see also Pettigrew, 1998a).

Nevertheless, we believe that frameworks such as the Common Ingroup Identity Model have both conceptual and applied value. Conceptually, approaches that focus on common *processes* provide more direct and parsimonious explanations than do approaches that simply identify a list of important contextual factors. The effects of diverse social and perceptual factors may be understood on the basis of their impact on fundamental psychological processes—in this case, on cognitive representations of the groups. In terms of practical considerations, in naturalistic intergroup situations it may be difficult to establish many of the specific conditions (e.g., equal status interaction) identified by the Contact Hypothesis. An understanding of the basic processes involved, however, permits the identification of alternative strategies that may be more feasible to implement but that have similar effects on representational processes. Thus, different techniques that are more suitable to a particular situation may be used to achieve the reduction of intergroup bias.

5
CHAPTER

Conditions of Intergroup Contact

For the past fifty years the "Contact Hypothesis" (Allport, 1954; Amir, 1969; Miller & Brewer, 1984; Cook, 1985; Hewstone & Brown, 1986; Watson, 1947; Williams, 1947; see also Hewstone, 1996; Pettigrew, 1998a) has represented a promising and popular strategy for reducing intergroup bias and conflict. It proposes that intergroup contact *under certain prerequisite conditions* promotes the development of more harmonious intergroup relations. Among these specific conditions are equal status between the groups (optimally within and outside of the contact setting), cooperative intergroup interaction, opportunities for personal acquaintance between outgroup members, and norms within and outside of the contact setting that support egalitarian intergroup interaction (Cook, 1985; Pettigrew, 1998a). Research within laboratory and field settings generally supports the efficacy of the list of prerequisite conditions for achieving improved intergroup relations (Blanchard, Weigel, & Cook, 1975; Cook, 1969, 1985; Deutsch & Collins, 1951; Green, Adams, & Turner, 1988; Schofield & Eurich-Fulcer, in press; Stephan, 1987, 1999; Weigel, Wiser, & Cook, 1975).

Structurally, however, the Contact Hypothesis has represented a list of loosely connected, diverse conditions rather than a unifying conceptual framework that explains *how* these prerequisite features achieve their effects. This is problematic because political and socioeconomic circumstances (e.g., real or perceived competitive, zero-sum outcomes) often preclude introducing these features (e.g., cooperative interdependence, equal status) into many contact settings. In the absence of an explanatory framework, it is not clear what alternatives could be substituted for these specific conditions that would produce similar psychological effects. The Common Ingroup Identity Model potentially provides an integrative framework, focusing on how these diverse situational factors operate through the convergent mechanism of changing cognitive representations of the groups.

Allport (1954, 1958) was aware of the benefits of a common ingroup identity, although he regarded it as a catalyst rather than as a product of the conditions of contact:

> To be maximally effective, contact and acquaintance programs should lead to a sense of equality in social status, should occur in ordinary purposeful pursuits, avoid artificiality, and if possible enjoy the sanction of the community in which they occur. While it may help somewhat to place members of different ethnic groups side by side on a job, the gain is greater if these members regard themselves as part of a *team*. (Allport, 1958, p. 489, emphasis added)

This chapter examines how four of the factors identified as critical in the Contact Hypothesis can improve intergroup relations. These four factors are intergroup cooperation, common goals, supportive norms, and equal status. Because the factor involving opportunities for personal acquaintance relates most directly to decategorization processes, we will consider it more thoroughly in Chapters 7 and 8 as we discuss how recategorization and decategorization processes may be complementary. Although the value of these factors is well-established empirically (see Pettigrew, 1998a), we focus on the mediating role of cognitive representations and some moderating factors (e.g., identity threat).

☐ Intergroup Cooperation

Despite substantial documentation that intergroup cooperative interaction reduces bias (Allport, 1954; Aronson, Blaney, Stephan, Sikes, & Snapp, 1978; Aronson & Patnoe, 1997; Cook, 1985; Deutsch, 1973; Johnson et al., 1983; Sherif, Harvey, White, Hood, & Sherif, 1954; Slavin, 1985; Worchel, 1979), it is not clear how cooperation achieves this effect. One basic issue involves the psychological processes that mediate this change.

The classic functional relations perspective by Sherif et al. (1954) views cooperative interdependence as a direct mediator of attitudinal and behavioral changes. However, several additional explanations have been proposed (see Brewer & Miller, 1984; Miller & Davidson-Podgorny, 1987; Worchel, 1979, 1986). For example, cooperation may induce greater intergroup acceptance as a result of dissonance reduction serving to justify this type of interaction with the other group (Miller & Brewer, 1986; see also Leippe & Eisenstadt, 1994); as a result of the positive, reinforcing consequences of mutual cooperation (Lott & Lott, 1965) or as a result of increases in knowledge about the other group, which reduces intergroup anxiety (Stephan & Stephan, 1984). An additional model that may account for the effects of cooperation is Tajfel's (1969) and Tajfel and Turner's (1979) work on social categorization. This approach proposes that intergroup cooperation promotes intergroup acceptance because it reduces the cognitive salience of the intergroup boundary (see also Wilder, 1986). A related position of Miller and Brewer (1984) proposes, in addition, that when cooperative interaction permits members' attention to focus on one another's personal qualities, it contributes to personalized rather than categorized interactions and thereby to reduced bias. Also, Neuberg and Fiske (1987) have shown more generally that cooperative interdependence increases motivation to form more individuated impressions.

Within the framework of the Common Ingroup Identity Model, we hypothesize that intergroup cooperation (with task-oriented interaction and common fate; see also Johnson, 1991) reduces bias, at least in part, because intergroup cooperation reduces the salience of the intergroup boundary. Specifically, we propose that intergroup cooperation induces the members to conceive of themselves as one (superordinate) group rather than as two separate groups, thereby transforming their categorized representations from "us" and "them" to a more inclusive "we" (see Brown & Turner, 1981; Doise, 1978; Feshbach & Singer, 1957; Hornstein, 1976; Turner, 1981; Worchel et al., 1978). Indeed, Sherif (Sherif & Sherif, 1969, p. 288; see also Sherif, 1966, p. 158) acknowledged the potential that intergroup interaction has toward facilitating the development of a common superordinate identity. This possibility, however, was conceived by Sherif and Sherif to represent the very gradual development of a highly structured superordinate group rather than the immediate creation of a social entity that may only exist more ephemerally within the perceptions of one or more of its members.

To test the hypotheses derived from the Common Ingroup Identity Model, we conducted an experiment involving two three-person groups in which cooperative interaction was manipulated independently of perceptions of the aggregate (Gaertner, Mann, Dovidio, Murrell, & Pomare, 1990). The design allowed the effects of cooperation to be experimentally separated from the effects of cognitive representations of the aggregate. Cooperation was manipulated by having two separately formed laboratory groups of three individuals interact to achieve a common goal which determined their shared fate; groups in the noncooperation condition merely sat together and listened to a recording of a third group's discussion. Perceptions of the two memberships (Group A and B) as two groups or one were manipulated through seating arrangements (AAABBB vs ABABAB), the use of the groups' different names or the assignment of a new group name to represent the six participants, and other structural factors used in an earlier study (see Chapter 4). Measures of bias ("How much did you like each participant?" "How cooperative, honest, and valuable was each person during the interaction?"), as well as perceptions of the aggregate (how much the aggregate of six felt like one group, two groups, or separate individuals) were the main dependent measures.

In the absence of cooperative interaction and shared fate, participants induced to feel like one group relative to those in the two group conditions reported that the aggregate did feel more like one group and they also had lower degrees of intergroup bias in their evaluations (likable, cooperative, honest, trustworthy) of ingroup and outgroup members. We regarded this as an important finding because it helps to establish the causal relation between the induction of a one-group representation and reduced intergroup bias even in the absence of intergroup cooperation.

Supportive of the basic proposition of the Common Ingroup Identity Model, among participants induced to feel like two groups, the introduction of cooperative interaction increased their perceptions of one group and also reduced their bias in evaluative ratings relative to those who did not cooperate during the contact period. As expected, reduced bias associated with introducing cooperation was due to enhanced favorable evaluations of the recategorized outgroup members. Consistent with Brewer's (1979) analysis, cooperation appeared to move people originally perceived as outgroup members closer to the self as they became recategorized as ingroup members. Consistent with our mediation hypothesis, cooperation induced a sense of group formation between the members of the two groups and also reduced bias.

More direct support for the mediation hypothesis was revealed by the multiple regression mediation approach (see Figure 5.1) suggested by Baron and Kenny (1986; see also Judd & Kenny, 1981). The multiple regression mediation approach (a form of path analysis) used three regression analyses involving the independent variable of cooperation (yes, no); the potential mediators of the extent (1–7) to which the aggregate was rated as One Group, Two Groups, Separate Individuals; the degree of perceived cooperativeness and competitiveness during the contact period, and the dependent variable, the evaluations of outgroup members or evaluative bias. The multiple regression mediation analysis uses a series of regression analyses to establish mediation. The first analysis tests whether the conditions of contact predict evaluations of outgroup members. This is similar to a main effect for the independent variable in an analysis of variance within an experimental design. The second analysis examines whether these conditions of contact also influence the proposed mediators (i.e., representations of the aggregate as One Group, Two Groups, and Separate Individuals). The third analysis considers the antecedent

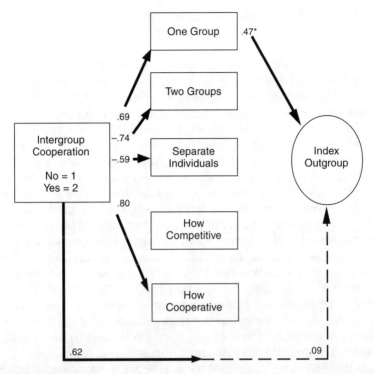

FIGURE 5.1. The effects of cooperation on the evaluation of outgroup members. Adapted from "How Does Cooperation Reduce Intergroup Bias," by S. L. Gaertner, J. A. Mann, J. F. Dovidio, A. J. Murrell, & M. Pomare, 1990, *Journal of Personality and Social Psychology, 59,* pp. 562–704.

conditions and the proposed mediators simultaneously and tests whether one or more of the proposed mediators relate to evaluative bias over and above the effects of the others variables. Also, in this third analysis, the effects of contact on the evaluation of outgroup members, independent of the mediators, should be weaker than before; with complete mediation, the conditions of contact would no longer relate directly to bias.

The results strongly supported the type of mediation proposed by the model. The thick, embolded arrows in Figure 5.1 indicate reliable relationships. Also, across all of our figures depicting mediation analyses, thick lines originating from a presumed causal variable (e.g., Intergroup Cooperation in Figure 5.1) that become thinner indicate that reliable direct paths became less reliable when the potential mediators are accounted for, and dashed lines represent direct paths that are no longer significant after the mediators are considered. For mediating variables (e.g., Two

Groups in Figure 5.1) nonsignificant paths are indicated by thin lines or, in more complex figures (such as this one), by the absence of lines.

Consistent with the hypothesized pattern of mediation in this study, first the independent variable of Cooperation does influence participants' ratings of how much it feels like one group (beta = .69), two groups (beta = −.74), and separate individuals (beta = −.59), as well how cooperative they were (beta = .80; see Figure 5.1). Second, the independent variable of cooperation, before consideration of the mediators, also causes changes in the evaluation of outgroup members (beta = .62). Because this is an experiment rather than a correlational study, we can speak about the direction of causality for each of the previously mentioned effects in un-ambiguous terms. That is, we can be certain that the cooperation ma-nipulation preceded respondents' representations of the groups and also their degree of intergroup bias. Third, when the ratings of outgroup mem-bers are regressed on the independent variable of Cooperation together with all of the potential mediators simultaneously (overall adjusted R^2 = .48), only the extent to which it feels like one-group is associated with higher evaluations of outgroup members (beta = .47), and also the inde-pendent variable of cooperation no longer predicts the evaluations of outgroup (beta = .09); note that the thick, embolded arrow from Coop-eration to evaluations of the outgroup becomes thinner to thereby depict this weaker relationship after the mediators are considered.

In this third analysis, the causal relation between participants' percep-tion of the aggregate as one group and their evaluations of outgroup mem-bers is more ambiguous because both variables were measured at the same time. In the current study, it is possible that manipulating coopera-tion initially influenced the evaluations of outgroup members, which in turn led to the different representations as one group or two groups. Only a longitudinal analysis could provide unambiguous evidence that partici-pants' representations preceded their evaluations of outgroup members. However, as we reported earlier, the fact that participants in the One Group relative to the Two Groups conditions in the absence of cooperation had lower degrees of intergroup bias in this experiment establishes the plausi-bility of a causal link between participants' perceptions of the aggregate as one group and their intergroup attitudes.

Because this study used an experimental design, we know that coop-eration preceded changes in members' conceptual representations of the aggregate from two group to one group and also changes in intergroup bias. Therefore, this experimental study is useful for establishing the overall plausibility of the direction of causality among the variables specified by the Common Ingroup Identity Model in subsequent survey studies.

One basic issue about the effects of intergroup cooperation, which was explored in this study, involves identifying the psychological processes that mediate reductions in bias. Another issue concerns which specific aspects of intergroup cooperation are necessary and sufficient to reduce intergroup bias. In the next section we examine this second issue.

☐ Common Fate and Interaction

Cooperation between groups is behavior that involves "sharing both the labor and the fruits of the labor" (Worchel, Wong, & Scheltema, 1989). Allport (1954) observed:

> only the type of contact that leads people to do things together is likely to result in changed attitudes. The principle is clearly illustrated in the multi-ethnic athletic team. Here the goal is all important; the ethnic composition of the team is irrelevant. It is the cooperative striving for the goal that engenders solidarity. (Allport, 1954, p. 264)

Whereas there is general agreement about the positive effects of inter-group cooperation, the identification of the specific elements of cooperative activity that are critical for reducing bias is less clear. Thus, one issue that we addressed in a study (Gaertner, Dovidio, Rust et al., 1999) involves examining two of the potentially separable elements of intergroup cooperative interdependence that may independently be sufficient to reduce bias. Allport's (1954) observation implies two different elements of cooperative contact. To "do things together" can include shared process (i.e., interacting together) and/or shared outcomes (i.e., common fate). A second issue that we pursued concerns the psychological processes that mediate the relations between elements of cooperative interdependence and the reduction of intergroup bias.

Although traditional definitions of intergroup cooperation do not explicitly specify that interaction between the groups is required, most implementations of intergroup cooperation in the literature involve interaction. Several theorists have proposed that the interaction between groups is the component of cooperation that is primarily responsible for reducing intergroup bias (e.g., Allport, 1954; Brewer & Miller, 1984; Cook, 1984; Miller & Davidson-Podgorney, 1987). However, other researchers, such as Brown and Wade (1987) and Deschamps and Brown (1983), have demonstrated that common fate and shared labor are together sufficient to reduce bias without intergroup interaction. In the present study, we therefore examined the potentially separable contributions of two elements of intergroup cooperation: (a) intergroup interaction and (b) common fate (i.e., shared outcomes).

Theoretically, interaction and common fate could have their effects through many of the same mediating processes. Several processes have been proposed: reinforcement, balance and cognitive consistency, and recategorization. Because of the potential for shared positive outcomes, intergroup interaction and common fate may both have reinforcing interpersonal consequences (Lott & Lott, 1965). Also, both can engage motives to restore attitudinal balance or cognitive consistency. Cooperative interaction, for example, may enhance evaluations of outgroup members so as to bring attitudes in closer alignment and greater balance with this positive behavior toward outgroup members (Worchel, 1986). These balance-restoring processes may also be engaged when groups are working for their mutual benefit—even in the absence of intergroup interaction. Intergroup interaction and common fate may also reduce bias by altering members' perceptions of the intergroup boundary (i.e., recategorization).

In addition, interaction uniquely offers the opportunity for intergroup attitudes to benefit from the development of more differentiated (i.e., less homogenized) and perhaps, personalized perceptions of outgroup members. Pettigrew (1998a) proposes that producing more individualized perceptions initially is a critical factor that facilitates the benefits of recategorization strategies in intergroup contact situations (see also Hewstone, 1996). Due to the information exchange, intergroup interaction (that is not hostile or competitive) can increase knowledge about outgroup members and reduce intergroup anxiety, which in turn broadens the perceptual field to allow impressions of outgroup members to become more accurate and more favorable (Stephan & Stephan, 1984; Islam & Hewstone, 1993). Because of the absence of individuating information, common fate without information exchange between the groups is unlikely to reduce bias through the differentiation of outgroup members.

In the experiment by Gaertner, Dovidio, Rust et al. (1999), two 3-person groups composed respectively of Democratic and Republican Party supporters were brought into contact under circumstances designed to vary, independently, common fate (two levels) and the degree of intergroup interaction (three levels). The manipulation of common fate involved whether the groups shared or had independent (but not competitive) opportunities to earn a $10.00-per-person monetary prize based partially on the quality of their labors. This manipulation occurred without information regarding the eventual outcome of their performances; the participants were not informed of their success or failure in obtaining the prize. Thus, as in our previous research (Gaertner et al., 1990), it is this explicit linking of goals, rather than the successful or unsuccessful attainment of goals, that is the essence of common fate in the present study.

The manipulation of intergroup interaction involved whether the groups worked together or separately on the same task during the contact period. In a Full Interaction condition, members of two groups interacted fully with free discussion and jointly reached a consensus solution to a problem facing the U.S. Government—namely which expenditures to cut and which taxes to increase. In a No Interaction condition, the contact conditions completely precluded interaction between the two member-ships. Members of each 3-person group worked on the problem sepa-rately, interacting only among themselves, but while together in the same room as the other group. In addition, a Partial Interaction condition was included that permitted a very restrictive type of intergroup interaction. In this condition, each participant shared the responsibility for communi-cating part of his or her 3-person group's rank-ordered solution to the problem at a time when neither group could benefit from learning of the other group's solution. A central purpose of this study is to determine whether the components of intergroup cooperation (interaction and com-mon fate) are separable. Yet, when groups interact fully to reach a con-sensus solution to the same problem, members may intrinsically experi-ence common fate with one another, regardless of whether other factors (e.g., a modest monetary prize) objectively determine mutuality or inde-pendence of fate. Therefore, we included the Partial Interaction condi-tion to separate more sharply the effects of interaction and perceptions of common fate.

To examine the processes by which the elements of cooperation reduce bias, as in our previous research (see Gaertner, Mann et al., 1989; Gaertner et al., 1990, 1993, 1994), dependent variables included evaluative ratings of ingroup and outgroup members and measures of potential mediating processes, such as participants' representations of the aggregate (e.g., the extent to which the aggregate feels like one group, two groups or sepa-rate individuals), how cooperative the two groups were perceived to be, and how much information about themselves each person revealed.

In addition, as a measure of spontaneous, less reactive reactions, mea-sures of facial affect were obtained in response to the contributions dur-ing the discussion of outgroup and ingroup members in the Full Interac-tion condition. Spontaneous, on-line measures can reveal intergroup biases that are undetected by self-report measures (e.g., Vanman et al., 1997). Each of the six participants wore a wireless microphone, ostensibly to allow us to record the interaction, that provided a record of who was speaking. A wall-mounted video camera provided a close-up image of one of the participants in each of these sessions. Subsequently, three rat-ers, unaware of the Common Fate or No Common Fate condition, viewed and rated each videotape of the facial expressions of the participant. These ratings were made without hearing the content of the interaction or know-ing whether an ingroup or outgroup member was speaking.

The major purpose of this study was to determine whether intergroup interaction and common fate are elements of cooperation that independently reduce intergroup bias. Independence of the effects of Interaction and Common Fate on bias would be indicated statistically by effects of Interaction or Common Fate on bias (but not an interaction involving both Interaction and Common Fate).

The results of the self-report measure of bias revealed only the predicted effect for Interaction (i.e., Full, Partial, None). As expected, each of the three Interaction treatment conditions differed significantly from each other. Bias (i.e., the difference between ingroup and outgroup evaluation) was lowest in the Full Interaction condition, followed in turn by the Partial and then the No Interaction conditions. The manipulation-check measures revealed that comparisons involving the Full Interaction condition were not completely independent of perceptions of common fate: Participants in Full Interaction had greater perceptions of common fate than did those in the partial interaction conditions. There was no difference, however, in the perception of common fate between the No Interaction and Partial Interaction conditions. Nevertheless, the comparisons between the Partial and No Interactions conditions clearly indicate that even very limited intergroup interaction, independent of common fate, is capable of reducing intergroup bias. Even this highly structured, impersonal, and relatively vacuous set of presentations produced the impression of interaction that ultimately was sufficient to reduce bias.

In this study, groups that interacted had lower intergroup bias than groups that did not interact regardless of the level of common fate. Even in the Partial Interaction condition in which there was no functional interdependence between the groups, bias was lower than when groups did not interact. Therefore, we can conclude on the basis of our study that interaction can be *sufficient* to reduce intergroup bias. However, there is also evidence (which we reviewed in Chapter 3) by Deschamps and Brown (1983) and by Brown and Wade (1987) that interaction *per se* is not *necessary* to increase positive evaluations of outgroup members. Based on assumptions of Social Identity Theory (Tajfel & Turner, 1979; Turner, 1981), Brown and Wade (1987) expected that members of groups working together would experience greater threat to the integrity of their group identities relative to those whose groups worked separately (see also Dovidio, Gaertner, & Validzic, 1998). Consequently, in order to re-establish positive, distinctive group identities, members of groups that worked together were expected to have higher levels of bias than those that worked separately.

Our own findings are very different, however. In the current study, the greater the level of intergroup interaction, the lower the level of intergroup bias, an apparent reversal of the findings of Brown and Wade (1987). Nevertheless, these results can be reconciled by considering some procedural differences across these two studies. For example, in our study the members of each group continued to wear their distinctively different group T-shirts throughout the interaction period. These conditions, therefore, may have precluded the arousal of threat to members' social identities when the groups interacted. Also, in our experiment, both groups always worked on all aspects of the problem and thus each group duplicated the work of the other. In Brown and Wade's study, however, when the groups worked separately, each group worked only on half of a newspaper article task (either, one page of a two-page article, or, on only the pictures or the text) that would later be combined to form the whole product (i.e., a two-page article with pictures and text). Thus, in the Brown and Wade (1987) study, the presence of the other group performing its half of the labor had immediate, tangible benefits to the members of each group. Each group only had its half of the work to accomplish. Also, in accord with Marcus-Newhall et al. (1993), task assignments in the current study were not related positively or negatively to either group's special competencies. In terms of functional utility, it would not have mattered whether the interacting groups were assigned comparable or noncomparable roles. Therefore, cooperative interaction did not threaten the effectiveness of the joint endeavor. Therefore, whether it is better for groups to interact and work together rather than separately without intergroup interaction, may depend on the degree to which the context threatens their respective group identities, and also on the perceived functional utility of the groups working together or separately.

Although the finding that people evaluate outgroup members more favorably after nonhostile, face-to-face, minimal degrees of interaction seems simple, the processes involved may be more complex. The minimal interaction in the Partial Interaction condition not only increased how much participants believed that they learned about members of the other group, but also it increased perceptions of cooperation and of superordinate connection between the groups. Regression analyses revealed that the difference in intergroup bias between the Partial Interaction and No Interaction conditions was mediated by the conceptual representation of the six participants as separate individuals (suggesting individuation) but also more strongly by conceptions of two subgroups within one group (suggesting recategorization). The separate individuals and the two subgroups within one group representations, along with one superordinate group representation, also mediated the reduction of bias between the Full Interaction and No Interaction conditions. Thus, communication—even minimal, nonhostile verbal exchange—between the members of two groups can produce substantial changes in the cognitive representations of the groups and consequently to the reduction of intergroup bias.

Contrary to the expectation that Common Fate would also reduce intergroup bias, no effect for Common Fate alone or in combination with Interaction was obtained on the self-report measures of intergroup bias. However, the analysis of the effect of Common Fate on facial expressions in the Full Interaction condition did yield evidence of significant bias. Ingroup favoritism (i.e., bias) was higher in the absence of common fate than in the presence of common fate between the groups. Contributions by outgroup members induced more pleasant facial expression in the Common Fate than in the No Common Fate condition while there were no differences between these conditions in response to the comments of ingroup members. The manipulation of common fate involving the potential to share the modest $10.00-per-person prize therefore reduced bias in facial reactions by more strongly influencing positive facial reactions toward outgroup members than toward ingroup members. These findings indicate that the Common Fate manipulation, in addition to its effect on the manipulation check, was sufficiently strong and effective to have a systematic and observable impact on participants and provides tentative evidence for Interaction and Common Fate as separate components of cooperation that are independently sufficient to reduce intergroup bias.

That more positive spontaneous, less voluntary, implicit, behavioral reactions to outgroup members did not translate directly into more positive evaluations on self-report measures is a complex issue. Nevertheless, there is precedent in the literature illustrating this lack of correlation (see also Greenwald & Banaji, 1995, for a general discussion). With respect to intergroup behavior, in particular, Vanman et al. (1997) reported a disparity between the results for facial EMG activity and self-reported preference for Black partners (see also Weitz, 1972). We believe that both types of responses (i.e., facial reactions and self-reported evaluations) are reflective of intergroup attitudes and can have important consequences for the course of intergroup relations. Dovidio and Fazio (1992; see also, Dovidio, Kawakami et al., 1997), for instance, demonstrated not only that there may be a fundamental dissociation between measures of implicit attitudes reflected in spontaneous reactions and self-reported explicit attitudes, but also that both can have a significant, but different, effects on the nature of intergroup relations and on the outcome of intergroup contact (Dovidio, Kawakami et al., 1997; Dovidio, Kawakami, & Beach, in press). Thus, interaction and common fate, which affected different types of measures of bias within the present study, may have different longer-term effects on intergroup relations, as well.

☐ Conditions of Contact: Perceptions of Supportive Norms, Interdependence, Interaction, and Status

The three correlational studies in this section investigate how perceptions of favorable intergroup contact, including supportive norms, may influence representations of the groups and thereby reduce bias. The first explores intergroup relations within a multi-ethnic high school. The second examines the model in the context of corporate mergers. The third study examines the quality of contact and stepfamily harmony.

Intergroup Relations in a Multi-Ethnic High School

A survey study was conducted in a multi-ethnic high school in the northeastern United States in which a sample of 1,357 Black, Chinese, Hispanic, Japanese, Korean, Vietnamese, and Caucasian students, closely matching the school's diversity, participated (see Gaertner et al., 1994; Gaertner, Rust et al., 1996). The primary theoretical question we pursued in this study was whether students' perceptions of the student body as one group or separate groups would mediate the proposed relation between their perceptions of the favorableness of the conditions of contact (e.g., cooperation, equal status) and their degrees of intergroup bias. Also, we explored the effects of the dual identity (in which subgroup identities are maintained within the context of a superordinate entity) using two different strategies. First, we included in the survey an item designed to tap this representation (i.e., "Although there are different groups at school, it feels like we are playing on the same team"). Second, we compared students who identified themselves as possessing a dual identity (e.g., some students indicated they were Korean and American) with those who reported their identity using only their subgroup name (e.g., Korean). We expected that, for both strategies, a dual identity would be associated with lower intergroup bias.

Questionnaire items that were modifications of those developed by Green et al. (1988) were designed to measure four distinct conditions hypothesized by the Contact Hypothesis (see Allport, 1954; Cook, 1984) to be necessary for successful intergroup contact: equal status, cooperative interdependence, the degree of interaction between the groups and egalitarian norms. Scores on these four scales were combined to form an overall measure of intergroup contact. Additional items, similar to those used in our laboratory work, were included to measure students' perceptions of the student body as one group ("Despite the different groups at school, there is frequently the sense that we are just one group"), separate groups ("At school, it usually feels as though we belong to different groups"), and separate individuals ("At school, it usually feels as though we are individuals and not members of a particular group"). Also, we included the dual-identity item.

An index of intergroup bias was obtained by including several items designed to assess feelings towards one's own ethnic group and towards each of the other ethnic groups (e.g., "How often do [name of ethnic group] make you feel (good, uneasy, badly, respectful)"). Evaluation of the "outgroups" was indexed by averaging feelings towards all ethnic groups to which students did not indicate membership. The index measuring bias in affective reactions was then obtained by calculating the difference between feelings for one's ingroup and feelings for the "outgroups." In addition, students rated the "overall favorability" of each ethnic/racial group on a modified "feelings thermometer" (see Abelson, Kinder, Peters, & Fiske, 1982) and an index of ingroup and outgroup overall favorability was derived in a manner similar to that for bias in affective feelings. Both affective feelings and overall favorability were included because there is converging support for the idea that overall attitudinal favorability toward groups are strongly determined by affect (Abelson et al., 1982; Stangor, Sullivan, & Ford, 1991).

Application of the multiple regression mediation approach revealed that the results of this study (see Figure 5.2a) closely paralleled the findings from the laboratory (overall adjusted R^2 = .12). The conditions of contact significantly predicted both cognitive representations of the groups and intergroup bias in affective feelings. Cognitive representations, in turn, predicted bias. The more the student body was perceived to be "one group" or "on the same team," the lower the bias in affective feelings (betas = −.08 and −.09, respectively), suggesting that each of these superordinate representations independently predict bias. While these relationships are relatively weak, they are statistically reliable. Furthermore, the relationship between conditions of contact and bias in affective feelings was significantly reduced (from beta = −.32 to beta = −.24) when cognitive representations were statistically controlled which provides further evidence of the partial mediating role of the cognitive representations.

When bias in overall attitudinal favorability was included in the analysis by regressing it on bias in affective reactions, the cognitive representations and the conditions of contact, simultaneously, there was evidence of further mediation (overall adjusted R^2 = .34). As revealed in Figure 5.2b, the relation between conditions of contact and bias in overall favorability (beta = −.28) is mediated by bias in affective feelings (beta = .53) and also by the extent to which the student body is perceived to be "different groups" (beta = .06). That is, the lower the bias in affective feelings and the weaker the "different groups" representation, the lower the bias in overall favorability. In terms of the role of the cognitive representations in this analysis, both the "one group" and "on same team" perceptions, in part, mediate the relation between contact conditions and bias in affective feelings which is a strong predictor of bias in overall favorability. Also, the "different groups" representation, in part, mediates the relation between conditions of contact and bias in overall favorability.

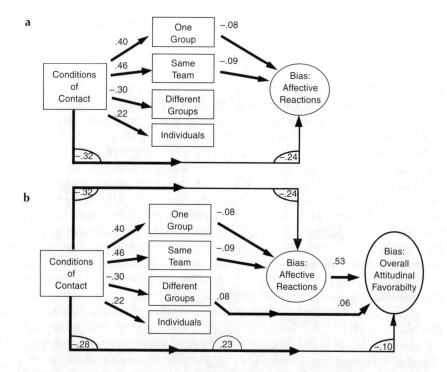

FIGURES 5.2a and 5.2b. Perceptions of conditions of contact in a multi-ethnic high school and (a) bias in affective reactions, and (b) attitudinal favorability. From "The Contact Hypothesis: The Role of a Common Ingroup Identity on Reducing Intergroup Bias Among Majority and Minority Group Members," by S. L. Gaertner, M. C. Rust, J. F. Dovidio, B. Bachman, & P. Anastasio, 1996. In J. L. Nye & A. M. Brower (Eds.), *What's Social About Social Cognition?*, pp. 230–260. Copyright 1996 by Sage Publications, Newbury Park, CA.

These results nicely support the ideas of Abelson et al. (1982) and Stangor et al. (1991) that overall attitudinal favorability may be determined by affective feelings. Also, the results are consistent with those of our laboratory study and indicate the applicability of the Common Ingroup Identity Model to naturalistic settings. In this multi-ethnic context, the "one-group" and the "the same team" representations *each* related positively to the conditions of contact and to lower degrees of bias in affective feelings. In addition, the lower the bias in affective feelings and the weaker the perceptions of the student body as "different groups," the lower the bias in overall favorability.

The beneficial effects of a superordinate identity is further revealed by the effects of a dual identity. Students who identified themselves on the survey as members of a minority group and also American had lower bias in affective reactions than minority students who did not use a superordinate American identity. Whereas there may be many differences between these two groups of students (e.g., American citizenship), they did have different cognitive representations of the student body. As we might expect if the item "different groups but on the same team" did measure a dual identity, minority students who identified themselves both as American and as a member of a minority group endorsed this "same team" item (but no other item) more strongly than students who only identified themselves using their minority group identities. These findings suggest that minority students who did *not* use a dual identity should more strongly perceive the student body as "different groups," relative to each of the other representations of the aggregate; whereas students who used the dual identity should most strongly perceive the student body as "different groups playing on the same team." Separate analyses conducted for these groups of students indicated that this expectation was generally supported. Thus, the perceptions of the student body by students who used a dual identity involving a minority subgroup and an American superordinate identity were generally less differentiated than students who used only a minority group identity. Furthermore, paralleling the mediation analyses of this study, the dual identity was also associated with perceptions of the conditions of contact that were favorable in terms of being closer to Allport's (1954, 1958) ideal, involving equal status, cooperative interdependence, personal interaction, and egalitarian norms.

Additional analyses of these data examined the moderating role of status, defined in terms of majority or minority group status (see Gaertner, Rust et al., 1996). Consistent with Islam and Hewstone's (1993) research and the idea that social-contextual factors influence intergroup attitudes, majority (i.e., Caucasian) students relative to the minority group students (disregarding whether they used a dual identity) perceived the conditions of contact more favorably. They also had stronger representations of the student body as "all playing on the same team" and had lower degrees of bias in affective reactions, primarily because their attitudes toward outgroup members were more favorable. These results suggest that status can moderate the processes involved in intergroup bias (see Sachdev & Bourhis, 1991), and as suggested by Fiske (1993), processes involved in stereotyping.

Overall, these findings offer further support for the Common Ingroup Identity Model in a rich and complex setting containing many different groups, so that bias involving ingroups and the outgroups was not limited to any specific pair possessing a unique history. The results also revealed that "one group" and "same team" cognitive representations each had independent effects in the reduction of bias. This is encouraging, for there may be situations in which facilitating the development of a dual identity or a conception of "different groups on same team" may be preferable to simply establishing a one-group representation without reference to prior group membership. Furthermore, generalization of positive feelings to other outgroup members outside of the common ingroup (for example, members of ethnic outgroups not attending one's school) is desirable in many circumstances and may best be facilitated by retaining some sort of associative link with the original outgroups. Keeping one's original group identity while simultaneously perceiving an inclusive superordinate group may create such an associative link.

In addition to demonstrating the generalizability of the processes outlined in the Common Ingroup Identity Model and illustrating the potential role of dual identities, our more recent analyses reconfirmed the importance of another aspect of the social context—the status of the groups (see Sachdev & Bourhis, 1991). Status is a fundamental form of social organization for both individuals and groups (Berger, Wagner, & Zelditch, 1985). In many social contexts it is the primary distinguishing factor. For example, in corporate mergers, the acquiring company, by virtue of its action, establishes its status relative to the company that was acquired. The following study tested the Common Ingroup Identity Model within such corporate structures where again groups are real and intergroup attitudes are rich and complexly determined.

Corporate Mergers and Ingroup Identity

In another effort to extend the model to situations outside of the laboratory, Bachman (1993; see also, Bachman & Gaertner, 1999) investigated the impact of intergroup processes in corporate mergers. Mergers embody in a rich and complex fashion the goals that we have attempted to study in our laboratory research—making two groups into one—and thus represent fertile ground for examining the processes of social categorization, stereotyping, and intergroup biases.

People who work in organizations that have merged are frequently resistant to post-merger integration (Marks & Mirvis, 1985). The negative consequences of these intergroup dynamics could be devastating for the newly formed organizational entity if allowed to go unchecked. After all, the survival and growth of any organization is dependent upon the commitment of all of its members to work together in order to achieve organizational goals. Research reveals, in fact, that many merged organizations experience lags in productivity, high turnover and absenteeism, and decreased profits (Jemison & Sitkin, 1986).

Categorization and its consequences are expected to be particularly influential during mergers because the process of merging is essentially a group-level phenomenon. Mergers increase the salience of group identity for organizational members because the focus of a merger is on the redefinition of organizational groups and their boundaries. Thus, awareness of the ingroup (own organization) and outgroup (the other organization) is heightened and likely to affect the judgments and interactions of merger participants. To protect self-esteem and to ensure the maintenance of a positive social identity in this context, employees may begin to perceive themselves (and their group) as "better" than the outgroup on important dimensions. Another important contextual dynamic that is quite prevalent in mergers—competition—should increase cohesion within groups and polarize perceived differences between them (Blake & Mouton, 1979). Given all of the pressures that tend to keep organizational groups apart, we wanted to investigate the factors that we hypothesized would promote more harmonious intergroup relationships.

The Common Ingroup Identity Model suggests that if group members' mental representations of separate groups could be recategorized into a "one group" representation, then the fundamental biases and conflicts between groups should diminish. Following the work in the multi-ethnic high school, Bachman et al. (1993) proposed that, to the extent that Contact Hypothesis variables were favorable in the merged organization, differentiation between groups would be reduced resulting in a more unified conceptualization of the merged organization. A more unified representation of the merged organization was predicted to be associated with lower levels of bias between the groups. Also as suggested by the high school study, the relative status of the groups in contact was expected to moderate members' perceptions and reactions to the merger. Within the context of the mergers, status relates to the roles each organization played in the merger. Because of group differences in power and control in the merged organization, acquiring organizations typically have higher status than organizations that were acquired. Some of the participants in our sample were members of an acquiring organization (high status group), some were from organizations that had been acquired (low-status group), while others indicated that theirs was a merger of equals. Bachman, Gaertner, Anastasio, and Rust (1993) proposed that status differentials between acquired and acquiring organizational members may affect their perceptions of the conditions of contact. Higher status groups may view the conditions of contact more favorably and thus may have a more inclusive representation of the merged organization and lower levels of intergroup bias.

The participants in this survey study were 229 banking executives who were students or alumni of a three-year long summer graduate banking program. We were fortunate to have the opportunity to study bankers because the banking industry has engaged in a high rate of merger activity over the past several years. Our participants came from many geographical locations and financial institutions across the United States. Some of the participants in our sample were members of an acquiring organization, some were from organizations that had been acquired, while others indicated that theirs was a merger of equals.

The merger survey measured (among other constructs) variables akin to those examined in the high school study: (a) the banking executives' assessment of contact conditions (i.e., the degree to which partners to the merger held equal status, the degree to which egalitarian norms existed, perceptions of positive interdependence among the banks, opportunities for interaction, and (b) the executive's mental representations of the merged organization (one group, two subgroups within a larger group [the dual-identity item], two separate groups, or separate individuals). The affective reactions component measured in this model was somewhat different from that used in the high school setting and was based on Stephan and Stephan's (1984, 1985) construct of intergroup anxiety. Here respondents were asked to rate their reactions to interacting with members of the "other" organization relative to how they felt when interacting with their own (including how awkward, self-conscious, accepted, confident, irritated, impatient, defensive and happy). As a measure of intergroup bias, participants rated the members of their original group relative to members of the other group on characteristics related to the corporate setting. Factor analysis indicated that our bias measure actually was composed of two distinct factors, which we interpreted as a "sociability" factor (sociable, helpful, and cliquish) and a "work-related" factor (intelligent, hard-working, reliable, organized, skilled, and creative). Consequently, the mediation analyses were executed separately for each of the two bias measures (see Figures 5.3a and 5.3b).

Overall, mediation analysis assessing the effects of contact conditions, mental representations of the group, and affective reactions (intergroup anxiety) on sociability bias (see Figure 5.3a) revealed a pattern of findings (overall adjusted R^2 = .25) that closely mirrored the results of the high school study. First, consistent with our previous findings, more favorable ratings of the conditions of contact were associated with lower intergroup anxiety (an affective response, beta = −.53) and in lower sociability bias (beta = −.44). Second, analyses confirmed that favorable conditions of contact significantly predicted participants' cognitive representations of the merged organization: as one group (beta = .53), two subgroups within one group (beta = −.32), separate groups (beta = −.57) and separate individuals (beta = −.22). Third, the relation between conditions of contact and intergroup anxiety was mediated by representations of the merged organization as one group (beta = −.26) and as separate individuals (beta = .14). The more the organization was perceived to be

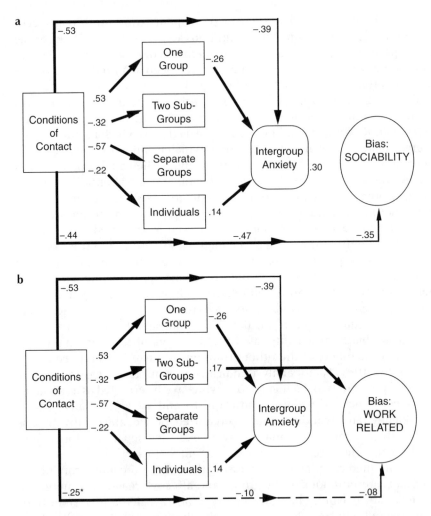

FIGURES 5.3a and 5.3b. Perceptions of conditions of contact in banking mergers and (a) in sociability bias, and (b) work-related bias. From "Revisiting the Contact Hypothesis: The Induction of a Common Ingroup Identity," by S. L. Gaertner, J. F. Dovidio, & B. Bachman, 1996, *International Journal of Intercultural Relations, 20,* pp. 271–290.

one group and the less as separate individuals, the lower the intergroup anxiety. Also, as in the high school study, the relation between perceptions of the contact conditions and bias was mediated by affective feelings involving intergroup anxiety (beta = .30); the lower the intergroup anxiety, the lower the bias in sociability. Thus, supportive of the Common Ingroup Identity Model, the superordinate, one-group representation, is associated with favorable perceptions of the conditions of contact, and lower intergroup anxiety. Also, as intergroup anxiety decreases, bias in sociability decreases as well.

The pattern of mediation for the work-related bias measure (see Figure 5.3b), while supportive of the general theoretical framework, provided us with what we consider to be a very interesting divergence from the previous results. Here we find the relation between favorable ratings of contact conditions and work-related bias is mediated directly by the dual identity representation, "two subgroups within one group" (beta = .17) rather than by intergroup anxiety as it was for bias in sociability (overall adjusted R^2 = .09). Furthermore, contrary to the findings of the high school study, the more favorable the perceptions of the contact conditions, the *less* the merged corporate entity was seen as "two subgroups within one group" (beta = −.32). The weaker this dual identity representation, the lower the work-related bias. Conversely, the more the merged entity was perceived as "two subgroups within one group," the *higher* the bias (beta = .17). In the high school study (see Figures 5.2a and 5.2b), the dual identity item "on the same team," in contrast, was related to *more* favorable perceptions of the contact conditions (beta = .46) and to *lower* intergroup bias in affective reactions (beta = −.09).

Additional analyses examined the moderating role of relative group status in more detail. While the results of this study were very interesting, they were also quite complex. Supportive of the assumed link between organizational role in a merger and status, participants rated their organizations as equivalent in status before the merger, but differences existed after the merger. Members of acquiring organizations perceived their group to be of higher status than did members organizations that were acquired. Members of organizations involved in mergers perceived to be of equals reported an intermediate degree of status, probably as a reflection of their greater power in the new organization. Furthermore, as expected and consistent with the high-school study, status was positively related to perceptions of the conditions of contact. Members of acquiring organizations rated the conditions of contact more favorably (i.e., more highly on the dimensions, such as equal status and cooperatively interdependent, that Allport [1954, 1958] identified as critical for successfully reducing bias) than did members of companies that were acquired in a merger. Members of organizations seen as equal partners in a merger viewed the conditions of contact at an intermediate level of favorability, although also more favorably than did members of acquired organizations.

In addition to perceptions of status and conditions of contact, members' representations of the merged organization also varied as a function of merger conditions. Members of organizations that acquired another company or who perceived the merger as involving equal partners had a less differentiated, more inclusive, one-group representation of the merged organization than did members of organizations that were acquired in a merger. These findings parallel the results of majority and minority status in the previous analyses of the high-school study.

As it did in the multi-ethnic high school, intergroup bias varied as a function of status. The picture is a bit more complex, however, because we divided the bias measure into two different indices based largely on the factor loadings of the items: sociability bias (including the traits of sociable, helpful, and cliquish), and work-competence bias (including the traits of skillful, creative, intelligent, and hard-working). When bias is measured in terms of sociability, members of acquiring organizations demonstrated lower levels of bias than members of the acquired organizations. Also members of groups perceived to be equal in status did not show significant ingroup favoritism. Thus, supportive of the processes hypothesized in the Common Ingroup Identity Model, lower levels of sociability bias corresponded with more favorable perceptions of the conditions of contact and more inclusive representations of the merged organization. When bias is measured in terms of work-competence, however, a different pattern emerges. In contrast to the results for sociability bias, members of acquiring organizations exhibited significantly higher levels of ingroup favoritism on the work-competence index than did either members of acquired organizations or members of equal-status organizations. Thus, higher work-related status, in terms of organizational role in a merger, was related to lower sociability bias but to greater ingroup bias in their perceptions of work-competence.

The effects of status on our bias measures are consistent with other studies that have found that high status groups tend to emphasize their superiority on power and competence dimensions (e.g., "We are more clever, richer, and stronger"), whereas low status groups tend to show "social creativity" in the terms of Social Identity Theory by emphasizing the importance of alternative social dimensions (e.g., "We are nicer"; see Cheyne, 1970; Doojse & Ellemers, 1997; Mummendey & Schreiber, 1983; Spears & Manstead, 1989). These effects of status suggest the importance of considering the relevance and centrality of the dimensions on which bias is assessed—that is, the social context of the dependent measures as well as the social context of the intergroup contact and the relative status of the groups. It is possible, for instance, that members of acquired organizations, recognizing their disadvantage in the work situation, were particularly motivated to seek positive distinctiveness on an alternative dimension—manifested in this case as higher levels of sociability bias than exhibited by members of acquiring organizations (see also Brewer, Manzi & Shaw, 1993; Mullen et al., 1992; Sachdev & Bourhis, 1991). In the next study, we explore these processes in a smaller, more personal *intergroup* context—the stepfamily.

Stepfamily Harmony

Families involve a fundamental form of group membership. Allport (1958), for example, states that the biological family "ordinarily constitutes the smallest and firmest of one's ingroups" (p. 41), and that "every society on earth" regards the child "as a member of his parents' groups" (p. 30). Biological, or first-married families, generally share memories, ancestral histories, traditions, daily rituals, and a common family name that contribute to a strong sense of family group identity (see Settles, 1993).

Given the importance of family group identity, stepfamilies represent an interesting domain to study intergroup relations. When the first-married family is fragmented by divorce or death and remarriage to a new partner occurs, the biological parents and children from the two families come together under new circumstances. Through remarriage, members of two separate "ingroups" with no common memories, histories, daily rituals, or even family name find themselves in an intensive intergroup context.

Relative to biologically-related, first-married families, stepfamilies have generally been described as more stressful and less cohesive. Stepfathers, for example, not only report being less satisfied with their own lives than do first-married fathers, but they also indicate that the lives of their stepchildren are less than satisfactory as well (Fine, McKenry, Donnelly, & Voydanoff, 1992). Bray and Berger (1993) found that, in couples remarried for 5 to 7 years, there were less positive wife-to-husband and biological parent/child interactions in stepfamilies than in their first-married counterparts. And, several studies have found that stepparent/stepchild relationships are more negative and conflict-ridden than are those between biological parents and children in first-married families (Anderson & White, 1986; Furstenberg, 1987; Sauer & Fine, 1988).

One reason why stepfamilies may experience less harmony is less than satisfactory contact among the stepfamily members. James and Johnson (1987) reported that competitiveness in stepfamilies is related to marital dissatisfaction and psychological pathology in both husbands and wives. Cooperativeness, however, relates to marital satisfaction for both partners, and to the husbands' positive psychological adjustment. Furthermore, the failure of stepchildren to respond in kind to their stepparents' positive behaviors toward them has been found to be associated with stepfamily dysfunction (Anderson & White, 1986; Brown, Green, & Druckman, 1990). A more positive relationship between the stepparent and stepchild, in contrast, is associated with more positive stepfamily functioning (Anderson & White, 1986) and stepfamily happiness (Crosbie-Burnett, 1984).

This study (Banker & Gaertner, 1998) examined, within the context of the Common Ingroup Identity Model, how those factors involved in positive contact among stepfamily members (e.g., cooperativeness) influence stepfamily functioning and harmony. Specifically, it was predicted that more favorable conditions of contact in the stepfamily home would relate to increased perceptions of the family as one group and to increased stepfamily harmony. The relationship between favorable conditions of contact and increased harmony were expected to be mediated by the one-group representation.

Undergraduate stepfamily members completed a questionnaire for this study. During pretesting, participants who were selected for this study reported that they lived at home with a married biological parent and stepparent and had at least one stepsibling. Each of these stepfamiles was therefore composed of at least four people who could view themselves initially as two separate groups (Aa and Bb). A measure of favorability of contact within the stepfamily was created by averaging together measures of cooperation, personalization, and equal status. Participants also rated the extent to which the stepfamily unit felt like one group, two subgroups within one (a measure of dual identity; see Chapter 3) two groups, and separate individuals. The measure of stepfamily harmony represented the average of four items, such as "Generally, there is a feeling of contentment in my house" and "I would characterize the environment in my house as 'harmonious'."

Compared to a separate sample of undergraduates from first-married families, participants from stepfamilies reported less favorable conditions of contact and representations as less like one group and more like two. Family harmony, however, was only nonsignificantly lower for stepfamilies than for first-married families. Of central importance to the model was the relationships among the variables for predicting stepfamily harmony (see Figure 5.4). As hypothesized, more favorable conditions of contact predicted higher one group ratings (beta = .80) and lower two groups (beta = −.74) and two groups within one (beta = −.65) ratings. Consistent with the hypothesized mediating role, one group representations, in turn, significantly predicted higher levels of stepfamily harmony (beta = .48).

The results of this study offer support for the Common Ingroup Identity Model and its utility for studying problems in stepfamilies. Moreover, the findings support and extend previous work in family research and suggests ways that harmony might be achieved within these families. The process of recategorization from two separate groups to one inclusive group is central to facilitating stepfamily harmony.

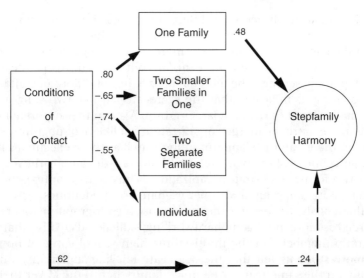

FIGURE 5.4. Perceptions of conditions of contact and stepfamily harmony. Adapted from "Achieving Stepfamily Harmony: An Intergroup Relations Approach, by B. S. Banker & S. L. Gaertner, 1998, *Journal of Family Psychology, 12*, pp. 310–325.

In summary, the results of the three studies reported in this section support the predictions derived from the Common Ingroup Identity Model. The results of the high school study, the corporate merger study, and the stepfamily study reveal that the conditions of contact reliably predict each of the measures of intergroup harmony and bias before the mediators are considered. Also, the conditions of contact do influence each of the participants' representations of the aggregate, as would be expected if one or more of these representations is a mediator. For example, the conditions of contact consistently predict the extent to which participants rate the aggregate as one group. In each case, the more favorable the conditions of contact are perceived, the more the aggregate feels like one group.

Moreover, consistent with the hypothesized mediating process, the relationships between the conditions of contact and bias in affective reactions, intergroup anxiety, and stepfamily harmony are substantially weaker after the mediators are considered than before. Furthermore, in each case, the extent to which the aggregate felt like one group was a primary predictor of affective reactions. Supportive of the model, the more it felt like one group, the lower the bias in affective reactions in the high school, the less the intergroup anxiety among the banking executives, and the greater the amount of stepfamily harmony.

In contrast to the consistent, significant effect for the one-group representation across these studies, we also observed that the role of the "dual identity" measure functioned differently across the high school study, corporate merger and stepfamily studies. In the high school setting, the better the conditions of contact the more students regarded the aggregate as "different groups on the same team." In contrast, in the corporate merger and stepfamily settings, the more favorable the conditions of contact, the less participants indicated that the aggregate felt like two subgroups or two smaller families within a larger group. Also, in the corporate merger context, the more the merged organization felt like two subgroups within a group, the greater the amount of ingroup bias these executives had in their perceptions of the work-related characteristics among the members of the two formerly separate organizations. Thus, in this context, the more strongly both subgroup and superordinate group identities were salient simultaneously, the greater the extent to which ingroup members were regarded as more intelligent, hardworking, skilled and creative than were outgroup members. In the multi-ethnic high school context, however, the more students felt that the aggregate felt like "different groups all playing on the same team" (the dual identity item), the lower their bias in affective reactions.

We suspect that contextual differences among these intergroup settings may alter the relative desirability and utility of maintaining a dual identity in lieu of a more inclusive one-group representation (see Gaertner, Dovidio, & Bachman, 1996). For example, maintaining strong identification with the earlier subgroup identities following a corporate merger may threaten the primary goal of the merger. Similarly, in stepfamilies, the salience of the former family identities, even with the simultaneous recognition of a more inclusive family identity, may violate members' expectations about what their ideal family should be like. Consequently, the salience of these subgroup identities may be diagnostic of serious problems—reflected, in part, by the fact that these "dual identities" become stronger in the merger and stepfamily contexts as the conditions of contact are more unfavorable. Of course, the direction of causality could actually be reversed. That is, it is possible that the stronger the experience of a dual identity, the worse people perceive the contact conditions to be. In either case, the relationship is quite different than in the high school context in which the salience of subgroup and superordinate identities would not be incompatible with the goals of the superordinate organization. Here, the salience of the subgroup identities, within the context of a superordinate entity that provides connection between the subgroups, may signal the prospects for good intergroup relations without undermining the goals of the school or those of the different ethnic or racial groups.

☐ Status and Intergroup Differentiation

One of the prerequisite conditions for successful intergroup contact, identified by the Contact Hypothesis, is that the groups should be of equal status in that context. As our earlier work on the conditions specified by the Contact Hypothesis suggests, equal status would be expected to facilitate the development of a common ingroup identity. However, bringing different groups together, particularly when they are similar on an important dimension (such as task-relevant status) might arouse motivations to achieve "positive distinctiveness" (Tajfel & Turner, 1979), which could exacerbate rather than alleviate intergroup bias (Brown & Wade, 1987). In this respect, establishing a common superordinate identity while simultaneously maintaining the salience of subgroup identities (i.e., developing a dual identity as two subgroups within one group) would be particularly effective because it permits the benefits of a common ingroup identity to operate without arousing countervailing motivations to achieve positive distinctiveness. We conducted two experiments investigating this hypothesis. The first study (Dovidio, Gaertner, & Validzic, 1998) was designed to extend this line of research by further investigating how the effects of equal status contact on the reduction of intergroup bias may be mediated by group representations and by exploring how contextual factors may moderate the effects of equal status contact on bias.

The consistent finding that perceptions of equal status and other conditions of contact specified by the Contact Hypothesis are associated with lower levels of bias does not necessarily imply that interventions that attempt to structure intergroup contact along these dimensions will successfully produce more inclusive intergroup representations or reduce bias. Theoretically, based on the assumptions of Social Identity Theory (Tajfel & Turner, 1979; Turner, 1981), under some conditions introducing equal status interventions in intergroup contact situations may produce threat to the integrity of members' separate group identities and needs for group distinctiveness. Consequently, to re-establish positively distinctive differences between the groups that are of equal status, members may develop relatively high levels of intergroup bias (Brown & Wade, 1987; Deschamps & Brown, 1983). Hornsey and Hogg (2000), for instance, found that a condition that emphasized students' common university membership produced even higher levels of bias between humanities and math-science students than did a condition that emphasized their separate group identities. Thus, under some conditions, intergroup interactions under conditions of equal status may not produce more inclusive group representations nor successfully reduce bias—and may, in fact, exacerbate bias.

Under other conditions, however, equal status contact can reduce bias. Hewstone and Brown's (1986; see also Hewstone, 1996) Mutual Intergroup Differentiation Model suggests that equal status interaction reduces intergroup bias when original group identities are salient and are not threatened by contact, such as when the groups have different areas of expertise. In particular, according to the Mutual Intergroup Differentiation Model, bias will be most effectively reduced when the groups are encouraged "to recognize mutual superiorities and inferiorities, and to accord equal values to dimensions favoring each group" (Hewstone, 1996, p. 334; see also Tajfel, 1981; Turner, 1981; van Knippenberg, 1984).

The present study thus examined how manipulations of relative status on the same and different dimensions can influence intergroup bias and how these effects may be mediated by cognitive representations of the groups. Two 3-person groups, composed of participants randomly assigned as overestimators or underestimators (supposedly on the basis of an earlier pretest in which they completed a series of estimation tasks), first worked separately on the Winter Survival Task. The groups were asked to determine the best solution on the same dimension (i.e., both groups assuming either that they would stay with the plane to be rescued or that they would be attempting to hike to safety) or on different dimensions (members of one group assuming that they would stay with the plane and the other group assuming that they would hike to safety).

Prior to engaging in the intergroup contact situation, two manipulations were introduced: (a) Same/Different Dimension and (b) Status. In the Same Dimension condition, each 3-person group was informed that the 6 participants would be asked to find the best solution based on the same assumption (stay or hike) that both groups worked under previously. In the Different Dimensions condition, the members of the 3-person groups were told that the 6 participants would be asked to come up with the best solution considering that the survivors could choose to stay with the plane or hike to safety (the separate alternatives that each group previously discussed). Status was manipulated, analogous to previous research (Ellemers, Doosje, van Knippenberg, & Wilke, 1992; Ellemers, van Knippenberg, DeVries, & Wilke, 1992), by providing the 3-person groups with false feedback about their performance and the performance of the other group on the initial problem-solving task. In the Equal Status condition, participants were informed that the two groups had initially performed equivalently (both in about the 50th percentile or the 90th percentile). In the Unequal Status condition, the groups were informed that one had performed in approximately the 90th percentile while the other group had performed in the 50th percentile. Then the groups were brought together in an intergroup contact situation to solve the problem. At the conclusion of this interaction, participants evaluated the members of the groups (see Gaertner, Mann et al., 1989; Gaertner et al., 1990).

Based on Hewstone and Brown's (1986) Mutual Intergroup Differentiation Model, it was hypothesized that equal status interaction would be primarily effective at reducing intergroup bias and improving attitudes toward the outgroup when the groups were differentiated by area of experience. Specifically, we predicted a pattern of means in which bias was expected to be lower (and outgroup attitudes more favorable) in the Equal Status/Different Dimension condition relative to the Equal Status/Same Dimension condition and to the conditions in which the groups were differentiated by status (i.e., Unequal Status/Different Dimension and Unequal Status/Same Dimension conditions). These latter three conditions were not expected to differ from one another. Furthermore, based on the Common Ingroup Identity Model (Gaertner et al., 1993), it was hypothesized that superordinate group representations would mirror this pattern and mediate the effects on the reduction of bias.

As predicted, the analyses revealed that when the groups were of equal status and task perspectives were different, intergroup bias was lowest (see Table 5.1). The Equal Status/Different Dimension condition displayed significantly less bias than the combination of these other three conditions. Analyses within each condition further demonstrated that intergroup bias was present within the Equal Status/Same Dimension condition; the Unequal Status/Same Dimension condition; and the Unequal Status/Different Dimension condition; but not, as expected, within the Equal Status/Different Dimension condition. Consistent with the Mutual Intergroup Differentiation framework, the difference in bias between the Equal Status/Different Dimension and the Equal Status/Same Dimension condition alone was significant.

TABLE 5.1. Group Evaluations (1–7) as a Function of Status and Task Differentiation

	Outgroup Evaluations	Ingroup Evaluations	Bias (Ingroup – Outgroup)
Equal Status			
Different Task	5.67	5.66	–.01
Same Task	5.29	5.61	.32
Unequal Status			
Different Task	5.34	5.62	.28
Same Task	5.29	5.49	.20

These effects appeared more due to differences in outgroup evaluations rather than in ingroup evaluations (see Table 5.1). Participants in the Equal Status/Different Dimension condition had more positive outgroup attitudes than did participants in the combination of the other three conditions. Also mirroring the pattern for bias, outgroup evaluations were significantly more positive in the Equal Status/Different Dimension than in the Equal Status/Same Dimension condition alone. In contrast to the results for bias and outgroup evaluations, ingroup evaluations showed no significant effects.

Consistent with the proposed mediating mechanism, the representation of the aggregate feeling like one group was higher than in each of the other three conditions (i.e., equal status–same task, unequal status–different task, and unequal status–same task). Furthermore, the one-group representation mediated the relation between the experimental manipulations of status and task perspective on intergroup bias. The significant predicted effects for bias and outgroup evaluations became nonsignificant once one-group representations were considered in multiple regression mediation analyses. These findings are consistent with the proposed value of equal status , primarily, as Hewstone and Brown (1986) propose, when the distinctiveness between groups is maintained.

An additional study using a different paradigm similarly revealed the importance of maintaining group distinctiveness when equal status groups interact cooperatively. In this study, we varied relative group status among actual employees of many different companies by asking them to imagine that their current organization was about to merge with another (Mottola, 1996). In one condition, their present company was described as higher in status than the other in terms generating greater sales and greater profits. In another condition, their company was lower in status on both dimensions. In a third condition, both companies were described as having equal status in terms of both sales and profit. In a fourth condition, their company was described as higher in status on one dimension (e.g., profit), but the other company was higher on the other dimension. Consistent with the hypothesis and the previous study, participants in the fourth condition in which one company had higher profit and the other higher sales anticipated that they would more strongly identify with the merged organization, that it would have higher levels of organizational unity and enjoy greater success than did participants in each of the other three conditions (which did not differ from one another). Thus, when groups have equal status and each group can maintain positive distinctiveness, we can anticipate greater acceptance of a superordinate identity from the members of both groups and more successful intergroup contact.

☐ Conclusion

In general, the results of the experiments and survey studies presented in this chapter offer evidence in support of the factors identified by the Contact Hypothesis to be critical for reducing intergroup bias. Across these studies, cooperative interdependence, and perceptions of cooperation, of supportive norms, of personalization, and of equal status consistently relate to more positive intergroup attitudes. However, supportive of social identity theory, equal status promotes more positive intergroup relations only when it does not engender threats to group identity; when it does, equal status groups show higher levels of bias than do unequal status groups.

Beyond previous studies of the Contact Hypothesis, our results also indicate the central role of superordinate, one group representations for mediating reductions of bias. For laboratory groups, stepfamilies, racial and ethnic groups, and corporate mergers, the more the groups feel like one and the less they feel like two, the lower the level of bias. Thus, theoretically, diverse situational factors may share a common mechanism for reducing bias.

In summary, the findings of our survey studies in natural settings converge with those of the laboratory study in offering support for the Common Ingroup Identity Model. Perceptions of more favorable conditions of contact predicted less differentiated, more superordinate representations of the memberships that, in part, seemed to contribute to reduced intergroup bias in affective reactions. These studies also offer provocative evidence for the role of a dual identity in intergroup bias. In intergroup contexts in which the formation of a single, more inclusive superordinate group is a desired goal, the continued existence of the earlier subgroup identities (even simultaneously with a superordinate identity) may be perceived as a sign that the amalgamation process is failing. Corporate mergers and the formation of blended families seem from our preliminary research to represent such contexts. In contrast, in contexts in which the two subgroups are conceived as working constructively toward a common goal—such as being on the "same team" in the high school study—a dual identity predicts more positive intergroup relations.

Our findings that factors identified by the Contact Hypothesis operate largely by creating one-group representations have relevance to enduring issues in intergroup relations. Although several structural integration patterns have historically characterized ethnic relations in societies in which different social and cultural groups have to coexist, we may begin to speculate about which pattern (i.e., assimilation, pluralism, or separatism) in any particular situational context would best encourage more positive beliefs, feelings and behaviors toward members of other groups. Assimilation comes closest to the melting pot metaphor to achieve homogeneity and integration. This pattern, however, in practice usually requires minorities to forsake their cultural distinctiveness as the price for acceptance into mainstream or dominant culture. This is closest to a one-group representation. Pluralism articulates the metaphor of a mosaic in which the cultural distinctiveness of all groups is visible and accepted within an integrated society. This resembles a dual identity. Separatism represents the metaphor of a mixture of oil and water in which each group remains structurally apart (i.e., segregated) from the others and each maintains its cultural distinctiveness. This is essentially a different-groups representation. Thus, consideration of the Contact Hypothesis and how it works may need to go beyond personal cognitive representations to encompass cultural values and goals.

Cognitive and Affective Priming: Antecedents and Consequences of a Common Ingroup Identity

As we have discussed in earlier chapters, the Common Ingroup Identity Model recognizes the central role of social cognition, specifically social categorization, in ameliorating as well as in creating intergroup bias. In two previous chapters, we considered how intergroup differentiation and the salience of intergroup boundaries (Chapter 4) and the nature of intergroup contact (Chapter 5) influence intergroup attitudes and how this effect is mediated by group representations. This chapter examines how cognitive and affective experiences, often apparently unrelated to intergroup interaction, can directly and indirectly facilitate more inclusive, superordinate representations and reduce intergroup bias.

Bodenhausen (1993) distinguished between *integral affect*, which is "elicited by the social group itself and the usual conditions and contexts with which that group is associated" (p. 14), and *incidental affect*, which involves emotions elicited by events unrelated to the intergroup context. Cognitive responses may similarly be elicited integrally, in terms of direct associations with a group or responses to the group's actions, or incidentally, in terms of responses to prior or contemporaneous events that are perceived to be unrelated to a group or its actions. In this chapter, we focus primarily on *incidental* cognitive and affective experiences.

Intergroup contact, particularly involving meaningful entities, can immediately elicit integral cognitive and affective associations (Dovidio &

103

Gaertner, 1993). Because these integral affective and cognitive responses are overlearned and "habitual," and often are supported by the shape of the intergroup interaction, direct attempts to alter them are particularly difficult, and often they meet with resistance and reactance (Dovidio, Kawakami, & Gaertner, 2000). Under these circumstances, incidental experiences that elicit favorable and inclusive associations and arouse positive affect may more effectively initiate—that is, prime—the types of thoughts, feelings, and actions that can begin to alter intergroup boundaries, facilitate the development of a common ingroup identity, and begin to improve intergroup relations. An understanding of how incidental cognitive and affective experiences influence intergroup attitudes can thus help in identifying alternate strategies for reducing bias when the nature of intergroup relations or the particular intergroup contact situation precludes more direct strategies.

The first section of the chapter explores how cognitive priming of ingroups and outgroups—specifically of "we's" and "they's"—can *automatically* activate favorable or unfavorable evaluative biases. This activation may also affect interaction with others in significant, but not always conscious, ways. Thus, positive connotations associated with the word "we" provide one mechanism by which the recategorization of outgroup members from "them" to "us" can improve attitudes toward former outgroup members. In addition, affect can either directly impact categorization or may moderate the impact of contextual factors (such as cooperation or competition) on social cognition and categorization (Isen, 1993). In the second section of this chapter, we report research that investigates how affect, specifically incidental positive affect, can shape intergroup attitudes.

☐ Cognitive Priming

The robustness and breadth of the consequences of the categorization of people into ingroups and outgroups, which we discussed in Chapter 3, argue for the importance of the ingroup/outgroup distinction in impression formation. As a consequence of the functional significance and prevalence of this distinction in everyday life, the categorization of people into ingroups and outgroup may spontaneously elicit systematic cognitive and affective responses. In this section on cognitive priming we therefore first investigate the automaticity of evaluative responses to stimuli indicating ingroup and outgroup membership.

We propose that words designating ingroup and outgroup status (such as the pronouns "we" and "they") may automatically introduce evaluative biases into the perception of new and unfamiliar people. In automatic processing, because of learned associations, the mere presence of a stimulus activates a concept or response, even if the person attempts to ignore the stimulus. Thus, simply using an ingroup designator (e.g., "we") in thought or speech to refer to a person may automatically establish a positive predisposition toward that person, whereas the use of an outgroup designator (e.g., "they") may elicit a less positive or even a negative predisposition.

In this section, we summarize four experiments that explored how ingroup and outgroup designators could systematically affect the way information is processed and how new evaluative associations are formed. In particular, two studies investigate how people develop new evaluations of stimuli (the first study) and expectations of people (the fourth study) when they are linked systematically with ingroup and outgroup pronouns. The two other experiments examine how the presentation of ingroup and outgroup pronouns can automatically and unconsciously activate evaluative associations.

Ingroup and Outgroup Associations

The question addressed in the first of this series of experiments (Perdue et al., 1990, Experiment 1) was whether, through classical conditioning, ingroup and outgroup designators (e.g., "we" and "they") could function to establish evaluative responses to novel, unfamiliar targets. The principles of higher-order conditioning predict that if a word with emotional meaning "is paired a number of times with a neutral stimulus, like a nonsense syllable, the meaningless word will in the process come to elicit the meaning response" (Staats, 1968, p. 25). Words such as "us" or "them" used consistently and contiguously with names for novel groups or target persons may therefore produce classically conditioned affective responses to those names (and, by extension, to those persons). For example, Staats and Staats (1958) found that a meaningless syllable (e.g., xeh) was rated as more pleasant if it had been consistently paired with real words having positive connotations; pairings with real words having negative connotations eventually produced an unpleasant rating of the nonsense syllable. In addition, in a related study, Staats and Staats (1958) conditioned evaluative responses to national labels (e.g., Swedish, Dutch) by pairing them with either positive words (e.g., sacred, happy) or negative words (e.g., ugly, failure). Ratings of the nationalities were more evaluatively positive when they had been paired with more evaluatively positive words. Thus, merely encountering the word "us" in association with a group label or with the name of an individual may, with repetition, condition a positive predisposition to that group or person—even if the person or group is novel or previously evaluatively neutral. The word "them" co-occurring with the name of a group or a person could establish less positive associations, or perhaps even some negative associations (Holtz, 1989; Rosenbaum & Holtz, 1985).

To evaluate this hypothesis, participants were repeatedly exposed to pairings of collective pronouns (e.g., "we") and nonsense syllables (e.g., "xeh") during a task in which participants were asked to indicate which letter string in a pair (e.g., "we" or "xeh") was an actual word. Among the 108 trials were 20 in which a nonsense syllable (e.g., "xeh") was paired with ingroup-designating pronouns (e.g., "us," "we," or "ours") and 20 in which another nonsense syllable was paired with outgroup-designating pronouns (e.g., "them," "they," or "theirs"). After the word identification task, participants rated the pleasantness of the nonsense syllable associated with the ingroup pronouns, the nonsense syllable associated with outgroup pronouns, and four control nonsense syllables that were not part of the identification task.

The results of these ratings, presented as standardized scores, are presented in Figure 6.1. As predicted, nonsense syllables paired with ingroup pronouns were rated more positively than the syllables paired with outgroup pronouns and the control syllables. The syllables paired with outgroup pronouns were rated somewhat, but not significantly less positively than the control pronouns. Furthermore, when debriefed, participants showed no awareness of the actual contingency between the se-

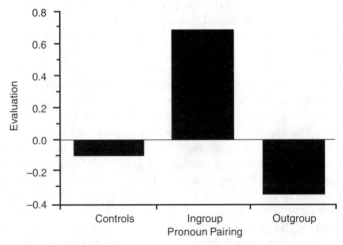

FIGURE 6.1. Ratings of target syllables as a function of pronoun pairing. From "Us" and "Them": Social Categorization and the Process of Intergroup Bias," by C. W. Perdue, J. F. Dovidio, M. B. Gurtman, & R. B. Tyler, 1990, *Journal of Personality and Social Psychology, 59,* pp. 475–486.

lected nonsense syllables and the group designating pronouns paired with them. Thus, ingroup and outgroup designation, even without reference to specific groups, elicited spontaneously different evaluative associations and conveyed these evaluations to new stimuli despite the fact that participants could not articulate the contingencies between them.

Semantic Priming

Whereas the previous experiment investigated classical conditioning of evaluative responses, a second experiment (Perdue et al., 1990, Experiment 2) examined the hypothesis that exposure to ingroup and to outgroup designators (e.g., "we" and "they") outside of awareness could bias the processing of any subsequently encountered information because of the effects of semantic priming (Meyer & Schvaneveldt, 1971). That is, this study explored implicit attitudes toward ingroups and outgroups. Implicit attitudes are evaluations that are automatically activated by the mere presence (actual or symbolic) of the attitude object (Greenwald & Banaji, 1995, p. 15). They commonly function in an unconscious fashion, without awareness and volition. Implicit attitudes (and stereotypes) develop with repeated pairings, either through direct experience (Fazio, Chen, McDonel, & Sherman, 1982) or social learning of the association (Devine, 1989) between the category or object and evaluative and semantic characteristics.

Response latency procedures and other techniques, often borrowed from cognitive psychology, have been frequently used in social psychology to assess implicit attitudes (Dovidio & Fazio, 1992; Fazio et al., 1995; Fazio, Sanbonmatsu, Powell, & Kardes, 1986), as well as the content of implicit stereotypes (Banaji & Greenwald, 1995; Dovidio, Evans, & Tyler, 1986; Gaertner & McLaughlin, 1983; Hense, Penner, & Nelson, 1995). Automatic attitude and stereotype activation has been found for a range of social groups, including Blacks (Devine, 1989; Dovidio, Kawakami et al., 1997; Lepore & Brown, 1997; Kawakami, Dion, & Dovidio, 1998, 2000; Fazio et al., 1995; Vanman et al., 1997; Wittenbrink, Judd, & Park, 1997), women and men (Blair & Banaji, 1996; Banaji & Greenwald, 1995; Banaji & Hardin, 1996; Banaji, Hardin, & Rothman, 1993), elderly people (Hense et al., 1995; Perdue & Gurtman, 1990), Asians (Macrae, Bodenhausen, & Milne, 1995), and a variety of other categories such as soccer hooligans, child abusers, and professors (Dijksterhuis & van Knippenberg, 1996; Macrae, Stangor, & Milne, 1994).

Specifically, in this study in intergroup attitudes more generally (Perdue et al., 1990, Experiment 2), ingroup and outgroup designators (e.g., "we" and "they") were presented briefly (55 msec) on a computer screen and then masked by positive or negative traits. Masking involves presenting a second stimulus immediately over the first, such that people are not consciously aware that the first stimulus was actually presented. In this case, the positive and negative traits masked the first stimulus, the pronouns, in such a way that participants had no conscious awareness of the presence of the ingroup and outgroup designators (see Perdue & Gurtman, 1990). Previous research has demonstrated that words presented outside of awareness can temporarily increase the accessibility of semantically (Fowler, Wolford, Slade, & Tassinary, 1981) and evaluatively (Perdue & Gurtman, 1990) related constructs. Participants in this study were asked to decide as quickly as possible whether each trait adjective was positive or negative, with decision latencies as the dependent measures. Shorter latencies are assumed to reflect greater association.

It was hypothesized that priming with ingroup and outgroup designators would automatically activate other highly associated constructs in memory. For example, Fazio et al. (1986) found that attitude objects with strong evaluative associations automatically facilitated responses to similarly valenced (positive or negative) trait adjectives. If ingroup-referent terms elicit more evaluatively positive associates, then the effect of such prior activation should be to prime subsequently encountered positive constructs, facilitating response times to positive trait information (e.g., helpful) in relation to those for negative trait information (e.g., clumsy). Response times to negative traits might also be facilitated following the presentation of an outgroup prime (Holtz, 1989).

Consistent with the predictions, the results of this study indicated that ingroup and outgroup pronouns at least transiently influence social information processing by altering the relative accessibility of constructs with similar evaluative connotations. In particular, participants were able to make decisions that a positive trait (e.g., helpful, competent) was a favorable one (rather than an unfavorable one) significantly more quickly after exposure to the masked words "us," "we," "ours," than after being primed by the masked words "them," "they," and "theirs." Conversely, participants made decisions that negative traits (e.g., impolite, wasteful) were unfavorable more quickly when they were preceded by masked outgroup designators than by masked ingroup designators. The conceptions of an individual as a "we" or a "they" may thus automatically and unconsciously bias the constructs used to construe that person.

Priming: Favoritism or Derogation?

Although the previous priming experiment demonstrated that ingroup- and outgroup-designating terms influenced the *relative* accessibility of positive and negative constructs, it remains unclear whether ingroup designators facilitate positive associations or inhibit negative associations, whether outgroup designators facilitate negative associations or inhibit positive associations, or whether some combination of these effects occurs. Thus, another experiment (Perdue et al., 1990, Experiment 3) was designed to examine the automatic effects of an ingroup designator and an outgroup designator in relation to a no-prime baseline condition in which the target trait words were preceded by a semantically meaningless control string (xxx) (see Fazio et al., 1986).

As in the previous priming study, participants were asked to make decisions concerning positive and negative adjectives after the presentation of a masked priming stimulus—that is, a word presented without the participant's awareness. The participant's task was quite different in this case, however. Shortly before (250 msec) the presentation of the positive or negative word (e.g., good or untrustworthy), they were presented visibly with a group of six letters symbolizing either a person (PPPPPP) or a house (HHHHHH). Their task was to indicate their decision, by pressing a "yes" or "no" key, about whether that word could ever describe a person (PPPPPP) or a house (HHHHHH). Responses to the person category were of central interest. The house primes and the use of test words that could describe houses but not people (e.g., drafty) were used to ensure that the correct answer was not always "yes." The central manipulation, however, involved a word presented subliminally before the person category (PPPPPP). Following the procedure of Bargh and Pietromonaco (1982), an ingroup or outgroup pronoun (e.g., "we" or "they") was presented for 75 msec and then immediately masked (i.e., hidden) by the PPPPPP or HHHHHH letter string, which limited exposure to the word (keeping participants unaware of its presence) and also cued participants to think about a specific category of targets (i.e., people or houses). The dependent measure was again response latency .

The results, which are illustrated in Figure 6.2, revealed the anticipated effects for ingroup and outgroup masked primes. Comparing the effects of just the ingroup and outgroup primes (i.e., "we" and the "they," but not the control prime, "xxx"), positive traits were responded to significantly faster following "we" than following "they;" negative traits were responded to somewhat, but not significantly, faster following "they" than following "we." Thus, as seen in the previous priming study, an ingroup-designating word (we) presented outside the perceiver's conscious awareness facilitated access to positive constructs in semantic memory in relation to the effects of an outgroup-designating word (they), as well as to the effects of the control (xxx) prime. In contrast, as seen in Figure 6.2, response latencies following the control (xxx) prime closely tracked the latencies following the "they" prime. This finding suggests that the

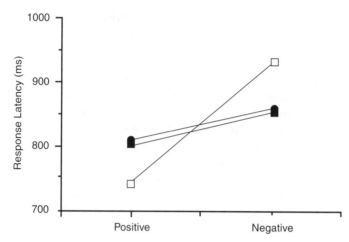

FIGURE 6.2. Response latencies to positive a'd negative traits as a function of prime type: we, they, and xxx. From "'Us' and 'Them': Social Categorization and the Process of Intergroup Bias," by C. W. Perdue, J. F. Dovidio, M. B. Gurtman, & R. B. Tyler, 1990, *Journal of Personality and Social Psychology, 59,* pp. 475–486.

outgroup prime was not actively promoting negative construct accessibility but instead that it was more neutral in priming consequences than was the ingroup designator. This interpretation is consistent with Brewer's (1979) conclusion that intergroup biases, at least in the minimal intergroup situation, are more a product of ingroup favoritism than of outgroup derogation.

   This fundamental and automatic ingroup favoritism bias also occurs when ingroup and outgroup membership is experimentally created using a minimal group task. Otten and Wentura (1999) assigned students in two studies, ostensibly on the basis of their task performance but actually randomly, as members of the concave or convex group (Study 1) or as members of the figure or ground group (Study 2). These labels were used in a subsequent priming task in which they were presented as primes out of awareness (i.e., presented very rapidly and then masked), and then participants were asked to make judgments about positive and negative words. Even though group assignment was random and the group membership had no previous or future material consequence, ingroup primes facilitated responses to positive words more so than did outgroup primes. Moreover, as indicated by a control prime condition, this effect was primarily due to facilitation of positive words by ingroup rather than by facilitation of negative words by outgroup primes. These findings thus conceptually replicate our work using ingroup and outgroup pronouns as primes. In the next study, we examined whether a person's use of ingroup pronouns when referring to other people systematically influences expectations of those others.

Priming Expectations

The first three experiments that we presented in this section have been highly cognitive and microscopic in nature. Ratings of nonsense syllables and response latencies were the dependent measures. In addition, the experimental contexts have been nonsocial; participants participated individually, often interacting primarily with a computer. The question we next asked, then, was whether the priming effects we observed have any implications for actual social interaction.

This study concerned the expectations that people form of others, with whom they expect to interact, on the basis of the ingroup and outgroup references (Dovidio, Tobriner, Rioux, & Gaertner, 1991). From our previous experiments, we hypothesized that referring to others in ingroup terms (i.e., using "we," "us," and "ours") compared to outgroup terms (i.e., using "they," "them," and "theirs") would elicit more positive expectations. Furthermore, in this study we explicitly considered the possibility that these more positive expectations would be due, at least in part, to the belief that these others are or are not members of one's own group.

Participants in this study began the session individually but were led to believe that they would be interacting with two other participants on a problem-solving task. After the participant completed some background information, the experimenter mentioned that the problem-solving session would be audio-recorded and that one person would be asked to identify briefly the session number and the task instructions so that the experimenter could "keep track of the conditions." Participants were informed that they were "randomly" selected to identify the session and then asked to memorize a brief script and to repeat it into a microphone. The key manipulation was the pronouns used to describe the participants. In half of the cases, ingroup designators were consistently used. The script read: "Subjects are participating in a study involving problem-solving. *We* have been asked to evaluate a given situation. *Our* task is to make decisions how *we* would respond in this situation." In the other half of the cases, ingroup pronouns were replaced by outgroup pronouns (e.g., "they" for "we"). Participants were next asked to rate what they thought their interaction would be like on two 7-point ("not at all" to "very much") scales ("feeling like one group" and feeling like "separate individuals") and to evaluate what they expected the "other two participants" to be like on scales representing the positive (e.g., good) and negative (e.g., bad) dimensions used in the priming studies and on a "similar to self" scale. Separate analyses examining how the use of pronouns influences feelings toward others were performed for positive and negative evaluative ratings.

The results of the mediation analysis for positive attributes of other participants prior to interaction are summarized in Figure 6.3 make arrow pronouns (bold arrows indicate significant paths, $p < .05$). In the initial regression equation, which did not consider the effects of the hypothesized mediators, use of pronouns was significantly related to positive evaluations (beta = .26; see the first segment of the uppermost pathway). Consistent with the priming research, even though they were unaware of the manipulation, participants who used ingroup pronouns had more positive expectations of the other participants than did participants who used outgroup pronouns. Subsequent regression equations in the mediation analyses revealed the expected pathways: Participants using ingroup pronouns reported that the interaction would feel more like one group and less like separate individuals than did participants who used outgroup pronouns; these ratings, in turn, influenced feelings of closeness. The more the interaction was expected to feel like one group and the less like separate individuals, the more they felt that the others would be similar to them. These feelings of similarity to the self then directly related to positive evaluations. Demonstrating the importance of the proposed mediating mechanisms, the direct path from pronoun use to evaluation was nonsignificant when the mediating variables were considered in the final regression equation. As illustrated in the uppermost path of Figure 6.3, whereas the path from pronoun use to positive evalu-

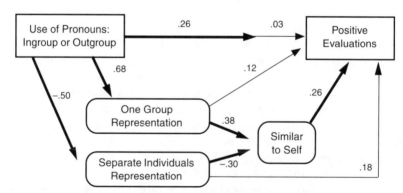

FIGURE 6.3. The direct and indirect effects of the use of ingroup and outgroup pronouns on interpersonal expectations. Adapted from "Stereotypes and Evaluative Intergroup Bias," by J. F. Dovidio & S. L. Gaertner, 1993. In D. M. Mackie & D. L. Hamilton (Eds.), *Affect, cognition, and stereotyping: Interactive processes in intergroup perception*, pp. 167–193. Copyright by Academic Press, Orlando, FL.

ations prior to interaction was significant *before* the mediators were considered (beta = .26; first segment), the path was nonsignificant *after* the mediators were considered (beta = .03; second segment). This result provides strong evidence of mediation of positive expectations of others. The analyses performed on the negative attributes, in contrast, were nonsignificant. In general, at least in terms of positive feelings, the overall pattern of the results suggests that the use of ingroup designating pronouns in thought and speech may be sufficient to generate more inclusive conceptions of group boundaries, which in turn lead to more positive expectations of others.

The importance of group conceptions of boundaries was also evidenced after participants had the opportunity to interact. Ratings of being like one group directly predicted evaluations on positive attributes (beta = .46) and indirectly predicted these evaluation through perceived similarity to the self (betas for those two paths were .52 and .37).

Cognitive Priming: Summary

In summary, many current theories of schema-based responding propose that the identification and classification of individuals as members of groups activates schema-relevant cognitions and evaluations. The results of the four studies we have presented in this section suggest that ingroup-outgroup categorization may have a basic, general effect. That is, the fundamental categorization of an individual as a member of one's own group or not in itself can give rise to differential affect and evaluation. These evaluative responses occur spontaneously and without conscious awareness, and, even without category-specific (i.e., stereotypic) cognitive representations, they can bias the nature of subsequent interactions. In the next section of this chapter, we explore how more general priming with positive affect can influence social categorization and intergroup attitudes.

☐ Affective Priming

Positive affect can significantly and systematically influence the inclusiveness of cognitive categories associated with both people and objects. Positive affect and its influence on *non*social categorization was initially investigated by Isen and Daubman (1984). In their study, participants were given the name of objects (e.g., belt) and were asked to rate how well these objects fit into categories (e.g., clothing). They found that people experiencing positive affect demonstrated broader, more inclusive categorization of objects than did people in an affect control condition. Specifically, compared to the control group, people experiencing positive affect were more likely to include nontypical exemplars as members of associated categories. People, regardless of the affect condition, identified typical exemplars as members of the categories, presumably because their membership was already well-defined. Isen and Daubman (1984) proposed that positive affect promotes the use of more material, particularly positive material, and more diverse information, thereby establishing a larger cognitive context in which more connections between nontypical exemplars and the categories can be identified. Our interest in this work relates to the potential of incidental positive affect for facilitating the impression that ingroup and outgroup members share a common identity.

Theoretically, these findings are consistent with Isen's (1987, pp. 234–235) hypothesis that positive affect influences the organization of cognitive material. Positive affect increases the accessibility of diverse ideas and produces a more complex associative context than normally occurs (Isen, Johnson, Mertz, & Robinson, 1985). As Tversky and Gati (1978) found, when people have more information and ideas about concepts, they are more likely to report similarities when they are motivated to perceive similarities and to report differences when they are motivated to perceive dissimilarities. Thus, when framed appropriately, positive affect can increase categorization breadth for neutral as well as positive stimuli (see also Murray, Sujan, Hirt, & Sujan, 1990).

Isen, Niedenthal, and Cantor (1992) extended these findings to social categorization; they hypothesized that positive affect would facilitate broader social categorization by leading people to associate what is usually seen as a neutral target with a positive category. Because positive affect primes positive material in memory, it facilitates a connection between the target and the positive category. As a consequence, people experiencing positive affect would be more likely to include nontypical exemplars into socially desirable categories. For instance, a grandmother and a bartender could both be considered examples of "nurturant people," but a bartender would be considered a nontypical (and relatively neutral) exemplar whereas a grandmother would be a typical exemplar. The results supported the predictions and the proposed mechanism. Positive affect increased the extent to which a nontypical exemplar was associated with a positive category. Also as predicted, positive affect did not increase the extent to which nontypical exemplars were associated with negative categories (i.e., emotionally unstable people and pretentious people), presumably because positive affect does not activate negative material and connections.

In general, the research on positive affect suggests that its influence on category breadth is moderated by the valence (positive or negative) of the category and by the valence and the strength (nontypical or typical) of the exemplars being considered. Isen (1993), for example, posited that positive affect has its effect by activating positive connections that exist between the category and the target being considered. As a consequence, with respect to the valence of the category, greater inclusiveness in categorization may be more likely to occur for more favorable social categories for which more positive connections exist. In contrast, positive affect would not be expected to increase the inclusiveness of categorization for negative categories, for which positive connections are rare or nonexistent (Isen et al., 1992).

With respect to the qualities of the target, the effect of positive affect has been found to facilitate the inclusion of nontypical but plausible examples into positive social categories more than typical examples (Isen et al., 1992). Typical exemplars are already highly associated with the social category. However, this effect occurs only for positive or neutral targets, for which potential positive connections exist, but not for negative targets for which associations are fundamentally unfavorable (Isen et al., 1992; Murray et al., 1990). Thus, when one has information about positively or even generally neutrally valenced others, positive affect may facilitate more inclusive, superordinate categorization because, as Isen et al. (1992) explain, "people who are feeling good may recognize aspects of ideas (especially neutral or ambiguous ones) that they do not normally think of, and these features will tend to be more positive than usual, as well" (p. 67). With respect to intergroup relations, attitudes toward outgroup members may be generally neutral for temporary laboratory groups with no current or past conflict; thus positive affect may be effective at producing the broader, more inclusive social categorizations that are hypothesized in the Common Ingroup Identity Model to be critical in reducing bias. In contrast, positive affect would not be expected to facilitate superordinate representations or to reduce intergroup bias between groups whose relations are generally negative—for which positive connections are unlikely to exist or to be activated. In addition, research involving neutral outgroups may have implications for understanding some "real-world" intergroup relations. For example, in Chapter 2 we speculated that the attitudes of aversive racists may reflect primarily pro-White rather than anti-Black sentiments such that, in an absolute sense, their feelings about Blacks may be relatively neutral.

The present series of studies that we present had three main objectives (see also, Dovidio, Gaertner, & Loux, in press). One objective was to understand how incidental positive affect—affect aroused by a source external and unrelated to the intergroup relations (Bodenhausen, 1993)—influences intergroup attitudes. The first study examined this issue for laboratory groups not in conflict. The second explored these effects for laboratory groups in the context of explicit intergroup cooperation and competition. The third study extends these findings to "real" groups with a history of competition and conflict. The second objective, related directly to the Common Ingroup Identity Model, was to examine the mediating role of superordinate group representations for more favorable attitudes toward outgroup members and for the reduction of intergroup bias. Across the studies presented, the degree to which the manipulations influenced the extent to which the aggregate was expected to feel like one group or two separate groups was assessed, and, in turn, the relationship between these representations and intergroup attitudes was tested. The third objective was to understand how positive affect influences information processing in intergroup relations. The fourth study, which tested the accuracy of incidental recall and within-group confusions of statements made, explored whether positive affect produces more rigid, stereotypic, and heuristic types of processes or might permit or even facilitate more elaborative types of processing.

These studies used, with some variation, the same general paradigm. Participants were initially categorized into groups on the basis of preliminary tasks (i.e., laboratory groups), assigned randomly to a group category but ostensibly on the basis of a pretest indicating the participant's orientation (e.g., as an overestimator or underestimator), or assigned on the basis of identification with an existing, "real" entity (e.g., liberals or conservatives). The next intervention involved variations in the anticipated intergroup contact: to simply meet one another, to cooperate, to compete, or to interact with independent outcomes. Affect was then manipulated across the three studies in three ways: an unexpected gift of candy (vs. no gift), a comedy videotape (vs. a travelogue), or a Velten (1968) procedure in which participants are asked to repeat positive (e.g., "It's great to be alive!") or neutral ("There are sixty minutes in an hour.") statements. Participants next viewed a videotape of the group with which they were going to participate perform a problem-solving task related to the anticipated group task (e.g., the Winter Survival Problem). The main dependent measures, besides manipulation checks for affect (e.g., happy) and intergroup relations (e.g., cooperative), included superordinate group representations (the more the group would feel like one group and the less like two groups) and intergroup attitudes (evaluations in terms of, for example, how likable and friendly the other group was). The first study we present examined the role of positive affect on relations between laboratory groups without conflict.

Positive Affect and Laboratory Groups

This experiment specifically investigated how positive affect can influence intergroup perceptions and evaluations among members of laboratory groups in ways outlined by the Common Ingroup Identity Model (Dovidio et al., 1995). Although the design was more complicated (see Chapter 4), we now focus on the affect manipulation. In particular, we hypothesized that positive affect would influence intergroup attraction by affecting the salience of group boundaries. Murray et al. (1990) found that positive affect increased participants' cognitive flexibility in approaching categorization tasks (about types of television programs) and representations. In addition, as we discussed earlier, Isen and her colleagues (Isen, 1987; Isen & Daubman, 1984; Isen et al., 1992) have found that positive feelings can facilitate broader and more inclusive positive categorization and reduce intergroup distinctions (see also Stroessner, Hamilton, & Mackie, 1992; Urada & Miller, 2000). Thus we predicted that participants in positive feeling states would be more likely to develop a more inclusive, superordinate representation of the aggregate than would participants in the affect control condition.

Participants in this experiment first formed a group and worked together on a problem-solving task. Then, in preparation for a combined-group interaction, they saw a videotape, ostensibly of the other group. The experimenter asked the participants to "try to get to know the group as well as its solution [because] you will be interacting with them later." The videotape portrayed three confederates performing a similar problem-solving task. An affective manipulation was intended to create positive feelings. After the small group interaction and before viewing the videotape of the other group, participants in the condition designed to produce positive affect were given a gift of candy, as has been done in previous research (e.g., Isen & Daubman, 1984); in the control condition, no mention of candy was made.

Research on interpersonal behavior indicates that simply the association of positive events, which may elevate one's mood, with another person enhances attraction (Veitch & Griffitt, 1976) through social conditioning (Byrne & Clore, 1970; Lott & Lott, 1974). In intergroup situations, rewards associated with pleasant, cooperative interaction or success may similarly directly create more positive impressions of outgroup members (Worchel, Andreoli & Folger, 1977). Positive affect has also been found to increase helping and generosity, which might also reflect a more favorable orientation to others engendered by positive feelings (Isen, 1970; Isen & Levin, 1972). We hypothesized that positive affect can also influence intergroup attraction *indirectly* by affecting the salience of group boundaries, facilitating broader and more inclusive categorization and reducing intergroup distinctions (Stroessner et al., 1992). Thus we predicted that participants in positive feeling states would be more likely to develop a more inclusive, superordinate representation of the aggregate than would participants in the affect control condition. The measure of this superordinate representation reflected stronger ratings of the extent to which the total aggregate would feel like one group and weaker ratings of the extent to which it would feel like two groups in later interaction. Furthermore, we hypothesized that more inclusive representations of the aggregate would, in turn, predict lower levels of intergroup bias.

The results supported the predictions. As expected, positive affect increased the extent to which participants formed inclusive group representations, anticipating that the members of two groups would feel more like one, superordinate group and less like two separate groups. Moreover, as anticipated, stronger superordinate group representations, in turn, predicted lower levels of intergroup bias. The direct path from the affect manipulation to intergroup bias was nonsignificant. Thus, in general, the reduction of bias occurred in the way proposed by the Common Ingroup Identity Model: Bias was reduced primarily by the more favorable ratings of the outgroup produced as a consequence of being recategorized from members of the outgroup to members of the superordinate ingroup.

Although consistent with the predictions, we recognize that the findings of this experiment may be limited in both practical and conceptual ways. In particular, the intergroup situation involved laboratory groups with an intergroup relationship that was not clearly defined. That is, the groups were not in either explicit cooperation or competition with one another, factors that can have a profound impact on intergroup dynamics (Sherif et al., 1954). Relatedly and pragmatically, this research also did not involve groups with enduring or meaningful boundaries or with current or past conflicts. The nature of intergroup bias may be quite different for ecologically meaningful social entities than for laboratory groups (Mullen et al., 1992). Conceptually, the manner in which affect influences cognitive processes may also vary as a function of the context of decision making (Isen, 1993). That is, if positive affect facilitates elaborative processing, then the nature of information available can moderate the influence of positive affect on attitudes and behavior. Thus, the effects we obtained in this experiment may not necessarily generalize to situations involving explicit competitive relations between groups or strong and meaningful intergroup boundaries, particularly when outgroup membership is associated with negative attitudes and feelings. The next two experiments therefore investigated first the influence of positive affect on bias as a function of the relationship between laboratory groups and then the influence of positive affect on intergroup attitudes in the context of relations between meaningful entities.

Cooperative Versus Competitive Interdependence

The impact of positive affect may be moderated by the nature of contemporary or historical intergroup relations. Bodenhausen (1993) reported research (Bodenhausen, Kramer, & Susser, 1994) that demonstrated that positive affect increased negative stereotypic judgments of outgroup members. There are alternative theoretical explanations for these and related findings (see Wilder & Simon, in press). Mackie and her colleagues have proposed that positive affect may reduce the capacity for deliberative information processing and thereby increase reliance on *heuristic cues* (Mackie et al., 1989; Mackie & Worth, 1989; Worth & Mackie, 1987). Other researchers have also proposed that positive affect may increase people's use of heuristic cues, but because of reduced *motivation* to process information systematically (Bodenhausen, 1993; Schwarz, Bless, & Bohner, 1991). With respect to intergroup relations, either of these views suggest that positive affect might increase reliance on general contextual cues in intergroup categorization and judgments. Framing potential intergroup contact in terms of cooperation or competition may provide one such contextual cue. To the extent that intergroup competition defines the relationship between two groups, positive affect could strengthen the two-group representations of these groups and thereby *increase* bias. However, when group interactions involve cooperative, friendly, or even neutral relations (as in the previous experiment), positive affect may increase the inclusiveness of one's group boundaries and consequently reduce bias. This reasoning suggests that the impact of positive affect on intergroup bias would be moderated by the competitive or cooperative nature of the intergroup contact and its effects substantially mediated by the salience of intergroup boundaries.

Alternatively, it is possible that positive affect by facilitating *elaborative* processes—that is, increased processing rather than decreased (Isen, Daubman, & Nowicki, 1987; Isen et al., 1985)—could increase bias between members of competing groups. Because positive affect promotes elaboration and flexibility in thinking, it could increase the perception of difference between groups when people are motivated to look for distinctions (e.g., Isen, 1987, p. 234; Murray et al., 1990). Furthermore, when groups have competitive or antagonistic relations, positive mood could increase sensitivity to threat and risk (Isen & Geva, 1987; Isen, Nygren, & Ashby, 1988; Isen & Patrick, 1983) and increase perceptions of difference and distrust, thereby enhancing bias. However, when group interactions involve cooperative, friendly, or even neutral relations (as in the previous experiment), positive affect may increase the inclusiveness of one's group boundaries and consequently reduce bias. Thus, both the Mackie et al. (1989) and Isen et al. (1988) perspectives suggest that the influence of positive affect on bias may be moderated by the nature of the context and that positive affect may exacerbate intergroup bias between directly competing groups or meaningful entities with traditionally competing vested interests. However, Isen's view suggests that, although increases in group biases may be mediated in part by group representations, these increases may occur substantially in other ways as well (e.g., increasing sensitivity to threat, independent of the recognition of separate group identities).

To explore the issue further, we conducted a study that utilized laboratory groups (participants randomly informed that they were over- and underestimators). We explicitly varied the cooperative or competitive relationship between these groups. Participants, who were identified randomly but ostensibly on the basis of a pretest, as overestimators or underestimators, viewed videotapes designed to produce positive affect (a comedy tape) or maintain neutral affect (a demonstration of wine corking). Then they individually viewed a videotape of a group reflecting the alternative orientation (underestimators or overestimators) and were led to believe that they would later be cooperating with or competing against this group for a monetary prize. The dependent measures included representations of the entities as two groups or one group and evaluations of the outgroup.

On the basis of the research suggesting that people experiencing positive affect would be more sensitive to the structure of the intergroup context than would neutral affect, control participants (Isen, 1993; Mackie et al., 1989; Schwarz et al., 1991), we predicted an interaction between affect and the cooperative-competitive task structure on outgroup evaluations. Specifically, on the cooperative task, we expected positive affect participants to evaluate the other group more favorably than would neutral affect participants; however, on the competitive tasks, we anticipated that positive affect participants would evaluate the other group less favorably. Furthermore, based on our previous work on the Common Ingroup Identity Model (Gaertner et al., 1993) and on affect and intergroup bias (Dovidio et al., 1995), we hypothesized that these evaluative responses would be mediated by representations of the entities as one group or two.

Preliminary analyses revealed that the manipulations of the competitive versus cooperative intergroup relations and of affect were successful. In addition, as expected, outgroup attitudes were more favorable when the groups were cooperatively rather than competitively interdependent. Moreover, as the predicted, positive affect had different effects in cooperative and competitive contexts. When cooperation was anticipated, positive affect participants had more positive attitudes toward the other group then did neutral affect participants; when competition was anticipated, positive affect participants had *less* positive attitudes toward the other group then did neutral affect participants.

Evidence of the intervening processes was also consistent with the hypotheses. As anticipated, superordinate group representations were stronger when participants anticipated intergroup cooperation than when they expected intergroup competition. Moreover, experienced positive affect had the expected moderating influence. When participants anticipated cooperation, those reporting higher levels of positive affect had higher superordinate group ratings ($r = .36$). In contrast, when participants anticipated competition, higher levels of positive affect tended to be negatively correlated with superordinate group ratings ($r = -.11$). These correlations were significantly different from one another. In turn, higher superordinate group ratings were related to more favorable outgroup evaluations ($r = .40$). Taken together, these results indicate that positive affect can enhance sensitivity to the nature of intergroup interdependence (either cooperation or competition), and consequently the salience of intergroup boundaries, which then can shape intergroup attitudes.

Overall, the findings from this experiment extend the results of our previous laboratory work on the influence of positive affect on intergroup relations. Also, the potential mediating role of perceptions of the memberships as an inclusive, superordinate group is consistent with the propositions of the Common Ingroup Identity Model. Furthermore, these results suggest that the findings of Dovidio et al. (1995) concerning the relationship between positive affect and the reduction of intergroup bias between members of laboratory groups may not necessarily generalize to some types of meaningful entities. In particular, enduring groups and meaningful social entities, particularly those for which intergroup relations is a problem, often have histories of conflict and competition. As a consequence, positive affect may increase, rather than decrease, bias between members of these types of groups.

However, it is further possible that positive affect could increase perceptions of similarity and common fate when a common group identity is made salient (Gaertner et al., 1990), and consequently reduce bias even between traditionally competitive groups. Isen et al. (1992) found that positive affect increased the extent to which exemplars, particularly nontypical exemplars (e.g., bartender), were perceived to be representative of positive superordinate categories (e.g., nurturant). In addition, positive affect has been found to increase the association of both the self and different others to the same positive categories (Rust, 1995). In a similar fashion, positive affect may enhance the effectiveness of interventions designed to create a positive superordinate identity (e.g., through superordinate goals), even while maintaining some degree of separate group identities (e.g., African Americans, White Americans). The next experiment in this series thus examined the hypothesis that positive affect would increase bias between meaningful entities with generally conflicting interests and explored the role that emphasizing a common ingroup identity could have in reducing this bias.

Positive Affect and Meaningful Social Entities

This experiment (see Dovidio, Gaertner, Isen, Rust, & Guerra, 1998) partially replicated the procedures of Dovidio et al. (1995, the first study in this section), except that it involved social categories of some importance to participants' identity (liberals, conservatives; pro-fraternity, anti-fraternity). Participants first interacted in 3-person groups on a problem-solving task. Then, in preparation for a combined-group interaction, they saw a videotape of another group. The videotape portrayed three confederates, ostensibly representing a historically competitive group (e.g., liberals, if participants were conservatives), performing a similar problem-solving task. Affect and the salience of group membership were independently manipulated. The affect manipulation was intended to create positive feelings. After the small group interaction and before viewing the videotape of the other group, participants in the conditions designed to produce positive affect were either given candy bars or viewed a comedy videotaped segment; in the control conditions, either no mention of candy bars was made or participants viewed a "neutral" videotape. The salience of group membership was varied by the labels participants used to refer to the two groups and themselves throughout the experiment. In a condition designed to reinforce existing group boundaries, participants referred to others in terms of their separate group memberships (e.g., liberals or conservatives). In a condition that emphasized the superordinate connection between the groups (the Common Identity condition) and their interconnection, the participants' common identity as a student of the university prefaced the references to their group membership (e.g., *Colgate* liberals, *Colgate* conservatives). This dual identity condition in which subgroup and superordinate identities were salient simultaneously was found in an earlier field study (see Chapter 5) to relate to reduced levels of intergroup bias in a multi-ethnic high school (Gaertner et al., 1994). The primary dependent measures were cognitive representations of the aggregate and group evaluations.

The analysis of outgroup evaluations and intergroup evaluative bias (i.e., favoring the ingroup over the outgroup in evaluations) demonstrated the predicted effects. As predicted, in the Two Groups context, participants in the positive affect condition, compared to those in the neutral affect condition, exhibited less favorable outgroup attitudes and higher levels of bias. However, in the Dual Identity condition, positive affect participants showed more positive outgroup attitudes and lower levels of bias than did neutral affect participants. This pattern is strongly supportive of the hypothesized influence of positive affect on intergroup relations. Consistent with our earlier work, the analysis of ingroup evaluations did not produce this interaction; the effect on the bias is primarily attributable to outgroup evaluations. As in the previous studies, stronger superordinate group ratings were substantially correlated overall with lower levels of bias ($r = -.55$) and more favorable evaluations of the outgroup ($r = .55$). Consistent with our earlier work, superordinate group ratings were not significantly correlated with ingroup evaluations ($r = .12$).

To evaluate the hypothesized processes contributing to reduced bias in the Dual Identity condition and increased bias in the Two Groups condition, path analyses were computed separately for each condition. In particular, for the Dual Identity condition the manipulation of positive affect was hypothesized to produce more inclusive group categorization (i.e., higher superordinate group ratings), which in turn was predicted to lead to reduced bias. As illustrated in the top panel of the Figure 6.4, the obtained results were highly consistent with the hypothesized pattern. The manipulation of positive affect created higher levels of self-reported positive affect. Self-reported positive affect predicted, as expected, more inclusive group representations, which then significantly predicted lower levels of intergroup bias. The direct path from manipulated affect to bias was not significant. In general, these results conceptually replicate the processes demonstrated by the path analysis reported in Dovidio et al. (1995).

The path analysis for the Two Groups condition, which is represented in the lower panel of the Figure 6.4, also demonstrates a pattern of results that generally conforms to the predictions. Specifically, it was hypoth-

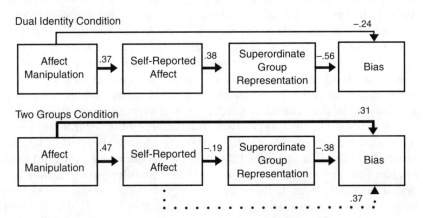

FIGURE 6.4. Paths from affect and representation to reduced bias in the Dual Identity and Two Groups Conditions. Adapted from "Positive affect, cognition, and the reduction of intergroup bias," by J. F. Dovidio, S. L. Gaertner, A. M. Isen, M. Rust, & P. Guerra, 1998. In C. Sedikides, J. Schopler, & C. Insko (Eds.), *Intergroup, cognition and intergroup behavior* (pp. 337–366). Copyright by Lawrence Erlbaum Associates, Hillsdale, NJ.

esized that for groups with meaningful social boundaries under conditions in which differences are salient, positive affect would lead to less inclusive group representations and therefore greater levels of bias. While the significant chi square value suggests that the originally proposed model (identified by solid-line paths) fits the obtained data marginally, the inclusion of an additional path from self-reported positive affect to bias (.37) significantly improves the fit of the model. The direct paths from the affect manipulation and from self-reported affect to bias suggest that positive affect may influence bias not only by increasing the degree to which participants perceived the groups as separate entities but also more directly by enhancing the salience and impact of different group identities on intergroup attitudes. In addition, directly supportive of the differential impact of positive affect, comparison of the paths between the two models revealed a significant difference (+. 38 vs. −.19) between the paths from self-reported affect to superordinate group representations between the Dual Identity and Two Groups conditions.

Overall, the results of this experiment demonstrated the predicted effect for positive affect on intergroup evaluations. When group boundaries are distinct and meaningful, positive affect may increase intergroup bias. Nevertheless, when a positive superordinate identity is made salient, positive affect can help reduce intergroup bias. These results are consistent with propositions of the Common Ingroup Identity Model, with the hypothesized processes by which positive affect influence cognitive processing (Isen et al., 1992), and with other recent research (Urada & Miller, 2000). For meaningful social entities, affect may influence the salience of features of the social context or the existing relationship that are involved in the analysis of the situation and in shaping one's reactions. For example, Isen proposes that, through enhanced deliberative processing, positive affect may increase *sensitivity* to threat. As a result, positive affect may tend to produce *less inclusive* group representations (that is, representations of the aggregate as two groups rather than as one group) and may make the potential *consequences* of that intergroup relation more salient (relating to the direct paths, independent of superordinate representations, from manipulated affect and self-reported affect to bias). Other research by Urada and Miller (2000) has also confirmed Isen's notion of broader categorization (as opposed to failure to differentiate) under incidental positive affect in the crossed categorization paradigm involving two categories differing in importance. We caution, though, that our findings can also still be viewed as consistent with a heuristic processing interpretation. That is, positive affect may increase reliance on the most salient group information available as a form of more simplified processing. The next study was designed to examine the cognitive processes more directly.

Intergroup Relations and Memory

This study was designed to provide a conceptual replication of the joint effects of affect and intergroup cooperation/competition we obtained earlier with laboratory groups—with four main differences. First, positive affect was manipulated in two ways, by videotapes and by a modified Velten (repeating positive or neutral statements) procedure. Second, instead of laboratory-formed groups, we used "real" social identities (pro-life/pro-choice). Participants were led to believe that the people on videotape were members of the other group. Third, in addition to cooperation and competition, we included an independent outcome condition. Fourth, to track the occurrence of more elaborative or diminished processing, we also included memory measures in this experiment.

With respect to memory, people recall fewer details about others classified as an outgroup member than as an ingroup member (Park & Rothbart, 1982), and categorization of others as an outgroup may increase intracategory errors in memory, such as confusions about which person in a group makes a specific comment (Taylor, Fiske, Etcoff, & Ruderman, 1978). Thus, we investigated the accuracy of recognition of the assignment of statements to specific individuals on the videotape and the number of intracategory (within-group) confusions in these attributions.

The measures of accuracy and type of errors in this study were included to examine, at least within this context, whether positive affect produces more elaborative or simpler processing. Participants were presented with a list of comments (half actual, half new) and asked to identify whether the comment was made by a member of the other group and, if so, by whom. To the extent that positive affect produces more deliberative processing, positive affect would be expected to relate directly to accuracy of statement assignment and inversely to intracategory confusions. That is, participants would be expected to show a high level of accuracy overall and to distinguish the unique contributions of each member of a group. To the extent to which positive affect promotes more heuristic processing, the opposite would be expected to occur, participants would be expected to be relatively inaccurate in recalling the details of the conversation, and they would be more likely to confuse the statements made by different members of the same group.

The affect manipulation was successful and comparably so for the videotape and Velten procedure. In addition, the nature of the intergroup context (cooperative, competitive, independent) had the anticipated impact on attitudes. In general, attitudes toward the outgroup were most positive in the cooperation condition, intermediately positive in the independent condition, and least positive in the competition condition. Furthermore, as predicted, affect significantly moderated these effects. Consistent with the previous studies, positive affect participants, compared to the control group, had more positive attitudes in the cooperation condition and less favorable attitudes in the competition and independent conditions. Also consistent with the previous work, the nature of the intergroup context influenced superordinate identities. Superordinate group ratings were highest in the cooperation condition, intermediate in the independent condition, and lowest in the competition condition. In addition, superordinate group ratings were significantly correlated with favorable outgroup attitudes ($r = .27$). This pattern of findings is consistent with the Common Ingroup Identity Model, in general, and with our previous research on positive affect, in particular.

The analyses of the identification of the statements made by members of the videotaped group members indicate that participants in positive moods were not less accurate overall (see also Bless, Clore et al., 1996; Bless, Schwarz, & Kemmelmeier, 1996; Forgas, 1998), but they did make more intracategory errors than did neutral mood participants. This latter finding suggests that positive-mood participants relied more than did neutral-mood participants on category information (group-based knowledge structures) relative to individualizing information (see Fiske & Neuberg, 1990). However, inconsistent with our expectations, this effect was consistent across the cooperative, competitive, and independent outcomes conditions.

In general, the findings of this study provide convergent evidence for the effects of positive affect on intergroup attitudes and help to illuminate some of the cognitive processes involved. The statement accuracy measures suggest that positive affect participants are not necessarily less able (i.e., because of limited capacity) or less motivated to process information about members of the other group. The intracategory error measure, however, indicates that they may be relying more on group-based than individuated impression processes. These findings are compatible with Bless, Clore et al.'s (1996) conclusion that happy moods do not "decrease either cognitive capacity or processing motivation, in general" but they do "increase . . . reliance on general knowledge structures" (p. 665). One important implication of the work of Bless, Clore et al. (1996) is that although positive affect people may typically rely on general knowledge structures, which often allow for efficient and parsimonious processing, their cognitive resources are flexible. Bless, Clore et al. (1996) propose: "If a situation is characterized as benign, individuals may rely on general knowledge structures, which usually serve them well. In contrast, if a situation is characterized as problematic, relying on one's usual routine is maladaptive, and attention to the specifics of the situation is called for" (p. 666). Isen's work (e.g., Isen, 1993) on positive affect and deliberative processing and findings related to positive affect and sensitivity to risk and threat indicate that positive affect participants may process "problematic" information in an even more detailed fashion than people not in positive moods. In general, then, these results support our previous research on the outcomes of positive affect on intergroup attitudes within competitive and noncompetitive situations. Moreover, they help to illuminate the psychological processes involved.

Priming with Positive Affect: Summary

The studies in this section of the chapter addressed three main objectives: (a) to understand how incidental positive affect influences intergroup attitudes; (b) to examine the mediating role of superordinate group representations for more favorable attitudes toward outgroup members and for the reduction of intergroup bias; and (c) to explore how positive affect influences elaborative and heuristic processing in intergroup relations.

With respect to the first objective, we found that incidental positive affect does influence intergroup attitudes, and that the effect is systematically moderated by the nature of intergroup contact. When groups have no previous history of conflict and when the immediate contact is nonthreatening (the first study in this section) or the groups are cooperatively interdependent (the third and fourth studies), positive affect can improve intergroup relations. Under these circumstances, positive affect produces more inclusive representations and increases the salience of actual or potential common identities. As a consequence, people experiencing positive incidental affect have more favorable attitudes and lower levels of bias than do those in neutral moods. However, when groups are in immediate competition or have histories of conflict and competition (the second, third, fourth studies), people experiencing positive affect have less favorable outgroup attitudes and higher levels of bias. This bias can be mitigated by making a common, positively valued identity salient (the second study). Thus, even in situations of perceived or actual group conflict, increasing the salience of a common ingroup identity—even when subgroup identities remain salient—represents a realistic strategy for potentially reducing bias, and incidental positive affect is a catalyst for reducing bias. As we have noted earlier, an understanding of the mechanisms by which intergroup bias can be reduced allows for the introduction of elements, such as reminders of shared group membership and affective inductions seemingly irrelevant to the group interaction, that can initiate a reduction of bias even when the immediate relations are perceived to be functionally competitive.

Moreover, this pattern of findings is conceptually consistent with the affective framework that guided the research. Specifically, Isen (1987,

1993) hypothesized that positive affect increases the accessibility of diverse ideas and produces a more complex associative context than normally occurs. As a consequence, people experiencing positive affect are more likely to report similarities when they are motivated to perceive similarities and to report differences when they are motivated to perceive dissimilarities.

With regard to our second objective, to understand how group representations mediate outgroup evaluations and intergroup bias, we found considerable evidence that is consistent with the central assumptions of the Common Ingroup Identity Model. Across all of the studies, more inclusive, superordinate representations predicted more positive attitudes toward the outgroup and lower levels of bias. In addition, the nature of the intergroup context influenced the inclusiveness of representations. As Gaertner et al. (1990; see Chapter 5) demonstrate, cooperative interdependence produces stronger one-group and weaker two-group representations of group memberships while also directly influence perceptions of the interaction. Across the present studies, expectations of cooperation also produced stronger superordinate group representations, whereas expectations of competition created weaker superordinate group representations (i.e., feeling less like one group and more like two groups).

Superordinate group representations, however, did not entirely mediate the effects of positive versus neutral affect. Whereas higher levels of positive affect generally significantly predicted more inclusive representations when group interaction was neutral (independent) or favorable (cooperative), the relationship tended to be negative when the relations were currently or historically competitive. Although the differences between these correlations were significant, in none of the studies was the negative correlation itself significant. In addition, interactions between the nature of the group interdependence (e.g., cooperative or competitive) and the manipulated affect on group representations only approached, but never fully attained, statistical significance. Thus, when intergroup relations are clearly defined and particularly when they are negative, positive affect has its influence in ways that are primarily independent of superordinate group representations. As we noted earlier, Isen's work (e.g., Isen et al., 1992) indicates that positive affect can increase the inclusiveness of categorization of exemplars that are reasonable but nontypical (e.g., a bartender for the category of nurturant people) but not for exemplars that are already highly typical (e.g., grandmother) or clearly not members of the category (e.g., drug addict). However, positive affect also has other effects, beyond its influence on categorization. It can increase *sensitivity* to risk or threat, but not necessarily the perceived degree of threat or difference between the groups (Isen, 1993). When intergroup relations are clearly competitive or negative the influence of positive affect may thus be more in terms of intensifying reactions to these conditions rather than through altering perceptions of group boundaries.

The third objective of this line of research was to explore how positive affect influences heuristic and elaborative cognitive processing. Our findings are consistent with those of Bless and his colleagues (Bless, Clore et al., 1996; Bless, Schwarz, & Wieland, 1996) who found that although positive affect can increase reliance on general knowledge structures ("top-down" processing such as the category-based processing in the fourth study), it does not necessarily produce inflexible and heuristic processing. Although the results for the memory measures for the fourth study did not directly support the Common Ingroup Identity Model, the systematic yet flexible nature of the information processing has implications for new tests of the model. For example, in intergroup contact situations with opportunity for interaction between the groups, we would expect that the development of a common ingroup identity would produce deeper and more individualized processing as others become recategorized from members of different groups to members of one's own group (see Chapter 3). As a consequence, people will rely less on original group membership for processing, producing fewer confusions among members within each original group (i.e., fewer intracategory errors along original group lines) and more confusions across members of the originally different groups (i.e., more intercategory errors). Thus, the findings related to positive affect suggest new ways to test the implications of our model more generally.

Overall, the four studies on affect in this section of the chapter indicate the importance of incidental positive affect on intergroup relations. Despite the obviously irrelevant source, incidental positive affect systematically influences how people think about intergroup interaction and how they respond to anticipated intergroup relations. Understanding how incidental affect shapes perceptions, cognitive processes, and impressions can also provide insight into the role of integral intergroup affect. To the extent that intergroup cooperation increases the likelihood of achieving valued goals, it is likely to produce consequent positive affect that should enhance inclusive representations and further reduce bias.

☐ Conclusion

This chapter examined how cognitive and affective priming can influence the accessibility and application of positive evaluations directly and indirectly through more inclusive group representations. Consistent with the Social Identity Theory and Brewer's (1979) theorizing, presentation of ingroup pronouns automatically elicits relatively positive responses; presentation of outgroup pronouns, at least in situations without conflict, does not necessarily produce relatively negative reactions. Of direct relevance to the Common Ingroup Identity Model, priming people with ingroup relative to outgroup pronouns and with positive affect can increase the likelihood that others will be considered as part of a common ingroup, which in turn can improve attitudes towards other people and groups. The influence of positive affect is relatively complex, however. The contemporary and historical relations between groups and the stereotypicality of individual group members can moderate the impact of positive affect on the ways people process information, the nature of group representations, and ultimately the favorability of intergroup attitudes. In the next chapter, we attempt to move beyond attitudes to examine the consequences of forming a common ingroup identity on other interpersonal and intergroup forms of behavior.

7

CHAPTER

Extending the Benefits of Recategorization

In the previous chapters we have examined the effects of intergroup differentiation, conditions of intergroup contact, and cognitive and affective priming on group representations and bias. Consistent with the Common Ingroup Identity Model, we have found evidence that aspects of intergroup contact that decrease intergroup differentiation promote an inclusive one-group representation, rather than a representation of two groups, and decrease intergroup bias (Chapter 4). Other research has indicated that factors identified by the Contact Hypothesis, such as cooperation as well as perceptions of equal status, supportive norms, and interpersonal interaction, also improve evaluations of outgroup members and decrease intergroup bias by changing members' representations of the aggregate from two groups to one group (Chapter 5). Both cognitive and affective priming, under appropriate conditions, can also enhance the inclusiveness of group representations and thereby reduce bias (Chapter 6).

For the vast majority of these studies, the main dependent measures were group evaluative biases and intergroup attitudes. This chapter examines how the benefits of recategorization extend to other measures of behavior and behavioral intentions, across time, and to the groups as a whole. We first consider other behavioral evidence of the effects of developing superordinate representations of the groups: how recategorization may be a catalyst for developing more personalized impressions of outgroup members through self-disclosure, and how it may facilitate helping and cooperation. After that, we examine how a sense of common community within a college setting influences students' support for the institution and their intentions to persist towards graduation. Then, the section that follows considers extensions of more positive attitudes across time and to the group as a whole (i.e., generalization).

☐ Behavioral Evidence

Direct evidence of the effects of recategorization on observable forms of behavior beyond self-reported attitudes comes from two studies. One investigated the effects on helping and self-disclosure; the other explored the influence of developing a common ingroup identity on intergroup cooperation.

Helping and Self-disclosure

Our field study of compliance with a request for assistance by Black and White interviewers at a football game as a function of whether they were members of the same or a different group (i.e., university) as the respondents (which we described in Chapter 3) provides initial evidence of the behavioral impact of forming a common ingroup identity. Research by Dovidio, Gaertner et al. (1997) further extended the Common Ingroup Identity Model by investigating the effects of a manipulation designed to induce recategorization on intergroup bias in helping and self-disclosure. Although the connection between positive intergroup attitudes and behaviors seems intuitive, the empirical extension from evaluative bias to intergroup behavior is not a trivial one. Much of the social categorization literature is based on self reports (e.g., trait ratings or hypothetical monetary or point distributions) without inclusion of behavioral measures. Even among self-report measures, there is often an inconsistency of results between positive and negative ratings. Bias on negative dimensions is less common and less pronounced than bias on positive dimensions (Wenzel & Mummendey, 1996).

The relationship between evaluative bias and actions also appears to be weak, in general. In a recent review of the literature regarding the relationship between racial prejudice and racial discrimination by Whites, Dovidio et al. (1996) found that the correlation was significant but relatively modest in magnitude ($r = .32$). In addition, Struch and Schwartz (1989) demonstrated that intergroup bias and intergroup discrimination were virtually unrelated ($r = .07$) and had different antecedents. The variables that predicted intergroup discrimination strongly, such as perceived conflict and trait inhumanity, predicted intergroup bias only weakly, if at all. Struch and Schwartz (1989) concluded, "These results make clear the danger of generalizing from research on in-group favoritism to intergroup aggression" (p. 371). The present research represents an initial examination of the consequences of promoting a common ingroup identity on positive behavioral interactions between groups.

Although, as Struch and Schwartz's (1989) work demonstrates, intergroup evaluative biases and intergroup discrimination may have different antecedents, the development of a common ingroup identity is likely to influence both evaluations and positive forms of intergroup interaction. With respect to helping, theoretically several factors could contribute to the effects of recategorization on intergroup helping. Recategorization could operate indirectly through several interpersonal processes. Recategorization of a person as an ingroup member increases perceptions of shared beliefs (e.g., Brown, 1984, 1995; Wilder, 1984). The perception of greater interpersonal similarity, in turn, typically facilitates helping (see Dovidio, 1984). In addition, recategorization may facilitate empathic arousal, whereby a person's motivational system becomes coordinated to the needs of another (Hornstein, 1976; Piliavin et al., 1981), which may motivate helpful and sometimes altruistic actions (see Batson, 1991).

Intergroup processes, as well as interpersonal processes, can promote helping. Hornstein and his colleagues (Flippen, Hornstein, Siegal, & Weitzman, 1996; Hornstein, 1976; Hornstein, Masor, Sole, & Heilman, 1971) have demonstrated that recognition of common group membership increases helping beyond the mere effects of interpersonal similarity or attraction. Hornstein and his colleagues (Hornstein, 1976; Sole, Marton, & Hornstein, 1975) proposed that factors such as similarity or common fate may give rise to a sense of "we-ness"—a sense of belonging to a common group. This sense of we-ness, in turn, leads to more positive behaviors such as helping, particularly under conditions of threat (Dovidio & Morris, 1975; Flippen et al., 1996). Sole et al. (1975) suggested that developing this sense of we-ness facilitated helping toward others independent of interpersonal attraction.

It is possible that the development of a common ingroup identity (the sense of we-ness) could also facilitate other forms of positive social interaction, such as the exchange of more self-disclosing information among members of the recategorized superordinate group. Recategorization fundamentally involves a more inclusive redefinition of the ingroup boundary, and self-disclosure is intimately involved in the regulation of interpersonal boundaries. According to Derlega, Metts, Petronio, and Margulis (1993), "It is useful to consider adjustments in self-disclosure outputs and inputs as similar to the opening and closing of 'boundaries'" (p. 67). Self-disclosure and interpersonal closeness are reciprocally related. Self-disclosure communicates a desire for intimacy and promotes closeness

(Altman & Taylor, 1973); in turn, as the closeness of the relationship between interactants increases, self-disclosure increases (Dindia & Allen, 1992) and can produce even greater involvement with the other person (Davis, 1976; Derlega & Chaikin, 1976; Shaffer, Pegalis, & Bazzini, 1996).

Aron and Aron (Aron & Aron, 1986; Aron, Aron, & Smollan, 1992; Aron, Aron, Tudor, & Nelson, 1991) have proposed that many aspects of close interpersonal relationships involve the inclusion of another person as part of the self—the incorporation of the other into one's self-concept. This process resembles those hypothesized for the development of a common ingroup identity. Brewer's (1979) analysis of the intergroup literature and Turner's (1985) self-categorization theory suggest that group formation brings ingroup members closer to the self. Smith and Henry (1996) observed, "With a relationship partner, as with an in-group that forms a significant social identity, people use the term we and share the other's perspective in important ways" (p. 636). Smith and Henry (1996) found evidence, paralleling Aron et al.'s (1991) results for close interpersonal relationships, that cognitive representations of the self and the ingroup are directly linked. Thus, creating a common ingroup identity may produce a bond of closeness that facilitates greater self-disclosure (Derlega et al., 1993), as well as greater trust, trustworthiness, and cooperativeness (Kramer & Brewer, 1984). We therefore hypothesized that recategorization from two groups to one superordinate group would increase both helping and self-disclosure between members of former outgroups.

The procedure used for developing a common superordinate representation or reinforcing a two-group representation was similar to that used in our previous research on group differentiation (e.g., Gaertner et al., 1989; see Chapter 4). Participants initially met in two three-person groups, ostensibly composed of overestimators or underestimators, in a study of group decision making. Following the 3-person group discussions, participants were informed of their subsequent contact with the other group. Aspects of the intergroup contact situation were manipulated to vary participants' cognitive representations as one group or two separate groups (e.g., integrated vs. segregated seating, common group name vs. different subgroup names, similar vs. different dress; see Gaertner et al., 1989; 1990). Under the conditions representing the one-group or two-group manipulations, the six participants worked again on the decision task and then completed questionnaires that assessed their cognitive representations of the aggregate and the impressions of the interaction and the interactants. Next, participants were introduced to the final phase of the experiment, which purportedly involved examining one-way and two-way interactions. These tasks provided the cover stories for assessing self-disclosure and helping.

To investigate self-disclosure, two pairs of participants were brought to separate cubicles. One dyad was composed of an overestimator and an underestimator; the other was composed of two members from the same original subgroup (i.e, two overestimators or two underestimators). Two different experimenters, unaware of dyad members' original subgroup identities, informed participants that they would be involved in an examination of "conversation preferences and interactions." Dyad members were asked to discuss a moderately disclosing topic, "What are you most afraid of?" These conversations were audio-taped and subsequently coded for level of intimacy.

To examine helping, the remaining two participants were escorted to separate rooms and informed that they had been chosen for the one-way communication condition and that they would be listening to a videotape of one of the previous participants in the two-way communication condition. One participant was informed that the person on the videotape was a member of their original subgroup category (e.g., an overestimator), whereas the other participant was told that the other person was from the opposite group. The audiotape presented a situation, modelled after that used by Dovidio, Allen, and Schroeder (1990) in their study of altruism, that involved the inability of the student to complete an important project because of illness. To provide the helping opportunity, following the procedure of Dovidio et al. (1990), at the conclusion of the session the experimenter handed the participant an envelope, explaining, "Since the person let us use his information, he asked us to distribute this note." The note contained an appeal to help by placing posters recruiting volunteers in various locations across campus. To help, participants were asked to identify the locations in which they would be willing to hang the posters. The dependent measure of helping was the number of locations indicated.

We predicted that in the two-groups condition, more favorable evaluations, more helping, and more self-disclosure would occur for same-group members than for different-group members. The condition designed to produce recategorization and enhance a one-group representation, however, was hypothesized to reduce and possibly eliminate this bias. The present research also explored whether cognitive representations of the aggregate as one group would mediate the reduction of bias in helping and self-disclosure as has been found for bias in evaluations (Gaertner et al., 1989, 1990).

As expected (see Table 7.1), the One Group manipulation produced more inclusive, one-group perceptions than did the Two Group manipulation, as well as more positive outgroup evaluations and lower levels of bias. Furthermore this manipulation had the predicted effect on the patterns of results for self-disclosure and helping. For self-disclosure, when

TABLE 7.1. Effects of the Group Manipulation on Ingroup and Outgroup
Evaluations and Behaviors

	Evaluations (1–7)	Self-disclosure (1–10)	Helping (Number of buildings)
Two-group condition			
Ingroup	5.76	5.38	4.83
Outgroup	5.35	4.41	2.25
Bias (ingroup – outgroup)	+0.41	+0.97	+2.58
One-group condition			
Ingroup	5.52	4.88	3.08
Outgroup	5.42	5.71	3.92
Bias (ingroup – outgroup)	+0.10	–0.83	–0.84

From "Extending the Benefits of Recategorization: Evaluations, Self-disclosure, and Helping," by J. F. Dovidio, S. L. Gaertner, A. Validzic, A. Matoka, B. Johnson, & S. Frazier, 1997, *Journal of Experimental Social Psychology, 33*, pp. 401–420.

separate group identities were reinforced by the Two Group manipulation, dyads composed of members of initially different groups exhibited less intimate self-disclosure than did dyads composed of members of the same original group. As predicted, however, the One Group manipulation eliminated this difference; in fact, under these conditions members of initially different groups were somewhat more intimately self-disclosing than were members of the same original groups. Furthermore, consistent with the prediction of the Common Ingroup Identity Model, the recategorization manipulation primarily affected behavior toward individuals who were initially members of the outgroup. Self-disclosure was significantly greater in dyads involving an original outgroup member (intergroup dyads) in the One Group manipulation condition than in the Two Group manipulation condition. There was no significant difference in self-disclosure between members of the same original groups (intragroup dyads) as a function of the One Group versus Two Group manipulation. Therefore, as hypothesized by the Common Ingroup Identity Model, establishing a superordinate identity reduces intergroup bias primarily by improving response to the outgroup.

The pattern of results for helping was similar but weaker and less fully consistent with the predictions (see Table 7.1). As anticipated, with the Two Group manipulation, participants were somewhat less helpful toward an original outgroup member than toward an original ingroup member. With the One Group manipulation, in contrast, there was no significant intergroup bias in helping. Paralleling the results for self-disclosure, participants were slightly more helpful to an original outgroup member than to an original ingroup member under these conditions. However, unlike the results for self-disclosure and inconsistent with predictions, participants were not significantly more helpful to original outgroup members as a consequence of recategorization: The difference in helping toward an original outgroup member was somewhat but not significantly greater in the One Group than in the Two Group condition. Overall, although less clear and strong than the findings for self-disclosure, this pattern of results for helping is generally consistent of the processes and consequences proposed in the Common Ingroup Identity Model.

To examine the hypothesized role of group representations, tests of mediation were performed on a composite score for each group that represented the average normalized score across the evaluation, helping, and self-disclosure measures (i.e., the mean of the z-scores for ingroup-outgroup differences on each measure for each group). The results of the mediation analysis for bias are supportive of the Common Ingroup Identity Model and replicate the results of Gaertner and colleagues (Gaertner et al. 1989, 1990). As illustrated in Figure 7.1, when the independent variable was considered by itself, the effect of the Group Manipulation on bias was substantially stronger (beta = −.60) than when the independent variable and the mediators were considered simultaneously (beta = −.37). Also, when the Group Manipulation and the mediators were considered simultaneously, higher one-group ratings tended to predict lower levels of bias. Similar tests for each of the measures of bias (i.e., bias in evaluations, self-disclosure, and helping) separately revealed the strongest evidence for mediation for evaluative bias, next most for helping, and least for self-disclosure.

In summary, the present research extends our previous work on the Common Ingroup Identity Model by demonstrating the effect of manipu-

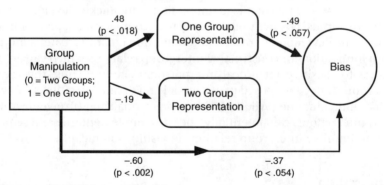

FIGURE 7.1. The Mediating Effect of One Group Representations on Bias. Adapted from "Extending the Benefits of Recategorization: Evaluations, Self-disclosure, and Helping," by J. F. Dovidio, S. L. Gaertner, A. Validzic, K. Matoka, & S. Frazier, 1997, *Journal of Experimental Social Psychology, 33*, pp. 401–420.

lations of cognitive representations of the aggregate on intergroup behaviors, as well as evaluations. Although Struch and Schwartz (1989) demonstrated that different factors may predict intergroup attitudes and behavior, the central mechanism of our model—the development of a superordinate identity—is hypothesized to affect both attitudes and behavior. Supportive of this hypothesis, the last experiment described in this chapter found that the manipulation of cognitive representations of the aggregate facilitated self-disclosing interactions between members of originally different groups and increased intergroup helping. These behaviors are particularly significant ones, because both self-disclosure and helping typically produce reciprocity. More intimate self-disclosure by one person normally encourages more intimate disclosure by the other (Archer & Berg, 1978). As the work of Miller, Brewer, and their colleagues (e.g., Miller et al., 1985) has demonstrated, personalized and self-disclosing interaction can be a significant factor in itself in reducing intergroup bias.

Considerable cross-cultural evidence also indicates the powerful influence of the norm of reciprocity on helping (Schroeder et al., 1995). According to this norm, people should help those who have helped them, and they should not help those who have denied them help for no legitimate reason (Gouldner, 1960). Thus, the development of a common ingroup identity can motivate interpersonal behaviors between members of initially different groups that can initiate reciprocal actions and concessions (see Deutsch, 1993; Osgood, 1962) that will not only reduce immediate tensions but can produce more harmonious intergroup relations beyond the contact situation.

As we proposed earlier (Gaertner et al., 1993), although finely differentiated impressions of outgroup members may not be an automatic consequence of forming a common ingroup identity, these more elaborated, differentiated, and personalized impressions can quickly develop because the newly formed positivity bias is likely to encourage more open communication. The development of a common ingroup identity creates a motivational foundation for constructive intergroup relations which can act as a catalyst for positive reciprocal interpersonal actions. Thus, the recategorization strategy proposed in our model and decategorization strategies, such as individuating (Wilder, 1984) and personalizing (Brewer & Miller, 1984) interactions, can potentially operate complementarily and sequentially to improve intergroup relations in lasting and meaningful ways.

Cooperation

Whereas helping is a unilateral action, cooperation usually involves immediate, bilateral reciprocity. However, intergroup cooperation may be particularly difficult to accomplish. Schopler and Insko (1992) have demonstrated a robust "discontinuity effect": the choices of groups on a prisoner's dilemma game are consistently less cooperative than are the choices of individuals. Schopler and Insko propose that fear of the other group and greed supported by one's own group underlie this effect. Thus, in a laboratory study (Gaertner, Rust & Dovidio, 1997) we examined whether a common ingroup identity, which can both reduce intergroup threat and increase prosocial behavior, can counteract the discontinuity effect and facilitate intergroup cooperation in a one-trial prisoner's dilemma game. In our experiment, two 3-person laboratory groups were induced to conceive of themselves as either one group or two groups (as in Gaertner et al., 1989, 1990). Following this representation manipulation (which was successful), the 3-person groups were led to separate rooms and presented with the prisoner's dilemma game. In addition, we manipulated the conditions of intergroup negotiation (similar to one study in the Schopler & Insko series of studies) whereby either the entire group or just one representative from each group met in a central area to discuss the task. After the negotiators returned to their respective rooms, each group made a collective decision on the prisoner's dilemma game. The results indicated that while bias on evaluative ratings in the One Group condition was lower compared to the Two Groups condition as we expected, prisoner's dilemma decisions in the One Group (55% cooperation) condition were not any more cooperative than those in the Two Groups (53% cooperative) condition. However, sessions in which negotiations involved all members of each group were more cooperative than when each group sent just a single representative (74% vs 35%). Representation and negotiation manipulations did not interact to influence cooperation.

Although these results did not support our prediction about the behavioral impact of manipulating a one-group representation, some internal analyses did suggest some support. Negotiations involving all six participants produced higher levels of cooperation than did those involving single representatives of the groups. The negotiations among all of the members also induced participants to feel more like one group and less like two groups. It was statistical evidence of direct mediation that was lacking. Thus, although there is evidence of some involvement of the one-group representation on prisoner's dilemma game decision making, it is not possible at this time to claim that it induced greater cooperation between the groups. However, we believe that this prisoner's dilemma game measure among groups that have been separated offers a powerful and challenging context to gauge the impact and durability of a common ingroup identity in establishing the trust and trustworthiness of groups to produce more immediate reciprocal intergroup prosocial behavior.

☐ College Support and Perseverance

Feelings of trust, intimacy, and connection can have enduring impact on people's personal goals and motivations. More positive interpersonal and intergroup relations, which predict more inclusive group representations, may not only relate to more positive attitudes toward others but also more favorable feelings about and commitment to one's organization or institution. Both individually and socially, this commitment can have important consequences. For instance, Mael and Ashforth (1992) found that people who identified more strongly with their college donated more money to it, participated in more alumni activities, and recommended the institution more highly to others. Identification with college may also influence perseverance and attrition. Attrition rate is a serious issue for students of color on college campuses (Steele, 1997) with between 50% and 60% of Black and Hispanic college students dropping out of college before receiving their degree (Carter & Wilson, 1997; Stangor & Sechrist, 1998). Institutional commitment may be an important predictor, over and above academic performance, of retention (Bennett & Okinaka, 1990).

To explore the applicability of the Common Ingroup Identity Model to this issue, we reanalyzed data from a racial climate survey of 140 Black and 345 White college students attending a midwestern state university (Snider & Dovidio, 1996). Students were asked about their satisfaction with student relations, with the local community, with the administration, and with teaching; their experience with classroom discrimination and personal discrimination outside the classroom; the quality of their high school academic preparation and their current grade-point average; and feeling part of the college community. Ratings of feeling themselves to be part of the college community represented common group identification. The primary outcome measures, related to institutional commitment, were their willingness to recommend the university to others and their intention to complete their degree at that institution. We predicted that measures of social satisfaction and feelings of discrimination would be related to recommendations and intentions to complete the degree, but that this effect would be primarily indirect and mediated by feeling part of the university community.

The results for willingness to recommend the university to others are summarized in Figure 7.2. Overall, Black students were less willing to recommend the university than were White students (beta = −.29). Black students were also less satisfied with student relations, the local community, the administration, and teaching. They reported higher levels of classroom and personal discrimination. Academically, Black students reported currently lower grade-point averages but not poorer high school preparation. Of central relevance to our model was evidence for mediation. Con-

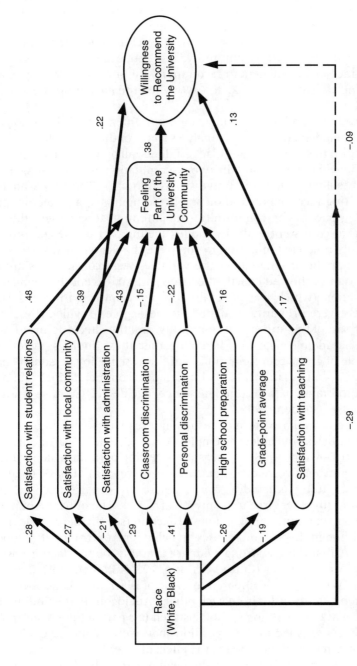

FIGURE 7.2. Feeling Part of the Community Mediates the Effects of Race and College Experience and Preparation on Students' Willingness to Recommend the University to Others.

sistent with the model, the satisfaction and discrimination measures all related significantly to feeling part of the community, which in turn strongly predicted willingness to recommend the university. Only satisfaction with the administration and with teaching had effects independent of feeling part of the community. Also supportive of mediation, the effect of race on willingness to recommend the university was substantially reduced (from beta = $-.29$ to $-.09$) when the mediating effects were considered.

Because Black and White students did not differ in their intentions to complete their degree, mediation analyses were conducted for these groups separately on this measure. For Black students, all of the satisfaction measures positively predicted and the two discrimination measures negatively predicted feeling part of the university community. The two academic measures (high school preparation and grade-point average) did not predict feeling part of the community (nor intention to complete the degree). Again consistent with the model, feeling part of the community significantly predicted intention to complete the degree; it was the only significant predictor when all of the variables were considered simultaneously. Whites showed exactly the same pattern, except that perceived discrimination (which was generally low) was not a significant factor. The effects were primarily mediated by the degree to which these students felt part of the university community, and the effects occurred over and above academic measures. Taken together, these findings suggest the central role of group representations—in this case feeling personally part of the group—on organizationally important recommendations and personally important goals to complete the college degree (see also Brewer, von Hippel, & Gooden, 1999).

We found a similar pattern of results in a reanalysis of data of White, Latino, and Black psychologists employed in academic departments (see Niemann & Dovidio, 1998). A measure of feeling part of the department was created from two related items in the survey: (a) "I have to prove myself to be fully accepted as a member of my department" (reverse scored), and (b) "I feel free to be myself at work." The outcome of interest, related to commitment, was job satisfaction (see Niemann & Dovidio, 1998). Although this section focuses on behavioral outcomes, it is important to note that there is strong evidence that low job satisfaction fosters high employee turnover (Cotton & Tuttle, 1986; Cramer, 1993). The responses of Whites were compared to those of Blacks and Latinos (which did not significantly differ from each other). Analogous to the findings for students, Black and Latino psychologists felt less part of their department and were less satisfied in their position than were White psychologists. Again, consistent with our model, the effect of race/ethnicity on job satisfaction was significantly mediated by feeling part of the department.

In general, these findings of the effects of developing a common organizational identity on organizational commitment are consistent with findings we reported earlier on organizational commitment in merged business organizations (e.g., Mottola et al., 1997, in Chapter 4; Mottola, 1996, Chapter 5), as well as with other work on mergers (Haunschild, Moreland, & Murrell, 1994). Furthermore, in business organizations, the degree of organizational unity experienced can have implications for the effectiveness and productivity of a merged organization—beyond generating more positive intergroup attitudes. For example, we have found that the extent to which members of two groups conceived of themselves as one superordinate group correlated with the actual effectiveness of their task solution ($r = .28$). This relationship is also consistent with the meta-analytic conclusions of Mullen and Copper (1994) who found that group cohesiveness significantly predicts group productivity ($r = .25$). Moreover, Mullen and Copper suggest that the relationship between cohesiveness and productivity may be bi-directional and thus iterative: cohesiveness may enhance productivity, and successful accomplishment, in turn, further increases cohesiveness. Indeed, the relationship between successful performance and subsequent cohesiveness is even stronger ($r = .51$) than the relationship between initial cohesiveness and productivity. Thus, the development of a common ingroup identity can help form a basis for more harmonious intergroup relations to develop through mutual success and achievement, which reinforces the common bond and identity between the groups.

Thus far, the studies we have reported in this chapter demonstrate the applicability of the basic principles and processes outlined in the Common Ingroup Identity Model to a range of behavioral responses. These studies generally focus on the effects for members directly involved in the contact situation. The measure of helping, however, suggests that the effects may generalize beyond the immediate contact situation over time and to other members of the group. The beneficiary of assistance was ostensibly a participant in an earlier session. In the next sections we address issues of generalizability, in terms of extending the benefits first across time and second to other members of the outgroup not directly involved in the intergroup contact situation.

☐ Generalizing the Benefits Across Time

Whereas laboratory experiments, including our own, typically involve immediate responses to others under highly controlled conditions, under naturalistic conditions intergroup relations extend over time. Moreover, individuals occupy multiple roles and are associated with multiple groups.

Consequently, how people categorize themselves and others may differ across situations and time (Brewer & Gardner, 1996). These variations may thus limit the benefits of developing a common group identity in a given contact situation beyond that context. Nevertheless, because of the primacy of ingroup membership; its positive effects on information processing, memory, and attributions; and its important affective and cognitive consequences (see Chapter 2), the impact of establishing a common ingroup identity may generalize across time even to situations in which alternative identities are more salient once again. We designed an experiment specifically to examine this issue (Gaertner, Dovidio, Mann & Anastasio, 1988).

This study began like other studies that we have discussed (e.g., Gaertner et al., 1989; see Chapter 4). Participants first interacted in two separate three-person groups on a problem-solving task, unaware of the existence of the other groups. This exercise facilitated the development of three-person group identities and allegiances. Then, as in the previous work, these three-person groups interacted with members of the other group under conditions designed to reinforce either different group identities (e.g., segregated seating with tables 36 inches apart, different colored T-shirts, interaction consisting of reporting earlier group solutions) or a common, one-group identity (e.g., integrated seating, same-colored T-shirts, interaction involving reaching a single, six-person group consensus solution to the earlier problem). However, unlike the previous studies, participants then participated in a third problem-solving session. This session also involved working under one of three conditions designed to emphasize different or common group identities.

The activities in these three sessions were systematically varied to produce three experimental conditions. In the One Group condition, after participating in the initial small-groups problem solving session, participants then interacted in the next two six-person sessions under circumstances designed to facilitate the development of a common ingroup identity. In the Two Groups condition, after the initial problem-solving task participants participated in the two six-person problem solving sessions with interventions supporting and reinforcing their different group identities (e.g., engaging in a competitive task with the other group). These two experimental conditions were similar to our One Group and Two Groups conditions in previous research, except that participants engaged in two (rather than one) six-person problem-solving tasks. The third condition (One Group/Two Groups Again) was designed to examine whether the benefits of developing a common ingroup identity in one six-person session would extend beyond a subsequent session in which the different group identities were reintroduced and reinforced. In this One Group/Two Groups Again condition, after the initial three-person group tasks, in the next, six-person session these groups worked under circumstances designed to induce a common ingroup identity but in the last session under the Two Groups conditions the original three-person groups were separated while they engaged in a competitive task with members of the other group. The dependent measure of interest was the level of intergroup bias after the third session.

The results for the One Group and Two Group conditions replicated our previous research. Participants in the One Group condition had significantly lower levels of intergroup bias than those in the Two Groups condition. Of primary interest were the results for the One Group/Two Groups Again condition. Would there be any "savings"? Would the effect of developing a common group identity extend to another situation in which the different group identities were salient? Yes, but not entirely. Participants in this condition had intermediate levels of intergroup bias. They also had intermediate levels of perceptions of the memberships being one group and two groups. Participants in the One Group/Two Group Again condition perceived the memberships most as "two subgroups within one group." Thus, the benefits of developing a common ingroup identity can linger, at least temporarily, even after the members return to their original group formations.

Both empirically and conceptually, these findings are consistent with Levine and Moreland's (1994; see also Moreland & Levine, 1982) model of socialization in groups. In their model, Levine and Moreland focus not only on stages in group membership but also the responses of ex-members to the group. Moreland and McMinn (1999), for example, proposed that "people remain loyal to their groups" (p. 4) and, as a consequence, they may favor members of their former group in evaluations and actions, even after the group has dissolved. Moreland and McMinn specifically asked, "Can a dissolved group still evoke loyalty when there is no contact among its former members? And what if the paradigm used by Gaertner and his colleagues were just reversed, so that instead of forming a large group by merging small groups, small groups were formed by dissolving a large group?" Their study did just that.

In the study by Moreland and McMinn (1999), laboratory groups performed an engaging task and then disbanded, with newer, small groups being created. Participants then evaluated the work of former ingroup and outgroup members and reacted to criticism of their own work, apparently from an ingroup or outgroup member. Consistent with the experimenters' hypothesis that people would still feel loyalty for former ingroup members and expect loyalty from them, participants evaluated former ingroup members' work more positively than comparable work by a former outgroup member. In addition, they were more upset by criticism of their own work when it came from a former ingroup than outgroup member.

Taken together, the findings from our own research and that of Moreland and McMinn (1999) indicate that the development of a common ingroup identity can still produce positive reactions to former ingroup members even after the group has dissolved and been replaced by another group. The benefits of a common ingroup identity linger over time. The duration of this effect is likely a function of a range of factors, such as the degree of identification with the groups (see Moreland & McMinn, 1999) and the compatibility of initial and subsequent group identities. Nevertheless, the convergence of these findings encouragingly indicates the perseverance of the benefits of a common group identity. In the next section, we consider the generalizability of these benefits to other group members not involved in the original group contact situation.

☐ Generalizing the Benefits to Others

Although research on the effects of intergroup contact has found support for the Contact Hypothesis for group members directly involved, these beneficial effects typically do not reliably generalize to the outgroup as a whole or to intergroup attitudes more generally (Stephan & Stephan, 1996). Nevertheless, the more circumscribed success for promoting harmony among the members of different groups in the contact situation is not a trivial accomplishment. In many intergroup contexts, this is precisely the major goal to be achieved.

One major reason why generalization fails is that the now positively evaluated outgroup members are regarded as exceptions and not necessarily typical of outgroup members more generally (Allport, 1954; Wilder, 1984). In this respect, the dual identity (e.g., African-American) may be a particularly promising mechanism for generalization to occur. In contrast to a separate individuals or purely one group representation, the dual identity maintains the associative link (see Rothbart, 1996; Rothbart & John, 1985) to additional outgroup members. This dual identity representation is also compatible with a "Mutual Intergroup Differentiation" model (Hewstone & Brown, 1986; Hewstone, 1996) that proposes that introducing a cooperative relationship between groups without degrading the original ingroup–outgroup categorization scheme is an effective way to change intergroup attitudes and to have these attitudes generalize to additional outgroup members.

Even models of personalization (e.g., Brewer & Miller, 1984) propose that group identities must be in conscious awareness for generalization to occur. The key issue from this perspective is the balance of the salience of identities. Miller and Harrington (1995; see also Harrington & Miller, 1993) argue that in real-world contact settings category identities characteristically are all too salient. The challenge, they suggest, is to create conditions in which personalized representations are weighed sufficiently relative to category representations to produce the positive interpersonal responses to generalize to the group as a whole.

Our "trade-off hypothesis" (Gaertner et al., 1993) also proposes that the balance of identities is crucial for generalization to occur. However, our focus (which we see as complementary to these other approaches) is on the relation between two-group and one-group representations. Specifically, we propose that people will develop more favorable attitudes toward other groups as a whole when they recognize both the common group membership and other group membership of group members in contact situations than if only the common group or other group membership alone were salient. However, compared to maintaining only a one-group representation, there is a "cost" for outgroup members present for recognizing both common and other group memberships: They will be responded to less favorably. Thus, we hypothesize a trade-off in which attitudes toward outgroup members present during contact would be less favorable with a dual identity than with a purely one group identity, but the modest change in attitude toward members present would more easily generalize to additional outgroup members.

Hewstone and Brown (1986) argue that generalization to the outgroup as a whole will be more likely when group identities are more rather than less salient during intergroup contact. Findings that pleasant contact with more typical rather than less typical outgroup members is associated with more favorable attitudes toward the outgroup more generally support Hewstone and Brown's position (Brown et al., 1999; Vivian et al., 1997; Wilder, 1984; see also Desforges et al., 1991). More specifically, Hewstone and Brown (1986) favor encouraging groups working together to recognize their mutual superiorities and inferiorities and to value equally the dimensions favoring each group. From the perspective of the Common Ingroup Identity Model, if Hewstone and Brown's recommendation could be realized, this would be ideal for keeping earlier group identities salient while simultaneously providing a superordinate connection between the groups.

While there is some evidence that inducing a superordinate identity without deliberately attempting to emphasize the outgroup members' subgroup identity can yield generalization in terms of the delivery of prosocial behavior (see Dovidio, Gaertner et al., 1997, discussed earlier in this chapter), there is also reason to believe that a dual identity may have even stronger potential for generalization. This idea was examined directly in an experiment by Hornsey and Hogg (2000). Although the groups never interacted, their instructions emphasized either students' individual identities, their separate group identities (as Humanities and Math-Science students), their superordinate University identity, or both their separate group identities as well as their superordinate University identities (i.e., a dual identity condition). These students were then asked a number of questions regarding how positive they would feel about working with students in each group (i.e., Humanities and Math-Science students).

Although students felt more positive overall about the prospects of working with students in their own group, supportive of the value of a "dual identity" for promoting more general positive outgroup attitudes, the least amount of bias occurred in the "dual identity" condition. Contrary to what we would have expected, however, the most bias did not occur in the separate groups condition, but rather when the superordinate identity alone was emphasized. Nevertheless, these results offer support for the value of a "dual identity" for promoting positive attitudes toward the outgroup more generally. Indeed, with a "dual identity" outgroup attitudes were more positive than those associated with a superordinate identity alone.

Testing the Trade-off

With respect to generalization, we propose (see also Hewstone & Brown, 1986) that if earlier group identities were completely abandoned, the associative links between former outgroup members who are present and outgroup members who are not present would be severed, and generalization of the benefits of intergroup contact would be minimal. However, there may be a "trade-off" between attitude change concerning members of the outgroup who are present and generalized attitude change to other outgroup members. Attitudes toward those outgroup members initially included within the common ingroup identity would be expected to be most positive when the salience of the previous group boundaries are completely degraded. In contrast, generalization would be most effective when the members conceive of themselves as two subgroups within a more inclusive superordinate entity (i.e., the dual identity). The strength of the superordinate group representation mediates positive attitudes toward outgroup members present; the strength of subgroup representations provides a mechanism for generalization to occur.

In one study of generalization and trade-off (Gaertner, Dovidio & Rust, 1997), two 3-person groups of Democratic and Republican Party members, interacted under experimental conditions that varied their representations of the six participants as One Group, Two Subgroups Within One Group (hereafter, Dual Identity condition), Two Separate Groups, and Separate (more personalized) Individuals (see Gaertner et al., 1989). As expected, evaluative bias toward ingroup and outgroup members present was low in the One Group, Separate Individuals, and Dual Identity conditions relative to the Two Separate Groups condition. Furthermore, consistent with positions that emphasize the importance of maintaining the salience of group identities for generalization to occur, bias toward members present and bias for the groups in general were correlated more positively when the memberships were in conditions designed to emphasize *group* boundaries rather than individual identity. The correlation between attitudes toward members present and toward the groups (Democrats or Republicans) as a whole were significantly positive in the One Group condition ($r = .25$) and in the Two Groups condition ($r = .27$). In the Dual Identity condition, the correlation was also positive, as expected, but it was weaker and nonsignificant ($r = .12$). In contrast, in the Separate Individuals condition, in which group boundaries were degraded, reductions of immediate levels of bias not only did not predict lower levels of bias in general, but also these measures were negatively correlated ($r = -.39$). The correlations between immediate and general levels of bias within each of the group representations conditions was significantly more positive than the correlation with the Separate Individuals condition. Although the generalizing effects for the Dual Identity condition were weaker than anticipated and the effects of the One Group condition were stronger than expected on the basis of the trade-off hypothesis, the findings are encouraging. Emphasizing a One Group or Dual Identity condition reduces bias in the immediate contact situation in a way that potentially facilitates generalization to the groups as a whole, whereas emphasizing a Separate Individuals representation reduces bias immediately but in a way that does not relate positively toward the groups in general. Emphasizing a Two Groups representation does produce a correlation between members present and the groups as a whole (Rothbart & John, 1985), but because outgroup members present were evaluated less positively than in the other conditions, this may not be the type of generalization we would want to promote.

Somewhat more support for the trade-off hypothesis is offered by a very recent experiment by Gonzalez and Brown (1999). As in the study by Hornsey and Hogg (2000), discussed earlier in this chapter, Gonzalez and Brown independently varied the salience of superordinate and subgroup identities in a 2 (Superordinate Group Salience: high vs. low) × 2 (Subgroup Salience: high vs. low) design. These investigators allowed two laboratory groups to interact while varying seating arrangements and perceptual cues, similar to our own work (e.g., Gaertner et al., 1990) to vary the salience of superordinate and subgroup representations. The combinations of high and low salient superordinate and subgroup identity produced four conditions similar to those in our previous work: One Group (i.e., high superordinate group and low subgroup salience), Dual Identity (or Two Subgroups Within One Group: i.e., high superordinate group and high subgroup salience), Two Groups (i.e., low superordinate group and high subgroup salience), and No Groups (or Separate Individuals; i.e., low superordinate group and low subgroup salience).

In terms of bias toward group members who were present during contact, bias in evaluative ratings in the Gonzalez and Brown (1999) study was eliminated in all conditions *except* when the groups appeared to be two separate groups (i.e., in the low superordinate, high subordinate group salience condition). These findings are consistent with the Common Ingroup Identity Model and supportive of our previous results (e.g., Gaertner, Dovidio, & Rust, 1997; Gaertner et al., 1989). In terms of generalization, bias in evaluative ratings of additional ingroup and outgroup members who were not present and only viewed on videotape was lower in the One Group (high superordinate, low subgroup salience) condition and the Dual Identity (high superordinate, high subordinate group salience) condition than in the other two conditions (i.e., Two Groups and No Groups). Furthermore, supportive of the trade-off hypothesis, although there was no significant bias (ingroup favoritism) toward group members viewed on videotape in the One Group condition, there appeared to be an even greater reduction of bias in the Dual Identity condition. In this condition, there was a tendency toward outgroup favoritism.

In addition to a dual identity in which subgroup composition is convergent with original ingroup and outgroup members, as we and Gonzalez and Brown (1999) considered in the previous studies relevant to the trade-off hypothesis, subgroup composition may *cross-cut* these original group boundaries. With the convergent composition, the subgroups are composed homogeneously of members from the originally separate groups, but these subgroups are associated with the same superordinate group identity: [(AA)(BB)]. With cross-cut composition, each subgroup is heterogeneously composed of members from different original subgroups, and these subgroups are connected by an overarching superordinate identity: [(AB)(AB)]. The next experiment investigated convergent and cross-cut subgroups, representations, evaluations, and generalizations.

Cross-cut and Convergent Boundaries

Building on earlier research by Marcus-Newhall et al. (1993), Rust (1996) varied the presence or absence of a superordinate group identity when First Year students (F) and Sophomores (S) were assigned preliminary tasks on the basis of cross-cut (FS)(FS) or convergent (FF)(SS) patterns. Replicating the findings of Marcus-Newhall et al. (1993), bias toward ingroup and outgroup members present was lower in the cross-cut than convergent conditions. Whereas the manipulation of a superordinate identity did not directly influence evaluations of outgroup members present nor outgroup members more generally, the greater extent to which participants perceived themselves as "crossed subgroups within a superordinate entity" [(FS)(FS)] did relate to more positive evaluations of outgroup members present and also to more positive evaluations of outgroup members more generally. The representation involving crossed groups without a superordinate connection (FS)(FS) did not relate to outgroup attitudes at all. Although the "convergent subgroups within a superordinate" representation [(FF)(SS)] did not relate directly to more general outgroup attitudes, it did relate marginally to outgroup members that were present. Furthermore, attitudes toward outgroup members in the contact situation predicted generalized outgroup attitudes. Thus, the "convergent subgroups within a superordinate" representation may lead to more positive generalized outgroup attitudes indirectly by influencing attitudes toward outgroup members present. Therefore, whether subgroups are constructed with a cross-cut or convergent configuration, the joint presence of a superordinate group connection seems to facilitate more positive evaluations of outgroup members.

A dual identity may be important for changing stereotypes as well as attitudes. Research by Anastasio, Bachman, Gaertner and Dovidio (1997) examined this possibility. In this study, we varied whether college students interacted with "Townie" outgroup members either as Individuals, as members of Two Separate Groups, or with a Dual Identity involving college students and townspeople from Newark, Delaware, who were competing against similarly composed groups representing Rhode Island. Students viewed a carefully scripted videotape depicting a single "Townie" outgroup member whose observed behaviors portrayed a somewhat typical outgroup member (e.g., loud and sloppy) who also possessed counter-stereotypic qualities (i.e., intelligent and creative). Whereas there were no differences across experimental treatments in the counter-stereotypic ratings of the "Townie" outgroup, the internal analyses were very suggestive of the value of a dual identity. First, participants perceived themselves as a "Newark, Delawarian" significantly more strongly in the Dual Identity condition relative to the other conditions. Second, the stronger this "Newark, Delawarian" identity, the more "Townie" outgroup members more were generally regarded with positive affect (e.g., liked), which in turn predicted stereotype change and reduction (in terms of more counter-stereotypical ratings the outgroup as a whole).

☐ Conclusion

In earlier chapters we demonstrated that a diverse range of cognitive, affective, and intergroup contact factors not only can reduce intergroup bias (in ways consistent with the Contact Hypothesis) but also can operate, at least in part, through the common mechanism of group representations. Across a substantial number of studies, factors that transformed members' representations of the memberships from two groups to one, superordinate entity consistently produced more favorable attitudes toward the outgroup and lower levels of intergroup bias. The purpose of this chapter was to explore how developing a common ingroup identity can facilitate other forms of positive social behavior and generalizable improvements of attitudes toward the outgroup as a whole.

The studies reported in this chapter offer direct evidence of the robustness and value of a common ingroup identity. Manipulations designed to produce more inclusive group representations were effective, and these representations in turn predicted greater intergroup helping, self-disclosure, and cooperation. As we noted, these are particularly important forms of social behavior because they each initiate reciprocal, positive actions that can further solidify intergroup relations. Thus, although creating a common ingroup identity may initially produce positive attitudes toward former outgroup members in a depersonalized, stereotyped, or heuristic manner, more elaborated, personalized impressions can soon develop within the context of a common ingroup identity because the newly formed positivity bias encourages more open and self-disclosing communication and reciprocal prosocial exchanges between members. Thus we view the Common Ingroup Identity Model and models of personalization (Miller & Brewer, 1984) and individuation (Wilder, 1986) as complementary rather than competitive strategies for reducing intergroup bias (see also Hewstone, 1996; Pettigrew, 1998a).

We also report in this chapter evidence that generalization of the benefits of intergroup contact to attitudes toward groups as a whole occurs as a function of the salience of group representations. Specifically, we presented some evidence in support of the hypothesis that there may be a trade-off between attitude change concerning members of the outgroup who are present and generalized attitude change to other outgroup members. Attitudes toward those outgroup members initially and specifically included within the common ingroup identity would be expected most positive when the salience of the previous group boundaries are completely degraded. When both common group and other group memberships are recognized, the relative strength of the superordinate group representation is hypothesized to be the primary predictor of reduced bias toward outgroup members present in the contact situation. As Urban and

Miller's (1998) meta-analytic review of the literature on crossed categorization effects revealed, the favorableness of responses to outgroup members under conditions when dual identities are salient approach those when only a common identity is salient when conditions facilitate the acceptance of common group membership (e.g., incidental positive affect; see also Chapter 6), permit the development of common group representations (e.g., lack of cognitive overload), or establish stronger positive connections to outgroup members (e.g., through personalizing interactions).

We further propose that generalization would be most effective when there is a balance between the salience of superordinate and subgroup identities, such as when the members conceive of themselves as two subgroups within a more inclusive superordinate entity. The strength of the superordinate group representation mediates positive attitudes toward members of the outgroup who are present; the strength of subgroup representations provides a mechanism by which generalization can occur. Thus, generalization would best be predicted by the interaction between the strength of subgroup and superordinate group representations, with the greatest generalization occurring when both identities are strong. Consistent with this reasoning, Scarberry, Ratcliff, Lord, Lanicek, and Desforges (1997) found that in a cooperative contact situation, which we have shown to increase a one-group representation, participants showed less generalization of the positive effects of intergroup contact to the group as a whole (in this case, homosexuals) when the confederate emphasized individuating information than when he did not. Individuating information reduces the salience of the confederate's subgroup identity and therefore, from our perspective, weakens the associative link for generalizing the benefits of positive intergroup contact to the entire group. Although the evidence is currently tentative, we believe that the results are sufficiently promising to merit future empirical study of the hypothesis.

Progress, Problems, and Promise

Thus far, we have considered the issues that stimulated our work on the Common Ingroup Identity Model, the theoretical underpinnings of the model, and empirical evidence for the various hypothesized processes and outcomes. We begin this chapter with a summary of the *progress* that has been made. We next move to *problems*: unfinished theoretical, empirical, and practical issues. Finally, we end both the chapter and the book by reflecting on the *promise* of our approach and alternative and complementary approaches for combating intergroup bias and resolving intergroup conflict.

☐ Progress

We began this book by describing the social problem that initially stimulated our interest—racism. As we explained in Chapter 1, Introduction and Overview, in our experiments we had found that contemporary forms of prejudice, particularly by Whites toward Blacks, were more subtle and indirect than traditional, "red-neck" forms. One form of contemporary bias, which captured our interest, was aversive racism (Kovel, 1970). Aversive racists consciously endorse egalitarian values, but, because of almost unavoidable cognitive, motivational, and sociocultural processes, they also develop unconscious negative feelings and beliefs about Blacks. These negative feelings are expressed in subtle, indirect, and rationalizable

155

ways that protect the aversive racist's nonprejudiced self-image yet ultimately disadvantage Blacks. In Chapter 2, Aversive Racism and Intergroup Biases, we reviewed how contemporary racial prejudice can be expressed more in terms of ingroup favoritism than outgroup derogation. Although its manner of expression is indirect and subtle, the consequences of aversive racism are as insidious as those of overt racism: the systematic restriction of social and economic opportunities for Blacks.

Moreover, because aversive racism is expressed subtly and typically unintentionally, and because aversive racists try to avoid wrongdoing by acting in a nonprejudiced fashion, traditional techniques for reducing bias may be largely ineffective for combating this form of bias. For instance, attitude-change techniques designed to convince people that prejudice is wrong and that they should be more egalitarian will not work for aversive racists. Aversive racists already *know* that prejudice is wrong, and they already embrace egalitarian principles. Thus, the problem here was developing new techniques for combating more subtle forms of prejudice. The Common Ingroup Identity Model represents one such approach.

In Chapter 3, Theoretical Background and the Common Ingroup Identity Model, we outlined the basic propositions of this model and described its theoretical foundation. Essentially, we hypothesized that a broad range of situational, structural, and social factors in intergroup contact situations reduce bias, at least in part, by changing cognitive representations of the memberships from two groups to one involving common ingroup membership, that is, by changing conceptions from "us" and "them" to a more inclusive "we." We sketched the basic elements and hypothesized relations of the model in Figure 3.1. In Chapters 4 through 7, we reviewed evidence for the model—the empirical and theoretical progress that has been made on this perspective. In this chapter, we reintroduce a version of that figure that identifies the relevant evidence in each of these chapters (see Figure 8.1).

Chapter 4, Altering the Perceptions of Group Boundaries, examined how factors that influence the salience of group differentiation and connectedness (see Group Differentiation in Figure 8.1) influence cognitive representations, and ultimately intergroup bias. The results of studies both with laboratory groups and real groups (i.e., racial groups) converged to demonstrate that interventions designed to facilitate the development of a common group identity and de-emphasize separate group identities produced more inclusive (one-group) representations and reduced bias primarily by producing more positive responses to others who would ordinarily be considered an outgroup member. For instance, we found that through similar dress or dress emphasizing common university affiliation, integrated seating arrangements, common group names and other manipulations designed to enhance conceptions of a single, common en-

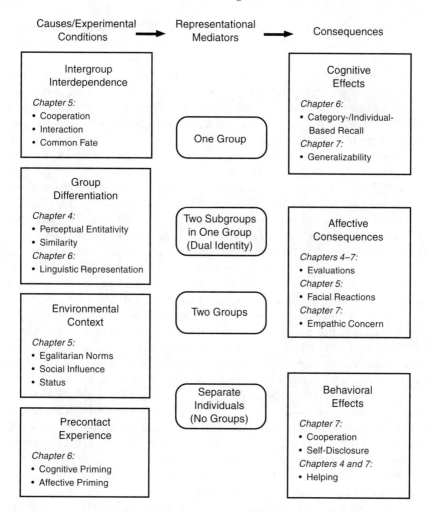

FIGURE 8.1. Evidence for the Common Ingroup Identity Model.

tity, participants were more likely to conceive of the groups as one group and less as two groups. They also had more positive evaluations of outgroup members and were more helpful toward them. Furthermore, consistent with a central proposition of our model, stronger one-group representations mediated more positive evaluations of outgroup members and lower levels of bias.

Chapter 5, Conditions of Intergroup Contact, explored how factors identified by the Contact Hypothesis (Allport, 1954,1958; Pettigrew, 1998a; Williams, 1947)—such as cooperative interdependence, equal status contact, interaction, egalitarian norms, and perceived support of authorities (see Figure 8.1)—can reduce bias by changing cognitive representations of the groups. Consistent with our perspective, experimental studies involving manipulations of cooperative interdependence and interaction showed the predicted relationships with more inclusive representations of the memberships and with reduced levels of intergroup bias. Common fate did not relate to self-report measures of bias, but it did produce lower levels of spontaneoues expressions of bias, in terms of facial reactions to contributions made by original ingroup and outgroup members. Survey studies across a variety of intergroup settings also revealed that perceptions of more positive conditions of intergroup contact along dimensions specified by the Contact Hypothesis predicted more inclusive representations and lower levels of intergroup bias. Moreover, evidence from both the laboratory experiments and the survey studies provided support for the mediating effect of an inclusive representation on lower levels of bias.

The evidence presented in Chapter 5 also identified a potentially important limiting condition of one key element of the Contact Hypothesis: intergroup status. To the extent that equal status interaction and related attempts to achieve a common ingroup identity threaten a person's positive group identity and feelings of positive group distinctiveness, these interventions will be ineffective at reducing bias and may, in fact, exacerbate negative intergroup attitudes. However, developing a common ingroup identity does not necessarily require abandoning one's original group identity. Both a superordinate identity and subgroup identity can remain salient simultaneously (see Two Subgroups in One Group representation in Figure 8.1). When this "dual identity" is compatible with the goals of the superordinate organization (e.g., a multicultural high school), it, too, can be an important mediator of lower levels of intergroup bias.

Chapter 6, Cognitive and Affective Priming: Antecedents and Consequences of a Common Ingroup Identity, considered how events and experiences often apparently unrelated to the nature of intergroup contact can significantly influence representations of the groups and ultimately affect intergroup bias and relations. Across a series of studies we demonstrated how ingroup and outgroup designators (e.g., the pronouns "we" and "they") can systematically influence the way information is processed and the way evaluative associations are formed. These effects occur spontaneously and without conscious awareness, and they can bias the nature of subsequent interactions. For example, in one experiment, inducing participants to use ingroup pronouns (e.g., "we") when referring to others led them to feel more like members of one group than separate individuals, which in turn influenced feelings of closeness, similarity, and positive evaluations (see Figure 8.1).

In addition, incidental positive affect—positive affect experienced as a consequence of a separate event (e.g., a comedy video)—can facilitate more inclusive representations, which in turn can improve evaluations of outgroup members and reduce intergroup bias. The nature of immediate and historical relations, for example cooperative or competitive, moderates the influence of positive affect. When groups have no previous history of conflict and when immediate contact is nonthreatening or cooperative, positive affect facilitates the development of positive outgroup attitudes. In contrast, when groups are historically in conflict or immediately in competition, positive affect increases the salience of separate group boundaries and exacerbates bias. Measures of accuracy of memory and confusions among the responses of different outgroup members (Figure 8.1) suggest that these effects are not necessarily due to stereotypic thinking or heuristic processing, but may instead reflect deliberative and elaborative types of processing.

Chapter 7, Extending the Benefits of Recategorization, investigates how the benefits of recategorization in terms of more positive intergroup attitudes extend to other measures of behavior and behavioral intentions, across time, and the groups as a whole. Research on intergroup attitudes and behavior toward members of other groups may have very different antecedents and bases, and the two types of responses may be only modestly correlated. Nevertheless, because of the varied, fundamental effects of categorizing a person as an ingroup member (e.g., on memory processes, attributions, evaluations), developing a common ingroup identity is likely to influence a range of cognitive, affective, and behavioral responses, to have relatively enduring impact, and to generalize to other members of the groups who are not physically present in the contact situation (see Figure 8.1). In Chapter 7 we reviewed evidence that interventions to produce a common ingroup identity not only improve attitudes but also facilitate prosocial behaviors and self-disclosing, personalized interactions. The behaviors, in turn, can initiate additional processes that can further encourage more harmonious relations between groups. Both helping and self-disclosing behaviors stimulate reciprocal responses in others, which can solidify positive relations. In addition, personalization represents a separate, independent route to reducing prejudice (Miller & Brewer, 1984), independent of recategorization. As we illustrate in this chapter, the benefits of recategorization can thus extend over time.

Because it emphasizes category membership rather than individual identity, recategorization may also be an effective strategy for developing generalizable positive intergroup attitudes—that is, more positive intergroup attitudes that extend beyond the contact setting to members who were not present in the intergroup contact situation. There is also reason to believe that a dual identity (Two Subgroups in One Group; see Figure 8.1) may be even more effective than a one-group representation for

achieving this objective. If earlier group identities are completely abandoned, the associative links between former outgroup members who are
present and outgroup members who are not present would be severed,
and generalization of the benefits of intergroup contact would be minimal. We presented research in Chapter 7 that provides initial evidence for
this proposition and examined how different types or dual identities (such
as cross-cut and convergent boundaries) can differentially facilitate generalization. Overall, the data considered in Chapter 7 suggest that the
processes outlined in the Common Ingroup Identity Model are valuable
not only for improving intergroup attitudes and relieving intergroup tensions among members present but also for producing more enduring and
generalizable reductions in intergroup bias and conflict.

In summary, the evidence presented in Chapters 4 through 7 provide
evidence of progress in understanding theoretical processes and pragmatic
interventions for reducing bias. By understanding the underlying processes, when some interventions (e.g., cooperative interdependence) are
precluded by situational constraints or the existing relations between
groups, it may be possible to identify and substitute alternative strategies
that are both pragmatic and effective. Nevertheless, as is frequently the
case, our progress still has limitations. Despite substantial evidence in support of the Common Ingroup Identity Model, conceptual, empirical, and
practical issues remain. We consider these "problems" in the next section.

☐ Problems

Although we are largely encouraged by the research involving the capacity of a common identity to reduce intergroup biases, a critical discussion
of the problems of this approach can help set priorities for further research and guide theoretical redrafting. Some of these problems we can
partially address at this time, but others create challenges for the future.
In particular, we consider three encompassing questions:

1. Is the development of a common ingroup identity a realistic strategy?
2. Is a dual-identity representation preferable to a one-group representation?
3. Does recategorization lead to generalization?

Is the Development of a Common Ingroup Identity a Realistic Strategy?

In the context of reviewing several category-based strategies for reducing
intergroup bias, Hewstone (1996) questioned whether the recategorization

process and the creation of a superordinate group identity can overcome powerful ethnic and racial categorizations on more than a temporary basis. We can also ask whether this strategy could effectively reduce intense conflict or ameliorate hostile, anti-outgroup feelings. If the rash of armed conflicts among the ethnic groups in Eastern Europe following the decentralization of the Warsaw Pact is to be any guide, it would appear that appeals to superordinate national identities of these combatants would not realistically decrease the ferocity of their fighting or quell their hostility for one another. What is difficult to determine, however, is whether this failure represents a theoretical boundary condition for the operation of recategorization processes or an applied social engineering problem involving how to build salient common ingroup identities in these contexts. That is, is the development of a common ingroup identity inherently ineffective in conditions of intense conflict, or is the problem difficultly in achieving a common ingroup identity under these circumstances? We suggest the latter.

While we must be cautious about over-interpreting the experimental evidence, we optimistically note that cooperation among Sherif et al.'s (1961/1988) groups of warring summer campers at Robbers Cave State Park (see Chapter 1) was associated with the development of greater intergroup harmony. When confronted with fundamental objectives (e.g., re-establishing the water supply) that could be achieved only by joint efforts (i.e., superordinate goals), the groups worked cooperatively, and bias and conflict were consequently reduced. This finding suggests that the problem with recategorization may be a practical engineering problem—introducing an intervention that is potent enough to achieve a common ingroup identity—rather than a conceptual boundary condition for the effectiveness of recategorization processes. Also, we are encouraged by our own laboratory and field experiments that has demonstrated that the development of a common identity increased positive evaluations and prosocial behavior across racial boundaries (e.g., among fans attending a football game; see Chapter 4). Also, the results of our survey studies among multi-ethnic high school students (Chapter 5) and college students (Chapter 7) provide reason to be optimistic that common ingroup identity can be associated with reduced bias among members of enduring groups involving consequential identities and potential realistic group conflict .

Whether a common superordinate identity can produce positive intergroup orientations for the long term or only temporarily also remains an important issue. On the one hand, evidence from our study (see Chapter 7) in which two three-person laboratory groups joined together as one group before becoming two groups again revealed that there was some residual benefit, in terms of reduced intergroup bias, to group members perceiving themselves as one group (see also Moreland & McMinn, 1999).

Whether such findings can extend beyond a single fifty-minute experimental session is a question we cannot address at this time. Nevertheless, given that the superordinate connections between the groups lasted only about 10 minutes, it is encouraging that there was any residual effect at all.

On the other hand, we do not believe that recategorization as one group, *at least by itself*, would be capable of sustaining favorable intergroup relations over the long term. Unless supported and sustained by group norms and the leadership structure, such an ephemeral superordinate connection between groups is unlikely to remain stable over time. Moreover, members' needs for both distinctiveness and inclusion (see Brewer, 1988) would favor the salience of smaller, less inclusive groups in the struggle among each person's multiple group identities for dominance. Hence, direct, long term benefits of inducing a one-group representation are not necessarily expected. Rather, as we discussed in Chapter 7, we believe that recategorization as one group, even temporarily, has the potential to initiate a chain of events including interpersonal processes and behaviors such as self-disclosure and helping among former outgroup members—which, in turn further increase the reduction of bias through independent and complementary routes.

At the moment, however, there is a fundamental, practical problem that is difficult to solve: how to activate recategorization processes when groups are engaged in mortal conflict. Who can step in, for example as Sherif et al.'s (1961/1988) investigative team did, to pose superordinate goals during such intergroup crises? In these circumstances, recategorization may theoretically be possible, but we too question whether it is realistic in many situations. Nevertheless, as Kelman (1997) has demonstrated, it is not necessary to create a common ingroup identity among all of the people involved in conflict to improve intergroup relations significantly. Kelman's work (e.g., Kelman, 1999) has focused on improving Palestinian-Israeli relations to achieve peace in the Middle East. His conflict resolution workshops (see Rouhana & Kelman, 1994) bring together 8 to 16 influential leaders from both sides in interactive, problem-solving exercises. As Pettigrew (1998b) observed: "The groups serve as laboratories and as a setting for direct interaction. They have the potential of initiating coalitions of peace-minded participants across conflict lines. And the workshops present a model for a new relationship between the parties" (p. 665). Thus even within the context of intense historical and contemporary conflict, it may be possible to be creative and to engineer the development of a common ingroup identity for a subset of group members with significant residual effects for the groups as a whole.

Is a Dual Identity Representation Preferable to a One-group Represenation?

A second point in Hewstone's (1996) critique was that the Common Ingroup Identity Model proposes a strategy that is analogous to assimilation models that blur group distinctiveness—a model of intergroup relations that is currently fairly uniformly rejected (e.g., Berry, 1984; Berry, Poortinga, Segall, & Dasen, 1992; van Oudenhoven, Prins, & Buunk, 1998). While we have articulated throughout this volume the benefits of a dual identity in which subgroups remain distinctive within the context of a superordinate identity, a dual identity is not necessarily always more effective than a one group representation for reducing bias. For example, Smith and Tyler (1996) found that a strong subgroup identity within the context of a strong superordinate identity did not interfere with group relations, but it also did not foster more positive intergroup attitudes. In addition, the evidence from our stepfamily and corporate merger studies (see Chapters 4 and 5) suggests that there are intergroup contexts in which the strength of a superordinate representation that blurs the original group boundaries may relate *more positively* to intergroup harmony than the dual identity representation. In our study of intergroup relations within a multiethnic high school (Gaertner et al., 1996; see Chapter 5), one group and a dual identity (different groups on the same team) representations correlated significantly with lower levels of bias both for Whites and for people of color. In the full sample, the one group and the dual identity representations independently predicted lower levels of bias (see Figure 5.2).

One problem to consider is just when the purely one group or the dual identity forms of recategorization would be preferable. Is the purely one group representation particularly advantageous only when the explicit goal is for the groups to merge together to form a single social entity? Perhaps other factors are involved as well. What if the goal of intergroup contact is perceived differently by each of the groups whereby one favors an assimilationist model while the other favors a pluralistic, multicultural approach? Indeed, in a recent study we have found that Whites most prefer assimilation, whereas racial and ethnic minorities favor pluralistic integration (Kafati, 1999). Moreover, these preferred types of intergroup relations models for majority and minority groups, a one-group representation for Whites and different groups on the same-team representation for people of color, may differentially mediate the consequences of intergroup contact for the different groups.

To explore this possibility, we examined how different types of cognitive representations might mediate the relationship between more positive perceptions of intergroup contact and higher levels of institutional commitment among White students and students of color (Kafati, 1999). As in the Snider and Dovidio (1996) survey study of college students considered earlier (Chapter 7), commitment was chosen as the main outcome variable because attrition rates by race/ethnicity are a widespread concern on college campuses. Perceptions of favorable intergroup contact were measured in the same way as in our multi-ethnic high school study (Gaertner et al., 1996) and included ratings on the dimensions of equal status, supportive norms, personal interaction, and intergroup interdependence (see Chapter 5). Commitment included items about students' intentions to complete their education at the institution and their willingness to recommend the institution to others, as well as questions about the academic and social climate. Whereas in the Snider and Dovidio (1996) survey, only a single item, feeling part of the university community, assessed recategorized representations, this study examined all four cognitive representations identified by the Common Ingroup Identity Model and hypothesized to represent different models of intergroup relations: perceptions of being (a) one group (assimilation), (b) separate groups (separatism), (c) separate individuals (decategorization/marginalization), and (d) different groups on the same team (integration/pluralism or multicultural). In addition, participants' identification with their racial or ethnic group was assessed.

We hypothesized that the positive relation between perceptions of more favorable intergroup contact and institutional commitment would be mediated by different representations of the groups. Whereas we expected that the relation for Whites would be mediated by one-group representations, reflecting an assimilation perspective, we anticipated that the relation for people of color would be mediated by different groups on the same-team representations, a multicultural perspective that recognizes both one's racial or ethnic group identity and a superordinate identity—a dual identity .

The results confirmed the hypothesis. For Whites, more positive perceptions of intergroup contact related to stronger perceptions of students consisting of one group, different groups on the same team, and separate individuals, as well as weaker perceptions of different groups. However, when considered simultaneously, only the one-group representation was significantly related to commitment (beta = .42; see Figure 8.2 top panel). Conditions of contact also significantly predicted each of the representations for students of color. In contrast to the pattern for Whites, though, the different groups on the same-team representation (beta = .34), but not the one-group representation (beta = .02), predicted commitment (see Figure 8.2, bottom panel). In general, these effects were stronger for people higher in racial ethnic identification, both for Whites and people of color. This suggests that the differences among minority and majority

White Students

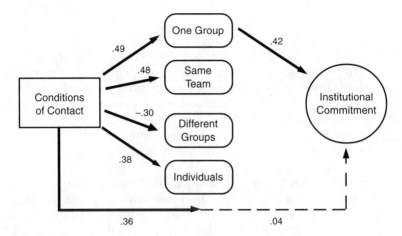

Students of Color

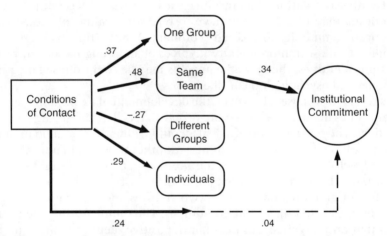

FIGURE 8.2. Conditions of contact, representations, and institutional commitment of White college students and students of color.

students were not simply due to stronger ethnic racial identities among minority than majority students.

Although these results do not fully address the dynamics of when and why a dual identity might be preferable to a one group representation, the finding that these representations can mediate commitment differently for people of color than for Whites has important practical implications. Strategies and interventions designed to enhance satisfaction need to recognize that Whites and people of color may have different ideals and motivations. Because White values and culture have been the traditionally dominant ones in the United States, American Whites may see an assimilation model, in which members of other cultural groups are absorbed into the "mainstream," as the most comfortable and effective strategy. For people of color, this model, which denies the value of their culture and traditions, may not only be perceived as less desirable but also as threatening to their personal and social identity—particularly for people who strongly identify with their group. Thus, efforts to create a single superordinate identity, although well-intentioned, may threaten one's social identity, which in turn can intensify intergroup bias and conflict.

Nevertheless when minorities do successfully adopt a superordinate group identity, there are benefits. Minorities who are more assimilated experience less stress and anxiety and have lower levels of failure in school and substance abuse (Burnam, Telles, Karno, Hough, & Escobar, 1987; Pasquali, 1985). However, there may also be psychological costs associated with assimilation. For instance, academically successful African Americans may feel that they have to reject the values of the African American community to succeed (Fordham, 1988). Thus, when the development of a common identity involves abandoning important racial or ethnic identities, the potential benefits may be compromised by other personal and psychological considerations.

As we have proposed, however, the development of a common ingroup identity does not necessarily require people to forsake their separate group identities. The consideration of a dual identity within the Common Ingroup Identity Model is, in fact, consistent with other models of cultural identity and well-being. For instance, the alternation model of second-culture acquisition (LaFromboise, Coleman, & Gerton, 1993) suggests that it is possible for an individual to know two cultures, identify with both, and draw on these identities at different times. The multicultural model suggests that an individual can maintain a positive identity while simultaneously participating in and identifying with a larger entity composed of many other racial and ethnic groups (Berry, 1984). Indeed, the development of a bicultural or multicultural identity is not only possible but can contribute to the social adjustment, psychological adaptation, and overall well-being of minority group members (LaFromboise et al., 1993; Ogbu & Matute-Bianchi, 1986; see also Crocker & Quinn, in press, for a general discussion of minority group well-being) in ways superior to full assimilation or acculturation. As a counterpoint to these benefits of a dual identity for minority group members, Wright (in press) proposed that identification with a superordinate group may reduce self-representations as members of their minority subgroup and obscure inequalities between minority and majority groups. Consequently, a dual identity may reduce minority group members' interests in collective action to redress social inequalities.

Contrary to strategies that seek to reduce bias by focusing primarily on the perpetrators rather than on their victims, the Common Ingroup Identity Model thus recognizes the importance of the participation and perspective of both group memberships. For example, majority-minority group relations frequently involve high levels of distrust and blame by both groups (Hochschild, 1995; see also Simon, Aufderheide, & Kampmeier, in press). As a consequence, minority group members may assume that only the majority group should actively participate in change, and they may be so distrustful that interventions to establish or emphasize common ingroup membership would be strongly resisted. When overtures to join together are resisted by one group, the prospects for developing more harmonious relations may be more tenuous than before. Moreover, majority group members, whose traditions usually dominate cultural landscapes, may resent minority group members' allegiance to their original heritage, even in the context of a dual identity. The loyalty or patriotism of these minorities to the superordinate group may be suspect. Thus, for the dual identity to provide positive intergroup consequences for both groups, it may be critical for minorities to demonstrate clearly their allegiance to the inclusive superordinate entity, a burden that they may not want disproportionately to bear. Perhaps, in our football study (Nier et al., 1999; see Chapter 4), one of the reasons that Black confederates who shared common team identity with the fans they interviewed elicited such positive reactions is that they were perceived to have intentionally decided to declare their allegiance to the superordinate University of Delaware entity by choosing to wear that group's signature clothing. Should they have chosen to wear signature clothing declaring their allegiance to both their superordinate university group and their racial group, they may not have been accorded such positive treatment.

A further potential problem when considering the value of a dual identity representation is that salient intergroup boundaries are usually associated with mutual distrust (Schopler & Insko, 1992) and intergroup anxiety (Greenland & Brown, 1999; Islam & Hewstone, 1993), whereby the potential for conflict along group lines remains high. Relatedly, in times of competition, threat, or political instability (e.g., within a country), the existence of a dual identity, when compared to a purely one group or separate individuals representation, provides a foundation for the reinstatement of separate group identities or the intensification of these identities in ways that can refuel intergroup conflict.

More generally, the relative salience of the subgroup and superordinate group boundaries (which may alternate as quickly as figure-ground perceptions when viewing reversible figures) is probably a crucial factor for determining the effects of the dual identity representation. When the superordinate group dominates the perceptual field, a dual identity is likely to be associated with harmonious relations between the subgroups. When subgroup identities are dominant and the superordinate group lurks only in the background, however, the effects of a dual identity is likely to approximate effects to a two separate groups representation.

Increasing the complexity of the problem further, Mummendey and Wenzel (1999) have proposed that a dual identity may *generally* be even more problematic for positive intergroup relations than a two separate groups representation. In addition to subgroup *similarity* that can threaten positive distinctiveness and thereby increase bias between subgroups (see Hewstone & Brown, 1986; see also Chapter 5), perceptions of subgroup *differences* can also exacerbate biases between subgroups. Specifically, Mummendey and Wenzel offer the provocative idea that a common identity under certain conditions can provoke social discrimination and intense conflict between subgroups. For example, they suggest that when subgroups possess different attributes (such as norms, values, goals), members of one group may begin to regard their subgroup's characteristics as more prototypical of the common, inclusive category compared to those of the other subgroup. As a consequence, they may assume that their group is more representative of the inclusive category and therefore superior to the other subgroup. Members of the other subgroup may be seen not only as inferior exemplars but also as deviants who justly deserve unequal and possibly harsh treatment.

A dual identity, therefore, may potentially serve as an instigator of intergroup bias and discrimination as well an effective strategy to ameliorate conflictual intergroup relations. The issue of when a dual identity representation is preferable to an undifferentiated, one group identity, is clearly a complex one that requires further inquiry and theoretical clarification.

Does Recategorization Lead to Generalization?

Hewstone's (1996) critique also questions whether recategorization effectively leads to generalization. Generalization, however, can take many forms. Generalization can mean that the benefits of interacting with specific members of the outgroup extend to additional members of that group (i.e., the outgroup as a whole), or to many other outgroups as well (see Pettigrew, 1997). Alternatively, these benefits can extend to those same outgroup members present during intergroup contact, but across time or across situations (e.g., at work and in social situations, or in the classroom and on the playground). In addition, generalization can involve changes across different types of responses. For instance, because of their common association to intergroup attitudes (Dovidio et al., 1996), changes in affective feelings (perhaps heuristically, as suggested in Chapter 3) during intergroup contact might generalize to altering stereotypic beliefs about either the same outgroup members present in the contact situation or additional outgroup members.

Besides considering different types of generalization, generalization can be measured in different ways. Generalization is frequently assessed in terms of changes in attitudes toward groups as a whole or toward specific members of a group who were not directly involved in the contact situation (Bettencourt et al., 1992; Scarberry et al., 1997). When participants in one contact condition have more favorable attitudes toward the outgroup category as a whole or toward other members not present, it is assumed that the contact experience had a more profound generalization effect than for participants in other treatment conditions. However, the *relationship* between responses to those members present and those not present in a contact situation or changes in group attitudes as a whole also merits consideration. That is, even while acknowledging that change scores may be less stable or reliable than single scores at one point in time, if generalization is occurring there should be a systematic relationship between the change elicited toward those outgroup members immediately present and other changes across time, situations or people. Thus, the answer about whether recategorization leads to generalization needs to consider how generalization is conceptualized and how it is measured.

We have proposed a trade-off hypothesis which expects differential consequences for the one group and the dual identity representations of common identity when we separately assess attitudes toward outgroup members present and toward the outgroup as a whole. Specifically, we hypothesize that as the one-group representation becomes stronger, attitudes toward immediate outgroup members will be more favorable, but because the associative link to additional members of the outgroup category has been potentially weakened (see Rothbart, 1996; Rothbart & John, 1985), these positive feelings would not generalize to the outgroup as a whole. However, as the strength of the dual identity becomes stronger (when both subgroup and superordinate identities are salient) attitudes toward outgroup members immediately present would not be as favorable as when only the superordinate boundary was salient, but whatever degree of favorability toward outgroup members present that does develop would have a greater likelihood of generalizing to other members of the outgroup or to the outgroup as a whole.

Although there are elements of theoretical and empirical support for the trade-off hypothesis, we have not yet observed evidence that is strongly supportive of this position. For example, Gonzalez and Brown's (1999; see Chapter 7) finding that the superordinate and the dual identity conditions were each associated with reduced bias toward outgroup members who were present during intergroup contact as well as those viewed on videotape (i.e., generalized bias reduction). Consistent with the trade-off hypothesis, generalized bias reduction was greater in the dual identity condition than the superordinate group condition, but the difference was not statistically significant. In other studies, (e.g., Rust, 1996; Gaertner, Dovidio, & Rust, 1997; see Chapter 7), we have found that attitudes toward members present did predict generalized outgroup attitudes more strongly in superordinate group and dual identity conditions than in conditions that created decategorized (separate individuals) representations. However, the relationships were not systematically stronger for dual identity than for superordinate group conditions. These findings offer promise that we may be approaching a theoretical understanding that can help guide interventions to produce generalized changes in intergroup attitudes, but they still reflect some problems for the trade-off hypothesis specifically. In the next section we discuss some additional work that offers promise for the future.

☐ Promise

The promise of the Common Ingroup Identity Model is *not* that, by itself, it offers *the* remedy for resolving intergroup conflict. Instead, we view the Common Ingroup Identity Model as one approach that can complement other perspectives and interventions to achieve more positive intergroup relations. Social relations between groups involve both group-level processes (e.g., social identity, realistic group conflict) and individual-level processes (e.g., motivation, memory). Thus, in this section on promise we consider the Common Ingroup Identity Model first within the theoretical context of other models of intergroup processes and then in relation to theories about individual motivation and social cognition.

Intergroup Processes

In Chapter 3, in particular, and throughout this volume we have discussed the potential of three category-based models for reducing intergroup bias and conflict: decategorization, recategorization, and mutual differentiation. Generally, each of these strategies has received empirical support. But a conceptual puzzle remains as to how we should conceptualize these alternatives that seem so very different, *even opposite* to one another? Are they incompatible competitors? Are they independent processes that reduce bias through different pathways? Or, are they different, but complementary processes that reciprocally facilitate each other? We believe that solving this conceptual puzzle offers promising insights that will have theoretical and applied value.

To illustrate the potential interrelationships among these processes, we now move beyond our data and the laboratory to reconsider the detailed account of the development and reduction of intergroup bias in the Robbers Cave experiment (Sherif et al., 1961/1988; see Chapter 1). Specifically, we attempt to understand how cooperation among Sherif et al.'s groups of summer campers reduced intergroup bias (see Gaertner, Dovidio, Banker et al., 2000). Was it through decategorization, recategorization, or mutual differentiation—or through all three processes? We focus on Sherif et al.'s work, not just to present an historical perspective, but for enlightenment regarding contemporary theoretical issues involving the possible interplay among these three category-based models. Although Sherif et al. did not provide many *p*-values for the effects they reported, they did provide a legacy of richly detailed observations of these boys' reactions to the planned interventions.

The work in our laboratories, Hewstone's (1996) review of category-based interventions, Pettigrew's (1998a) recent *Annual Review of Psychology* chapter, and Sherif et al.'s (1961/1988) richly detailed descriptions converge to suggest that *when viewed over time* decategorization, recategorization, and mutual intergroup differentiation strategies for reducing intergroup bias are not competitors. Rather they can each contribute to the reduction of intergroup bias and also they can reciprocally facilitate each other (see also, Hewstone, 1986). Thus, recategorization can lead to more interpersonally friendly, self-revealing interactions. Hewstone (1996) speculated that, "common ingroup identity can affect decategorization (and possibly, over time, differentiation, too)" (p. 354). This is illustrated most clearly in Sherif et al.'s account. Personalized, self-revealing interactions, however, can also lead to recategorization. Similarly, mutual intergroup differentiation, under specifiable circumstances (such as when groups share equal status, see Chapter 5), can also lead to recategorization. Thus, these processes are not necessarily independent.

As we detail the events at Robbers Cave, note some of the following characteristics that mark the occurrence of each of these category-based processes:

1. *Decategorization* can include: (a) Friendly interactions in which people relate to one another in terms of their personal interests and abilities rather than interests that are important to their respective groups; (b) Self-other comparisons that replace group-on-group comparisons; (c) Self-revealing interactions; and (d) Lack of uniformity among ingroup

members in their views about how outgroup members should be treated.

2. *Recategorization* can involve: (a) Use of pronouns "us" and "we," whose meaning is inclusive of the memberships of both groups; (b) Arrangement of the memberships in space—such as an arrangement that reduces the salience of separate group boundaries (e.g., an alternating seating pattern: ABABAB), which could be characteristic of decategorization as well; and (c) Activities that celebrate common superordinate groups to which the members actually belong (e.g., singing songs symbolic of superordinate group memberships).

3. *Mutual Intergroup Differentiation* can include: (a) Maintenance of original boundaries in the use of space; (b) More respectful appreciation of differences between the groups; and (c) Solutions to collective problems that respectfully recognize the group boundaries.

As we described in Chapter 1, in the Robbers Cave study (Sherif et al., 1961/1988) 12-year-old boys at a summer camp in Oklahoma were initially assigned to different groups. To permit time for the groups to form and develop, they were kept apart for the first week. During the second week, the groups engaged in a series of competitive activities (e.g., tug-of-war, baseball, and touch football), which generated negative intergroup attitudes, stereotypes, and verbal and physical conflict. Sherif and his colleagues then introduced a series of superordinate goals intended to elicit intergroup cooperative activity among the conflicting groups. Quite literally, with control over environmental features of the camp, the researchers successively placed these groups in common predicament requiring their mutual cooperation. For our purposes, the focus of this return to Robbers Cave involves the detailed observations of the patterns of behavior during and following these cooperative intergroup activities.

In the first superordinate goal of the series, the investigators sabotaged the camp's water supply by clogging the faucet valve on the water tank located some distance above the camp's facilities. To mobilize the boys' cooperation, the staff announced to the assembled campers that there may be a leak in the pipe somewhere between the reservoir and the camp and that about 25 people (i.e., just about everyone present, including the staff) would be needed to locate the source of the problem. Upon hearing this information that was specifically intended to enlist their assistance, both groups of boys volunteered to help. Four homogeneous search parties, each composed exclusively of Eagles or of Rattlers set off to locate the problem. Thus, even during this cooperative activity initiated by the camp's staff, the boys were split in separate groups divided along their group lines. Eventually, all of the boys wound up at the water tank and identified the problem, and—with Eagles and Rattlers working together now—remedied the situation. Sherif et al. reported:

When the water finally came through, there was common rejoicing. The Rattlers did not object to having the Eagles get ahead of them when they all got a drink, since the Eagles did not have canteens with them and were thirstier. No protests or "Ladies first" type of remarks were made. . . . When the first enthusiasm for the work . . . died down, individuals drifting away from the faucet increased. Among these boys there was a noticeable increase of mingling across group lines in such activities as catching lizards and making wooden whistles. . . . This was the first striking instance in which we observed friendly interaction among the members of the two groups on a general scale. (Sherif et al., 1961, [pp. 163–164; reprinted 1988])

It is clear that friendly interpersonal relations among these boys occurred immediately upon their achieving their common goal, but not before or even during the last stages of the cooperative episode when members of both groups were working together at the sabotaged water tank. That friendlier interpersonal relations between the groups emerged only *after* but *not during* this activity, which the investigators described as highly task-focused, is consistent with more recent findings suggesting that a strong task focus is not optimally conducive to personalizing processes even during intergroup cooperation (Bettencourt et al., 1992; Brewer & Miller, 1984). The friendlier, decategorized interpersonal relations across group lines that occurred after achieving the superordinate goal were transitory, however. The negative intergroup attitudes were again full-blown at supper that very evening. The investigators wrote, "During the meal, members of both groups started throwing left-overs, bottle caps, and paper that started in a rather good-natured way, but, in time, took on serious proportions" (Sherif et al., 1961, p. 164).

The second superordinate goal introduced by the staff involved the boys securing the highly desirable movie, "Treasure Island." The staff explained that renting this appealing film would cost $15.00 and that the camp could not afford to pay the whole amount. Because two boys became homesick and left camp early, there were 11 Rattlers and only 9 Eagles at this time. Although more grossly unfair solutions were initially considered, the boys decided that each group would pay $3.50 and the camp would pay $8.00. What is interesting about this solution is that since there were 11 Rattlers, each would pay 31 cents and each of the 9 Eagles would contribute 39 cents. Sherif et al. (1961) remarked, "It is worth noting that in individual terms this . . . was not equitable. But it was an equitable solution between the two groups" (p. 166). This solution was considered fair by both groups, which is supportive of mutual intergroup differentiation processes because the groups were cooperative and they were beginning to treat each other fairly at the group level. The fact that it was inequitable at the individual level was not important. Also, the boys sat along group lines while viewing the movie, further suggesting that at this time neither decategorization or recategorization processes were operating. But, relative to the week before, these groups treated each other fairly—and this carried over to the next morning: "While waiting in line for breakfast...the two groups discussed and reached an agreement that the Rattlers would go into breakfast first, and at lunch the Eagles would be first. . . . Thus the notion of 'taking turns' was introduced . . . on the intergroup level to regulate matters of mutual concern" (Sherif et al., 1961, p. 168).

The next day the groups departed in separate trucks for an overnight camping trip to Cedar Lake. Shortly after their arrival, it was time for lunch which set the stage for the introduction of the third superordinate goal. The driver of one of the trucks indicated that he would drive down the road to get the food. But, as planned, the truck would not start and the boys were very hungry. Some Rattlers suggested pushing the truck, but the truck was facing uphill. Someone suggested, uphill. Someone suggested,

> Let's get "our" tug-of-war rope and have a tug-of-war against the truck.
> . . . Someone said, "20 of us can pull it for sure." (Sherif et al., 1961, p. 171)

The use of the collective pronouns "our" and "us" at this point reveals that recategorization actually *preceded* actual intergroup cooperative activity in this instance. This is interesting because it suggests that the earlier episodes of intergroup cooperation among the boys may have resulted temporarily in recategorization processes that could re-emerge when they once again faced a common predicament. Thus, although there was no direct evidence of recategorization occurring during or following the earlier two instances of intergroup cooperative activity, the collective pronouns used by the boys *prior* to this third instance suggests the potentially lingering effects of their earlier cooperative experiences. Following this third episode of intergroup cooperation, recategorization again seemed to initiate decategorization revealed by the friendlier, interpersonal interactions across group lines.

> Mills [Rattler] ran over to get the rope [which was planted by the staff in full sight near the truck] and started to tie it to the front bumper of the truck. An Eagle said it would be too long, and suggested pulling it half-way through the bumper, thus making 2 pulling ropes. Harrison [Rattler] suggested that the Eagles pull one rope and the Rattlers the other. Barton [Rattler] said, "It doesn't make any difference." . . . The line-up pulling on the two ends of the rope was Eagles on one side and Rattlers on the other. . . . The first pull did not "start" the truck . . . On the second pull, the members of both groups were thoroughly intermixed on both ropes. . . . Finally the truck started. . . . Allen [Rattler] shouted: "We won the tug-of-war against the truck!" Bryan [Eagle] repeated, "Yeah! We won the tug-of-

war against the truck." This cry was echoed with satisfaction by others from both groups.

Immediately following this success, there was much intermingling of groups, friendly talk, and backslapping. Four boys went to the pump and pumped water for each other. . . . Thus the successful, interdependent efforts of both groups in pulling the truck, which was to get their food, had an immediate effect similar to that of superordinate goals introduced on previous days at the camp—intermingling of members of the two groups and friendly interaction between them. (Sherif et al., 1961, p. 171)

In this instance, it is clear from the use of the pronoun "We" that intergroup cooperation led immediately to recategorization which preceded intermingling, helping across group lines, and friendly interpersonal interactions. When it came time to begin preparing food for lunch, however, there was still tension about whether the groups wanted to remain apart or together. Among the Eagles, for example, some were in favor of alternating meal preparation such that one group would prepare lunch and the other would handle dinner. Others objected to the alternating arrangement and wanted to cook just for themselves. As it turned out, as discussions continued, food preparation suddenly began in which boys from each group prepared lunch together as a single group:

McGraw, the customary meat-cutter in the Eagle group, began cutting the meat. He received much advice from everyone, and Mills [Rattler] stood at his elbow for a time and helped him. In the meantime, Simpson [Rattler] and Craig [Eagle] poured Kool Aid into a bucket . . . and Meyers [Eagle] poured in what he thought was sugar. Unfortunately, it turned out to be salt; but Meyers was not berated by either Eagles or Rattlers for his mistake. . . . Harrison [Rattler] pointed out that it wasn't really Meyers' fault since the salt was in a sugar sack. (Sherif et al., 1961, p. 172)

This display of compassion, interpersonal sensitivity and protectiveness by Harrison toward Meyers, a former enemy, surely signals the magnitude of the shift in the relationship between the members of these two groups. That evening, just before supper, the truck "stalled" again, but this time, with hardly any discussion, the boys acted as a single, recategorized unit as they pulled the rope through the bumper and lined up on the two ropes thoroughly mixed together. Thus, throughout the series of superordinate goals, there was marked transformation in just how mutual cooperation between the groups was initiated and whether it was executed by the groups working separately or together as a single unit. Initially, when the camp's water supply was threatened, intergroup cooperation had to be gently coaxed by the investigators, and it was executed with the boys divided along group lines. In contrast, in this last instance in which the truck was stalled a second time, the groups spontaneously joined together as a single unit. Meal preparation as one group followed this last cooperative effort accompanied by much intermingling and helping without regard to former group membership.

The next day, however, joining together as one group did not come easily and there was obvious tension between whether the boys should recategorize or remain mutually differentiated. Upon planning a trip to the nearby Arkansas border, there was still some tension as to whether the groups should travel separately: "Whether or not group lines would be followed was coming to depend more and more on factors in the immediate situation" (Sherif et al., 1961, p. 176). As it worked out, the boys all did go in one truck:

> Clark [Eagle] began to whistle the Star Spangled Banner and was joined by several boys . . . without any discussion, the members of both groups now continued singing for about half-an-hour, alternating a song which had become associated with the Eagles with one which the Rattlers had adopted. . . . The truck stopped . . . to allow the boys to have cool drinks . . . and the seating arrangement at the tables, which seated four or five boys each, reflected little of the group demarcations. (Sherif et al., 1961, p. 177)

This type of seating, which was unrelated to prior group membership, also occurred during the evening meal the last day at camp when the staff rearranged the dinning hall so that seating arrangement would not simply reflect habitual patterns—unless that was desired by the boys. The final evening's campfire program "was a striking demonstration of the cumulative effectiveness of . . . interdependent activities toward common superordinate goals. The notion of 'taking turns,' which had started as a way of regulating activities in which a conflict of interests was involved (going in to meals), had been extended to joint singing of the two groups . . . in entertaining one another, as groups and as individuals" (Sherif et al., 1961, p. 177).

During breakfast and lunch on the last day of camp, the seating was without regard to earlier group membership as it was on the bus ride home to Oklahoma City. The boys crowded close together toward the front of the bus singing "Oklahoma."

Throughout the period following the introduction of superordinate goals, the change from hostile to friendly relations between these groups reveals the emergence of decategorization, recategorization and mutual differentiation processes, although not necessarily in that order. Clearly, nothing substantively materialized in terms of reducing hostility between these groups until, together, they achieved their first superordinate goal involving the camp's water supply. At that moment, the conditions of contact (Allport, 1954) were favorable. The groups were cooperatively interdependent, they enjoyed equal status, the camp authorities supported harmonious relations between these groups, and there was opportunity for personal interaction.

Pettigrew (1998a) proposed that the conditions of intergroup contact reduce prejudice over time by initiating a sequence of strategies for reducing bias. He suggested that the sequence unfolds beginning with decategorization, followed in turn by mutual differentiation and recategorization. According to this reformulated contact theory, this combination, over time, can maximally reduce prejudice toward outgroup members and also generalize across situations, to different outgroup members, and even to different outgroups (see Pettigrew, 1997).

The order in which these category-based processes unfold, however, probably depends upon specific features of the contact situation, such as whether contact emphasizes group-on-group interaction (as at Robbers Cave) or interaction among individuals from different groups (as among neighbors). Nevertheless, the cogency of Pettigrew's (1998a) general perspective receives converging support from Sherif et al.'s (1961/1988) detailed descriptions of the events at Robbers Cave and from recent laboratory studies that were designed to examine how these conditions of contact (e.g., cooperation and equal status) reduce intergroup bias and to explore the possible interplay between decategorization, recategorization and mutual differentiation processes.

Our analysis reveals that at Robbers Cave the introduction of superordinate goals instigated a sequence of category-based social processes that alternated between decategorization, recategorization, mutual intergroup differentiation and categorization as two conflicting groups. Indeed, Sherif and his colleagues emphasized that intergroup harmony was achieved gradually, only after the groups cooperated on a series of superordinate goals. Sherif et al.'s report of the detailed description of these events reveals that the alternation pattern among the different categorization processes was evident throughout the gradual transition from conflict to harmonious relations between the groups. After the groups jointly moved the stalled truck carrying their food, the boys immediately rejoiced, chanting repeatedly, "We won the tug-of-war against the truck." The inclusive pronoun "we" signaled the recategorization of these groups— and this was followed by the boys intermingling across group lines with friendlier, more interpersonal interactions.

Recent Evidence for Reciprocity
Between the Category-based Processes

Some recent experiments in our laboratories further explored the processes that by which intergroup cooperation and reduces bias and conflict and illustrates potential interrelationships among recategorization, decategorization, and mutual intergroup differentiation.

The sequence which proceeded from recategorization to friendlier interpersonal relations observed at Robbers Cave was replicated in a laboratory experiment (Dovidio et al., 1997, see Chapter 7) in which the members of two groups were induced to conceive of themselves as one group or two groups and then given the opportunity to self-disclose or to offer assistance to an ingroup or outgroup member. As expected, the degree of bias in self-disclosure and prosocial behavior favoring ingroup members was generally lower among participants in the one-group relative to the two-groups condition. Self-disclosure and prosocial behaviors are particularly interesting because they elicit reciprocity which can further accelerate the intensity of positive interpersonal interactions across group lines even when the initial recategorization process lasts only temporarily. In terms of a longitudinal analysis, these increasingly positive interpersonal relations can fuel the progression to next stage in the sequence (e.g., mutual differentiation or the formation of a more permanent recategorized bond between the memberships). This possibility is illustrated in a laboratory study in which personalized, self-disclosing interactions among the members of two groups meeting group-on-group transformed their perceptions of the aggregate from two groups to one group (Gaertner, Rust & Dovidio, 1997).

Within an alternating sequence of categorization processes, mutual differentiation may emerge frequently to neutralize threats to original group identities posed by the recategorization and decategorization processes. As suggested by the laboratory experiment reviewed in Chapter 5 (Dovidio, Gaertner, & Validzic, 1998), however, mutual differentiation can facilitate recategorization among equal status groups which may otherwise experience threats to the distinctiveness of their group identities. Thus, recategorization, decategorization and mutual differentiation processes seem to share the capacity to facilitate each other, supporting the view that when viewed over time, these processes are complementary and reciprocal. Conceptualizing these strategies in this way offers promise both theoretically and pragmatically for designing interventions to reduce intergroup conflict and bias.

Interventions, such as activities that are planned and the spatial configuration of the groups in the setting, may provide the opportunity to influence which process begins the sequence or the pattern with which the processes alternate. However, which categorization-based process to emphasize initially may depend upon structural features of the contact situation, the nature of intergroup relations, and intragroup processes. Structural aspects of the contact situation may relate to, for example, whether contact is group-on-group or among individuals. The nature of intergroup relations can involve whether groups are in overt conflict or bias is less direct.

When the level of conflict between groups is very high, it may be best to begin with decategorization, which promotes more friendly relations between individuals, one-on-one, to inhibit the recurrence of perceptions of the memberships as two competing groups (Hewstone, 1996). As the details of Sherif et al.'s (1961/1988) Robbers Cave study reveal, the introduction of superordinate goals, which initiates recategorization processes, can also be an effective strategy when conflict between groups is high—but we also recognize that in some circumstances it would not be realistic. In contrast, some contemporary forms of White racism, such as aversive racism (Dovidio & Gaertner, 1998; Gaertner & Dovidio, 1986a), may involve primarily a lack of a sense of connection to outgroup members rather than conscious hostility (Gaertner, Dovidio et al., 1997). For these types of biases, recategorization may be a particularly effective strategy because it extends the cognitive and motivational processes involved in ingroup favoritism to people who would otherwise be considered only outgroup members.

With respect to intragroup considerations, the degree to which people identify with their group may be a particularly important factor. When group identities are very strong (but the level of conflict is not very high), contact situations that initially facilitate mutual intergroup differentiation, which emphasizes similarities and differences between groups, would reduce threats to members' social identities and thereby facilitate more favorable intergroup attitudes. This can become very complex, however; groups in contact can have different levels and types of identities. For example, intergroup contact frequently involves members of minority groups who have a strong sense of ethnic identity and who may consequently prefer intergroup contact that emphasizes mutual differentiation, and members of a majority group, who prefer a more assimilationist, recategorization model for contact (see Dovidio, Kawakami, & Gaertner et al., 2000; Dovidio, Gaertner, & Kafati, in press). Thus, choosing one strategy for both groups could be problematic. In this type of situation, integrative strategies, such as the dual identity form of recategorization that emphasizes both the salience of the superordinate group identity and ethnic subgroup identities simultaneously, may be most effective.

Understanding intergroup bias and identifying strategies for reducing it involves not only looking ahead to new theoretical insights but also looking back to the important field studies of Sherif and his colleagues (1961/1988) as well as to other classic works in the field (e.g., Allport, 1954; Tajfel & Turner, 1986; Williams, 1947). These sources continue to offer timeless insights into intergroup relations, and they often also provide valuable descriptions and analyses of events that would be difficult to reconstruct or replicate today. Reflecting on these events in the context of contemporary theory can further illuminate psychological processes that would be difficult to observe with the spatial and temporal constraints of the typical laboratory study. Moreover, developing a more comprehensive understanding of these processes in this way has practical, as well as theoretical benefits. In particular, although the Contact Hypothesis (Allport, 1954; Williams, 1947) identifies a number of necessary and facilitating conditions of intergroup contact for reducing bias, the reality often is that these conditions are difficult to introduce in many actual contact situations. Having a theoretical understanding of the psychological processes that can reduce bias, both individually and sequentially, can help to identify alternatives that can be introduced when these particular conditions of contact can not be fully implemented. Thus, classic work in the field, such as the Robbers Cave study, can offer rare, detailed analyses of complex social relationships over time that complement current research, methods, and theory in ways that leave a truly enduring legacy to the field.

Individual Motivation and Social Cognition

As we have argued in this volume and elsewhere (e.g., Dovidio & Gaertner, 1999), intergroup bias is an individual-level as well as group-level phenomenon. It needs to be combated at both levels, and we believe that the theoretical processes hypothesized in the Common Ingroup Identity Model offer promise on both fronts. In this section, we consider the model in the context of personal motivations and social cognitive processes. In particular, we return to where we began—the topic of aversive racism (see Chapter 2), an issue that initially stimulated our work on the Common Ingroup Identity Model.

According to the aversive racism framework, many Whites who believe they are nonprejudiced and sincerely embrace egalitarian values also harbor unconscious negative feelings and beliefs about Blacks. These negative feelings and beliefs are based on almost unavoidable cognitive (e.g., ingroup–outgroup categorization), motivational (e.g., needs for status), and socio-cultural (e.g., socialization) processes. Aversive racists thus have negative feelings and beliefs, but they are normally able to suppress them. This proposition is consistent with other theories and findings of motivation and social cognition. In particular, there is considerable empirical evidence that, when sufficiently motivated and with sufficient cognitive resources, people can avoid the influence of stereotypes in the conscious evaluations of others (Bargh, 1999; Devine, 1989; Fiske, 1989). In addition, there is evidence that people might be able to moderate the activation of unconscious negative attitudes and stereotypes, at least temporarily (Blair & Banaji, 1996; cf. Bargh, 1999).

We propose, in addition, that the negative feelings and beliefs will often be expressed subtly and indirectly—in ways that are not readily attributable (by others or themselves) to racial bias and thus do not threaten an aversive racist's nonprejudiced self-image. From this perspective, a major motive of Whites in interracial situations is to *avoid wrong-doing*. Supportive of this view, we have found across a variety of different studies that Whites typically do not discriminate against Blacks in situations in which norms for appropriate behaviors are clearly defined. Thus, Whites can, at least under some circumstances, successfully suppress negative beliefs, feelings and behavior toward Blacks when it is obvious that expressing such expressions reflects racial bias. That some people are motivated by cultural values to avoid thinking, feeling or behaving in a prejudicial way is a positive quality that can limit or lessen social conflict. However, aversive racism also has negative consequences.

In Chapter 2 we noted that the motivation to avoid or suppress wrong-doing has two important potential costs for interracial interactions. First, this concern about avoiding wrong-doing increases anxiety that can motivate avoidance or premature withdrawal from the interaction. This avoidant reaction precludes the opportunity for meaningful, self-revealing exchanges between ingroup and outgroup members. For example, in one of our initial studies of aversive racism (Gaertner, 1973; see Chapter 2) Liberal Party members who were telephoned "by mistake" hung-up prematurely more frequently on Black than on White callers (and more so than Conservative Party members did) in ways that prevented them from understanding the full nature of the caller's predicament and need. Second, in view of recent work on stereotype suppression and rebound (e.g., Bodenhausen & Macrae, 1996), it is possible that once this self-imposed suppression is relaxed, negative beliefs, feelings and behaviors would be even more likely to occur than if they were not suppressed initially.

In the search for strategies that could eliminate the indirect, rationalizable ways that aversive racists discriminate we considered the importance of establishing positive interpersonal and intergroup motivations rather than simply suppressing negative motivations. The Common Ingroup Identity Model, because it focuses on redirecting the forces of ingroup favoritism, offers such promise. Specifically, the recognition of a common ingroup identity potentially changes the motivational orientation of aversive racists from trying to avoid wrong-doing to trying to *do what's right*.

Although this change is subtle, it can have fundamental benefits. For instance, it may relieve intergroup anxiety (see Stephan & Stephan, 1985) and reduce the likelihood of negative consequences of effortful attempts to avoid wrong-doing, such as the increased accessibility of negative thoughts, feelings and behavior that occur when suppression is relaxed (Monteith, Sherman, & Devine, 1998; Wegner, 1994). Some recent preliminary evidence from our laboratory suggests the potential promise of a common ingroup identity to alter motivation in just such a positive way (Dovidio, Gaertner, & Kawakami, 1998).

In this experiment, White participants who were about to interact with a White or a Black confederate were either asked to try to avoid wrong doing, instructed to try to behave correctly toward the other person, informed that they were part of the same team with their partner and competing against a team at a rival institution, or were given no instructions. The dependent measure of interest was the relative accessibility of negative thoughts, as assessed by changes in responses on a Stroop color-naming task after the interaction relative to responses on a baseline Stroop task administered before the interaction (see Lane & Wegner, 1995). A rebound effect would be reflected in greater accessibility (operationalized in terms of longer color-naming latencies) of negative relative to positive words on the post-test Stroop task.

We hypothesized that, because the primary motivation of aversive racists in interracial interaction is to avoid wrong doing and thus to suppress negative thoughts and feelings, participants explicitly instructed to avoid wrong doing and those given no instructions would show relatively strong accessibility of negative thoughts after interacting with a Black confederate. In contrast, we expected participants instructed to behave correctly and those in the "same team" condition (who were hypothesized to adopt a positive orientation on their own) would escape such a rebound effect.

The results, while preliminary are very encouraging. When the confederate was White, the experimental conditions did not differ significantly in the accessibility of negative thoughts from one another or from baseline. When the confederate was Black, however, the increased accessibility of negative relative to positive characteristics (from the pre-test to the post-test) in the avoid wrong doing (+ 25 msec) and no instructions (+33 msec) conditions was significantly greater than in the do right (−32 msec) and same team (−5 msec) conditions ($p < .05$). The pattern of these findings strongly suggests that the development of a common ingroup identity can alter motivation in interracial situations from one of suppressing negative thoughts, feelings, and actions to one that is positive and prosocial— and in a way that does not ironically result in further increases in negative thoughts. These findings are particularly encouraging to us because they illustrate the effectiveness of the Common Ingroup Identity Model for addressing individual-level biases and particularly the underlying dynamics of aversive racism—which, as we said in Chapter 1, "was the start and is at the heart of it all."

☐ Conclusion

We began this chapter by summarizing the chapters in this book and the progress we have made in our research exploring the potential of a particular category-based strategy namely, the creation of a common ingroup identity, to reduce intergroup bias. We then examined some important theoretical, empirical, and practical challenges to this approach and potential problems to address in future work. In the third section of this chapter, we considered the promise of the Common Ingroup Identity Model in the context of other theoretical approaches for improving intergroup relations and combating bias.

The promise of our model is not that it offers *the solution* to intergroup bias and conflict but that it provides one perspective—one that offers alternatives to and may be complementary with other approaches. Sherif et al.'s (1961/1988) descriptions of the events at Robbers Cave and data from our own laboratories converge to support Hewstone (1996) and Pettigrew's (1998a) ideas that decategorization, recategorization and mutual intergroup differentiation processes each contribute to the reduction of intergroup bias and conflict. Furthermore, particularly when the processes are viewed over time, these categorization-based approaches not only can reduce bias individually, they can also facilitate each other reciprocally. Therefore, strategies and interventions to reduce intergroup bias and conflict may consider these processes both independently and collectively. They are potentially complementary and alternating routes to more positive intergroup relations.

In conclusion, we recognize that bias and conflict are complex phenomena having historical, cultural, economic, as well as psychological roots. In addition, these are dynamic phenomena that can evolve to different forms and manifestations over time. A debate about whether a societal, institutional, intergroup, or individual level of analysis is most appropriate, or a concern about which model of bias or bias reduction accounts for the most variance, may thus be not only futile but may distract scholars from a more fundamental mission. Our ultimate goal has been to understand the nature of bias and to develop ways of combating this bias and improving intergroup relations. We acknowledge that the work we have reviewed in this book has its limitations; we do not suggest that we have achieved our objective. Nevertheless, we offer this work as one piece which, in combination with the contributions of others, can provide a fuller picture of individual and intergroup dynamics and offer promise of more positive interpersonal, intergroup, interracial, inter-ethnic, and international relations.

REFERENCES

Abelson, R. P., Kinder, D. R., Peters, M. D., & Fiske, S. T. (1982). Affective and semantic components in political person perception. *Journal of Personality and Social Psychology, 42,* 619–630.

Abrams, D. (1985). Focus of attention in minimal intergroup discrimination. *British Journal of Social Psychology, 24,* 65–74.

Adorno, T. W., Frenkel-Brunswik, E., Levinson, D. J., & Sanford, R. N. (1950). *The authoritarian personality.* New York: Harper.

Allport, G. W. (1954). *The nature of prejudice.* Cambridge, MA: Addison-Wesley.

Allport, G. W. (1958). *The nature of prejudice* (abridged). Garden City, NY: Doubleday.

Altman, I., & Taylor, D. A. (1973). *Social penetration: The development of interpersonal relationships.* New York: Holt, Rinehart, & Winston.

Amir, Y. (1969). Contact hypothesis in ethnic relations. *Psychological Bulletin, 71,* 319–342.

Anastasio, P. A., Bachman, B. A., Gaertner, S. L., & Dovidio, J. F. (1997). In R. Spears, P. J. Oakes, N. Ellemers, & S. A. Haslam (Eds.), *The social psychology of stereotyping and group life* (pp. 236–256). Oxford, UK: Blackwell.

Anderson, J. Z., & White, G. D. (1986). An empirical investigation of interaction and relationship patterns in functional and dysfunctional nuclear families and stepfamilies. *Family Process, 25,* 407–422.

Archer, R. L., & Berg, J. H. (1978). Disclosure reciprocity and its limits: A reactance analysis. *Journal of Experimental Social Psychology, 14,* 527–540.

Aron, A., & Aron, E. N. (1986). *Love as the expansion of self: Understanding attraction and satisfaction.* New York: Hemisphere.

Aron, A., Aron, E. N., & Smollan, D. (1992). Inclusion of the Other in the Self Scale and the structure of interpersonal closeness. *Journal of Personality and Social Psychology, 63,* 596–612.

Aron, A., Aron, E. N., Tudor, M., & Nelson, G. (1991). Close relationships as including the other in the self. *Journal of Personality and Social Psychology, 60,* 241–253.

Aronson, E., Blaney, N., Stephan, C., Sikes, J., & Snapp, M. (1978). *The jigsaw classroom.* Beverly Hills, CA: Sage.

Aronson, E., & Patnoe, S. (1997). *The jigsaw classroom.* New York: Longman.

Ashmore, R. D. (1970). Prejudice: Causes and cures. In B. E. Collins (Ed.), *Social psychology: Social influence, attitude change, group processes and prejudice* (pp. 245–339). Reading, MA: Addison-Wesley.

Bachman, B. A. (1993). *An intergroup model of organizational mergers.* Unpublished Ph.D. Dissertation, Department of Psychology, University of Delaware, Newark, DE.

Bachman, B. A., & Gaertner, S. L. (1999). *An intergroup model of organizational mergers.* Unpublished manuscript, Department of Psychology, Siena College, Loudenville, NY.

Bachman, B. A., Gaertner, S. L., Anastasio, P. A., & Rust, M. C. (1993, March). *When corpo-*

rations merge: Organizational identification among employees of acquiring and acquired organizations. Paper presented at the 64th Eastern Psychological Association Convention, Crystal City, VA.

Banaji, M. R., & Greenwald, A. G. (1995). Implicit gender stereotyping in judgments of fame. *Journal of Personality and Social Psychology, 68,* 181–198.

Banaji, M. R., & Hardin, C. D. (1996). Automatic gender stereotyping. *Psychological Science,* 7, 136–141.

Banaji, M. R., Hardin, C. D., & Rothman, A. (1993). Implicit stereotyping in person judgment. *Journal of Personality and Social Psychology, 65,* 272–281.

Banker, B. S., & Gaertner, S. L. (1998). Achieving stepfamily harmony: An intergroup relations approach. *Journal of Family Psychology, 12,* 310–325.

Bargh, J. (1999). The cognitive monster: The case against controllability of automatic stereotype effects. In S. Chaiken & Y. Trope (Eds.), *Dual process theories in social psychology* (pp. 361–382). New York: Guilford Press.

Bargh, J. A., & Pietromonaco, P. (1982). Automatic information processing and social perception: The influence of trait information presented outside of awareness. *Journal of Personality and Social Psychology, 43,* 437–449.

Baron, R. M., & Kenny, D. A. (1986). The moderator-mediator variable distinction in social psychological research: Conceptual, strategic, and statistical considerations. *Journal of Personality and Social Psychology, 51,* 1173–1182.

Batson, C. D. (1991). *The altruism question: Toward a social-psychological answer.* Hillsdale, NJ: Erlbaum.

Batson, C. D., Polycarpou, M. P., Harmon-Jones, E., Imhoff, H. J., Mitchener, E. C., Bednar, L. L., Klein, T. R., & Highberger, L. (1997). Empathy and attitudes: Can feeling for a member of a stigmatized group improve feelings toward the group? *Journal of Personality and Social Psychology, 72,* 105–118.

Bennett, C., & Okinaka, A. M. (1990). Factors related to persistence among Asian, Black, Hispanic and White undergraduates at a predominantly White university: Comparisons between first and fourth year cohorts. *The Urban Review, 22,* 33–60.

Berger, J., Wagner, D. G., & Zelditch, M., Jr. (1985). Introduction: Expectation States Theory. In J. Berger & M. Zelditch, Jr. (Eds.), *Status, rewards, and influence* (pp. 1–72). San Francisco: Jossey-Bass.

Berkowitz, L., & Daniels, L. R. (1963). Responsibility and dependency. *Journal of Abnormal and Social Psychology, 66,* 429–436.

Berry, J. W. (1984). Cultural relations in plural societies. In N. Miller & M. B. Brewer (Eds.), *Groups in contact: The psychology of desegregation* (pp. 11–27). Orlando, FL: Academic Press.

Berry, J. W., Poortinga, Y. H., Segall, M. H., & Dasen, P. R. (1992). *Cross-cultural psychology: Research and applications.* Cambridge, UK: Cambridge University Press.

Bettencourt, B. A., Brewer, M. B., Croak, M. R., & Miller, N. (1992). Cooperation and the reduction of intergroup bias: The roles of reward structure and social orientation. *Journal of Experimental Social Psychology, 28,* 301–319.

Billig, M. (1988). Social representations, objectification and anchoring: A rhetorical analysis. *Social Behaviour, 3,* 1–16.

Billig, M. G., & Tajfel, H. (1973). Social categorisation and similarity in intergroup behavior. *European Journal of Social Psychology, 3,* 27–52.

Blair, I., & Banaji, M. R. (1996). Automatic and controlled processes in gender stereotyping. *Journal of Personality and Social Psychology, 70,* 1142–1163.

Blake, R. R., & Mouton, J. S. (1979). Intergroup problem solving in organizations: From theory to practice. In W. Austin & S. Worchel (Eds.), *The social psychology of intergroup relations* (pp. 19–31). Monterey, CA: Brooks/Cole.

Blanchard, F. A., Weigel, R. H., & Cook, S. W. (1975). The effects of relative competence of group members upon interpersonal attraction in cooperating interracial groups. *Journal of Personality and Social Psychology, 32*, 519–530.

Bless, H., Clore, G. L., Schwarz, N., Golisano, V., Rabe, C., & Wölk, M. (1996). Mood and the use of scripts: Does a happy mood really lead to mindlessness? *Journal of Personality and Social Psychology, 71*, 665–679.

Bless, H., Schwarz, N., & Kemmelmeier, M. (1996). Mood and stereotyping: Affective states and the use of general knowledge structures. In W. Stroebe & M. Hewstone (Eds.), *European review of social psychology* (Vol. 7, pp. 63–93). London: Wiley.

Bless, H., Schwarz, N., & Wieland, R. (1996). Mood and the impact of category membership and individuating information. *European Journal of Social Psychology, 26*, 935–959.

Bobo, L. (1999). Prejudice as group position: Micro-foundations of a sociological approach to racism and race relations. *Journal of Social Issues, 55*(3), 445–472.

Bodenhausen, G. V. (1993). Emotions, arousal, and stereotypic judgments: A heuristic model of affect and stereotyping. In D. M. Mackie & D. L. Hamilton (Eds.), *Affect, cognition, and stereotyping: Interactive processes in group perception* (pp. 13–37). San Diego, CA: Academic Press.

Bodenhausen, G. V., Kramer, G. P., & Susser, K. (1994). Happiness and stereotypic thinking in social judgment. *Journal of Personality and Social Psychology, 66*, 621–632.

Bodenhausen, G. V., & Macrae, C. N. (1996). The self-regulation of intergroup perception: Mechanisms and consequences of stereotype suppression. In C. N. Macrae, C. Stangor, & M. Hewstone (Eds.), *Stereotypes and stereotyping* (pp. 227–253). New York: Guilford.

Bray, J. H., & Berger, S. H. (1993). Developmental issues in stepfamilies research project: Family relationships and parent-child interactions. *Journal of Family Psychology, 7*, 76–90.

Brewer, M. B. (1979). Ingroup bias in the minimal intergroup situation: A cognitive-motivational analysis. *Psychological Bulletin, 86*, 307–324.

Brewer, M. B. (1988). A dual process model of impression formation. In T. S. Srull & R. S. Wyer (Eds.), *Advances in social cognition: Vol. I: A dual process model of impression formation* (pp. 1–36). Hillsdale, NJ: Erlbaum.

Brewer, M. B. (1991). The social self: On being the same and different at the same time. *Personality and Social Psychology Bulletin, 17*, 475–482.

Brewer, M. B. (1999). The psychology of prejudice: Ingroup love or outgroup hate? *Journal of Social Issues, 55*(3), 429–444.

Brewer, M. B., & Gaertner, S. L. (in press). Toward reduction of prejudice: Intergroup contact and social categorization. In R. J. Brown & S. L. Gaertner (Eds), *Blackwell handbook of social psychology: Intergroup processes*. Oxford, UK: Blackwell.

Brewer, M. B., & Gardner W. (1996). Who is the "We"? Levels of collective identity and self representations. *Journal of Personality and Social Psychology, 71*, 83–93.

Brewer, M. B., Ho, H., Lee, J., & Miller, N. (1987). Social identity and social distance among Hong Kong school children. *Personality and Social Psychology Bulletin, 13*, 156–165.

Brewer, M. B., Manzi, J. M., & Shaw, J. S. (1993). In-group identification as a function of depersonalization, distinctiveness, and status. *Psychological Science, 4*, 88–92.

Brewer, M. B., & Miller, N. (1984). Beyond the contact hypothesis: Theoretical perspectives on desegregation. In N. Miller & M. B. Brewer (Eds.), *Groups in contact: The psychology of desegregation* (pp. 281–302). Orlando, FL: Academic Press.

Brewer, M. B., & Miller, N. (1996). *Intergroup relations*. Buckingham, UK: Open University Press.

Brewer, M. B., & Schneider, S. (1990). Social identity and social dilemmas: A double-edged sword. In D. Abrams & M. Hogg (Eds.), *Social identity theory: Constructive and critical advances* (pp. 169–184). London: Harvester Wheatsheaf.

Brewer, M. B., von Hippel, W., & Gooden, M. P. (1999). Diversity and organizational entity:

The problem of entrée after entry. In D. A. Prentice & D. T. Miller (Eds.), *Cultural divides: Understanding and overcoming group conflict* (pp. 337–363). New York: Russell Sage Foundation.

Brigham, J. C. (1993). College students' racial attitudes. *Journal of Applied Social Psychology, 23*, 1933–1967.

Brown, A. C., Green, R. J., & Druckman, J. (1990). A comparison of stepfamilies with and without child-focused problems. *American Orthopsychiatric Association, Inc., 160*, 556–566.

Brown, R. J. (1984). The effects of intergroup similarity and cooperative vs. competitive orientation on intergroup discrimination. *British Journal of Social Psychology, 21*, 21–33.

Brown, R. J. (1995). *Prejudice*. Cambridge, MA: Blackwell.

Brown, R. J., & Turner, J. C. (1981). Interpersonal and intergroup behavior. In J. C. Turner & H. Giles (Eds.), *Intergroup behavior* (pp. 33–64). Chicago: University of Chicago Press.

Brown, R. J., Vivian, J., & Hewstone, M. (1999). Changing attitudes through intergroup contact: The effects of group membership salience. *European Journal of Social Psychology, 29*, 741–764.

Brown, R. J., & Wade, G. (1987). Superordinate goals and intergroup behavior: The effect of role ambiguity and status on intergroup attitudes and task performance. *European Journal of Social Psychology, 17*, 131–142.

Buono, A. F., & Bowditch, J. L. (1989). *The human side of mergers and acquisitions: Managing collisions between people, cultures, and organizations*. San Francisco: Jossey-Bass.

Burnam, M. A., Telles, C. A., Karno, M., Hough, R. L., & Escobar, J. I. (1987). Measurement of acculturation in a community population of Mexican Americans. *Hispanic Journal of the Behavioral Sciences, 9*, 105–130.

Byrne, D., & Clore, G. L. (1970). A reinforcement model of evaluative responses. *Personality: An International Journal, 1*, 103–128.

Cadinu, M. R., & Rothbart, M. (1996). Self-anchoring and differentiation processes in the minimal intergroup setting. *Journal of Personality and Social Psychology, 70*, 661–677.

Campbell, D. T. (1958). Common fate, similarity and other indices of the status of aggregates of persons as social entities. *Behavioral Science, 3*, 14–25.

Campbell, D. T. (1965). Ethnocentric and other altruistic motives. In D. Levine (Ed.), *Nebraska symposium on motivation* (Vol. 13, pp. 283–311). Lincoln, NE: University of Nebraska Press.

Carter, D. J., & Wilson, R. (1997). *Minorities in higher education*. Washington, DC: American Council on Education.

Cheyne, W. M. (1970). Stereotyped reactions to speakers with Scottish and English regional accents. *British Journal of Social and Clinical Psychology, 9*, 77–79.

Cook, S. W. (1969). Motives in a conceptual analysis of attitude-related behavior. In W. J. Arnold & D. Levine (Eds.), *Nebraska symposium on motivation* (Vol. 18, pp. 179–236). Lincoln, NE: University of Nebraska Press.

Cook, S. W. (1984). Cooperative interaction in multiethnic contexts. In N. Miller & M. B. Brewer (Eds.), *Groups in contact: The psychology of desegregation* (pp. 291–302). Orlando, FL: Academic Press.

Cook, S. W. (1985). Experimenting on social issues: The case of school desegregation. *American Psychologist, 40*, 452–460.

Cotton, J. L., & Tuttle, J. (1986). Employee turnover: A meta-analysis and review with implications for research. *Academy of Management Review, 11*, 55–70.

Cramer, D. (1993). Tenure, commitment, and job satisfaction of college graduates in an engineering firm. *Journal of Social Psychology, 33*, 791–796.

Crisp, R. J., & Hewstone, M. (1999). Differential evaluations of crossed category groups: Patterns, processes, and reducing intergroup biases. *Group Processes & Intergroup Relations, 2*, 307–333.

Crocker, J., & Quinn, D. M. (in press). Psychological consequences of devalued identities.

In R. J. Brown & S. L. Gaertner (Eds), *Blackwell handbook of social psychology: Intergroup processes*. Oxford, UK: Blackwell.

Crocker, J., & Schwartz, I. (1985). Prejudice and ingroup favoritism in a minimal intergroup situation: Effects of self-esteem. *Personality and Social Psychology Bulletin, 11*, 379-386.

Crosbie-Burnett, M. (1984). The centrality of the step relationship: A challenge to family theory and practice. *Family Relations, 33*, 459–463.

Crosby, F., Bromley, S., & Saxe, L. (1980). Recent unobtrusive studies of black and white discrimination and prejudice: A literature review. *Psychological Bulletin, 87*, 546–563.

Darley, J. M., & Latané, B. (1968). Bystander intervention in emergencies: Diffusion of responsibility. *Journal of Personality and Social Psychology, 8*, 377–383.

Davis, J. D. (1976). Self-disclosure in an acquaintance exercise: Responsibility for level of intimacy. *Journal of Personality and Social Psychology, 33*, 787–792.

Derlega, V. J., & Chaikin, A. L. (1976). Norms affecting self-disclosure in men and women. *Journal of Consulting and Clinical Psychology, 44*, 376-380.

Derlega, V. J., Metts, S., Petronio, S., & Margulis, S. T. (1993). *Self-disclosure*. Newbury Park, CA: Sage.

Deschamps, J. C., & Brown, R. J. (1983). Superordinate goals and intergroup conflict. *British Journal of Social Psychology, 22*, 189–195.

Deschamps J. C., & Doise, W. (1978). Crossed-category membership in intergroup relations. In H. Tajfel (Ed.), *Differentiation between social groups* (pp. 141–158). London, UK: Academic Press.

Desforges, D. M., Lord, C. G., Ramsey, S. L., Mason, J. A., Van Leeuwen, M. D., & Lepper, M. R. (1991). Effects of structured cooperative contact on changing negative attitudes toward stigmatized groups. *Journal of Personality and Social Psychology, 60*, 531–544.

Deutsch, M. (1973). *The resolution of social conflict*. New Haven, CT: Yale University Press.

Deutsch, M. (1993). Educating for a peaceful world. *American Psychologist, 48*, 510-517.

Deutsch, M., & Collins, M. (1951). *Interracial housing: A psychological evaluation of a social experiment*. Minneapolis, MN: University of Minnesota Press.

Devine, P. G. (1989). Stereotypes and prejudice: The automatic and controlled components. *Journal of Personality and Social Psychology, 56*, 5–18.

Devine, P. G., Plant, E. A., & Blair, I. B. (in press). Classic and contemporary analyses of racial prejudice. In R. J. Brown & S. L. Gaertner (Eds.), *Blackwell handbook of social psychology: Intergroup processes*. Oxford, UK: Blackwell.

Dijksterhuis, A., & van Knippenberg, A. (1996). The knife that cuts both ways: Facilitated and inhibited access to traits as a result of stereotype-activation. *Journal of Experimental Social Psychology, 32*, 271–288.

Dindia, K., & Allen, M. (1992). Sex differences in self-disclosure: A meta-analysis. *Psychological Bulletin, 112*, 106–124.

Dion, K. L. (1974, September). *A cognitive model of ingroup-outgroups bias*. Paper presented at the American Psychological Association Meeting, New Orleans, LA.

Doise, W. (1978). *Groups and individuals: Explanations in social psychology*. Cambridge, UK: Cambridge University Press.

Doise, W., & Sinclair, A. (1973). The categorization process in intergroup relations. *European Journal of Social Psychology, 3*, 145–157.

Doosje, B., & Ellemers, N. (1997). Stereotyping under threat: The role of group identification. In R. Spears, P. J. Oakes, N. Ellemers, & S. A. Haslam (Eds.), *The social psychology of stereotyping and group life* (pp. 257–272). Oxford, UK: Blackwell.

Dovidio, J. F. (1984). Helping behavior and altruism: An empirical and conceptual overview. In L. Berkowitz (Ed.), *Advances in experimental social psychology* (Vol. 17, pp. 361–427). New York: Academic Press.

Dovidio, J. F., Allen, J., & Schroeder, D. A. (1990). The specificity of empathy-induced helping: Evidence for altruism. *Journal of Personality and Social Psychology, 59*, 249–260.

Dovidio, J. F., Brigham, J. C., Johnson, B. T., & Gaertner, S. L. (1996). Stereotyping, prejudice, and discrimination: Another look. In C. N. Macrae, C. Stangor, & M. Hewstone (Eds.), *Stereotypes and stereotyping* (pp. 276–319). New York: Guilford.

Dovidio, J. F., Evans, N., & Tyler, R. B. (1986). Racial stereotypes: The contents of their cognitive representations. *Journal of Experimental Social Psychology, 22,* 22–37.

Dovidio, J. F., & Fazio, R. H. (1992). New technologies for the direct and indirect assessment of attitudes. In J. Tanur (Ed.), *Questions about survey questions: Meaning, memory, attitudes, and social interaction* (pp. 204–237). New York: Russell Sage Foundation.

Dovidio, J. F., & Gaertner, S. L. (1983). The effects of sex, status, and ability on helping behavior. *Journal of Applied Social Psychology, 13,* 191–205.

Dovidio, J. F., & Gaertner, S. L. (1986). *Prejudice, discrimination, and racism.* Orlando, FL: Academic Press.

Dovidio, J. F., & Gaertner, S. L. (1991). Changes in the nature and expression of racial prejudice. In H. Knopke, J. Norrell, & R. Rogers (Eds.), *Opening doors: An appraisal of race relations in contemporary America* (pp. 201–241). Tuscaloosa, AL: University of Alabama Press.

Dovidio, J. F., & Gaertner, S. L. (1993). Stereotypes and evaluative intergroup bias. In D. M. Mackie & D. L. Hamilton (Eds.), *Affect, cognition, and stereotyping: Interactive processes in intergroup perception* (pp. 167–193). Orlando, FL: Academic Press.

Dovidio, J. F., & Gaertner, S. L. (1996). Affirmative action, unintentional racial biases, and intergroup relations. *Journal of Social Issues, 52(4),* 51–76.

Dovidio, J. F., & Gaertner, S. L. (1998). On the nature of contemporary prejudice: The causes, consequences, and challenges of aversive racism. In J. Eberhardt & S. T. Fiske (Eds.), *Confronting racism: The problem and the response* (pp. 3–32). Newbury Park, CA: Sage.

Dovidio, J. F., & Gaertner, S. L. (1999). Reducing prejudice: Combating intergroup biases. *Current Directions in Psychological Science, 8,* 101–105.

Dovidio, J. F., & Gaertner, S. L. (2000). Aversive racism and selection decisions: 1989 and 1999. *Psychological Science, 11,* 319–323.

Dovidio, J. F., Gaertner, S. L., Anastasio, P. A., & Sanitioso, R. (1992). Cognitive and motivational bases of bias: The implications of aversive racism for attitudes toward Hispanics. In S. Knouse, P. Rosenfeld, & A. Culbertson (Eds.), *Hispanics in the workplace* (pp. 75–106). Newbury Park, CA: Sage.

Dovidio, J. F., Gaertner, S. L., & Bachman, B. A. (in press). Racial bias in organizations: The role of group processes in its causes and cures. In M. Turner (Ed.), *Groups at work: Advances in theory and research.* Hillsdale, NJ: Erlbaum.

Dovidio, J. F., Gaertner, S. L., Isen, A. M., & Lowrance, R. (1995). Group representations and intergroup bias: Positive affect, similarity and group size. *Personality and Social Psychology Bulletin, 21,* 856–865.

Dovidio, J. F., Gaertner, S. L., Isen, A. M., Rust, M., & Guerra, P. (1998). Positive affect, cognition, and the reduction of intergroup bias. In C. Sedikides, J. Schopler, & C. Insko (Eds.), *Intergroup cognition and intergroup behavior* (pp. 337–366). Hillsdale: NJ: Erlbaum.

Dovidio, J. F., Gaertner, S. L. & Kafati, G. (2000). Group identity and intergroup relations: The Common Ingroup Identity Model. In S. Thye & E. J. Lawler, M. Macy, & H. Walker, (Eds.), *Advances in group processes* (Vol. 17, pp. 1–35). Stamford, CT: JAI Press.

Dovidio, J. F., Gaertner, S. L. & Kawakami, K. (1998, October). *Multiple attitudes and contemporary racial bias.* Paper presented at the annual meeting of the Society for Experimental Social Psychology, Lexington, KY.

Dovidio, J. F., Gaertner, S. L., & Loux, S. (2000). Subjective experiences and intergroup relations: The role of positive affect. In H. Bless & J. Forgas (Eds.), *The message within: The role of subjective states in social cognition and behavior* (pp. 340–371). Philadelphia: Psychology Press.

Dovidio, J. F., Gaertner, S. L., & Validzic, A. (1998). Intergroup bias: Status, differentiation, and a common ingroup identity. *Journal of Personality and Social Psychology, 75*, 109–120.

Dovidio, J. F., Gaertner, S. L., Validzic, A., Matoka, K., Johnson, B., & Frazier, S. (1997). Extending the benefits of recategorization: Evaluations, self-disclosure, and helping. *Journal of Experimental Social Psychology, 33*, 401–420.

Dovidio, J. F., Kawakami, K., & Beach, K. R. (in press). Implicit and explicit attitudes: Examination of the relationship between measures of intergroup bias. To appear in R. Brown & S. L. Gaertner (Eds.), *Blackwell Handbook of Social Psychology: Intergroup Processes*. Oxford, UK: Blackwell.

Dovidio, J. F., Kawakami, K., & Gaertner, S, L. (2000). Reducing contemporary prejudice: Combating bias at the individual and intergroup level. In S. Oskamp (Ed.), *Reducing prejudice and discrimination* (pp. 137–163). Hillsdale, NJ: Erlbaum.

Dovidio, J., Kawakami, K., Johnson, C., Johnson, B., & Howard, A. (1997). The nature of prejudice: Automatic and controlled processes. *Journal of Experimental Social Psychology, 33*, 510–540.

Dovidio, J. F., Mann, J. A., & Gaertner, S. L. (1989). Resistance to affirmative action: The implication of aversive racism. In F.A. Blanchard & F.J. Crosby (Eds.). *Affirmative action in perspective* (pp. 83–102). New York: Springer-Verlag.

Dovidio, J. F., & Morris, W. N. (1975). The effects of stress and commonality of fate on helping behavior. *Journal of Personality and Social Psychology, 31*, 145–149.

Dovidio, J. F., Tobriner, M., Rioux, S., & Gaertner, S. L. (1991). *Say "we": Priming interpersonal expectations.* Unpublished manuscript, Department of Psychology, Colgate University, Hamilton, NY.

Eagly, A. H., & Chaiken, S. (1998). Attitude structure and function. *The handbook of social psychology* (4th ed., Vol. 1, pp. 269–322). New York: McGraw-Hill.

Eisenberger, R., Huntington, R., Hutchinson, S., & Sowa, D. (1986). Perceived organizational support. *Journal of Applied Psychology, 71*, 500–507.

Ellemers, N., Doosje, B., van Knippenberg, A., & Wilke, H. (1992). Status protection in high status minority groups. *European Journal of Social Psychology, 22*, 123–240.

Ellemers, N., van Knippenberg, A., DeVries, N., & Wilke, H. (1992). Social identification and permeability of group boundaries. *European Journal of Social Psychology, 18*, 497–513.

Faranda, J., & Gaertner, S. L. (1979, March). *The effects of inadmissible evidence introduced by the prosecution and the defense, and the defendant's race on the verdicts by high and low authoritarians.* Paper presented at the annual meeting of the Eastern Psychological Association, New York, NY.

Fazio, R. H., Chen, J., McDonel, E. C., & Sherman, S. J. (1982). Attitude accessibility, attitude-behavior consistency, and the strength of object-evaluation association. *Journal of Experimental Social Psychology, 18*, 339–357.

Fazio, R. H., Jackson, J. R., Dunton, B. C., & Williams, C. J. (1995). Variability in automatic activation as an unobtrusive measure of racial attitudes: A bona fide pipeline? *Journal of Personality and Social Psychology, 69*, 1013–1027.

Fazio, R., Sanbonmatsu, D., Powell, M., & Kardes, F. (1986). On the automatic activation of attitudes. *Journal of Personality and Social Psychology, 50*, 229–238.

Ferdman, B. M. (1995). Cultural identity and diversity in organizations: Bridging the gap between group differences and individual uniqueness. In M. M. Chemers, S. Oskamp, & M. A. Costanzo (Eds.), *Diversity in organizations: New perspectives for a changing workplace* (pp. 37–61). Thousand Oaks, CA: Sage.

Ferguson, C. K., & Kelley, H. H. (1964). Significant factors in over-evaluation of own groups' products. *Journal of Abnormal and Social Psychology, 69*, 223–228.

Feshbach, S., & Singer, R. (1957). The effects of personality and shared threats upon social prejudice. *Journal of Abnormal and Social Psychology, 54*, 411–416.

Fiedler, K., & Schmid, J. (in press). How language contributes to persistence of stereotypes as well as other, more general, intergroup issues. In R. J. Brown & S. L. Gaertner (Eds.), *Blackwell handbook of social psychology: Intergroup processes*. Oxford, UK: Blackwell.

Fine, M. A., McKenry, P. C., Donnelly, B. W., & Voydanoff, P. (1992). Perceived adjustment of parents and children: Variations by family structure, race, and gender. *Journal of Marriage and the Family, 54*, 118–127.

Fiske, S. T. (1989). Examining the role of intent: Toward understanding its role in stereotyping and prejudice. In J. Uleman & J. Bargh (Eds.), *Unintended thought* (pp. 75–123). New York: Guilford.

Fiske, S. T. (1993). Controlling other people: The impact of power on stereotyping. *American Psychologist, 48*, 621–628.

Fiske, S. T., & Neuberg, S. L. (1990). A continuum of impression formation, from category-based to individuating processes: Influences of information and motivation on attention and interpretation. In M. Zanna (Ed.), *Advances in experimental social psychology* (Vol. 23, pp. 1–74). Orlando, FL: Academic Press.

Fiske, S. T., & Taylor, S. E. (1991). *Social cognition* (2nd ed.). New York: McGraw-Hill.

Flippen, A. R., Hornstein, H. A., Siegal, W. E., & Weitzman, E. A. (1996). A comparison of similarity and interdependence as triggers for ingroup formation. *Personality and Social Psychology Bulletin, 22*, 882–893.

Fordham, S. (1988). Racelessness as a factor in Black students' school success: Pragmatic strategy or pyrrhic victory. *Harvard Educational Review, 58*, 54–58.

Forgas, J. P. (1998). Mood effects on the fundamental attribution error: On being happy and mistaken. *Journal of Personality and Social Psychology, 75*, 318–331.

Fowler, C. A., Wolford, G., Slade, R., & Tassinary, L. (1981). Lexical access with and without awareness. *Journal of Experimental Psychology: General, 110*, 341–362.

Frey, D., & Gaertner, S. L. (1986). Helping and the avoidance of inappropriate interracial behavior: A strategy which perpetuates a non-prejudiced self-image. *Journal of Personality and Social Psychology, 50*, 1083–1090.

Furstenberg, F. F., Jr. (1987). The new extended family: The experience of parents and children after remarriage. In K. Pasley & M. Ihinger-Tallman (Eds.), *Remarriage and stepparenting: Current research and theory* (pp. 42–61). New York: Guilford.

Gaertner, L., & Insko, C. A. (in press). Intergroup discrimination in the minimal group paradigm: Categorization, reciprocation, or fear? *Journal of Personality and Social Psychology*.

Gaertner, L., & Schopler, J. (1998). Perceived ingroup entitativity and intergroup bias: An interconnection of self and other. *European Journal of Social Psychology, 75*, 695–711.

Gaertner, S. L. (1973). Helping behavior and racial discrimination among liberals and conservatives. *Journal of Personality and Social Psychology, 25*, 335–341.

Gaertner, S. L., & Dovidio, J. F. (1977). The subtlety of white racism, arousal, and helping behavior. *Journal of Personality and Social Psychology, 35*, 691–707.

Gaertner, S. L., & Dovidio, J. F. (1986a). The aversive form of racism. In J. F. Dovidio & S. L. Gaertner (Eds.), *Prejudice, discrimination, and racism* (pp. 61–89). Orlando, FL: Academic Press.

Gaertner, S. L., & Dovidio, J. F. (1986b). Prejudice, discrimination, and racism: Problems, progress and promise. In J. F. Dovidio & S. L. Gaertner (Eds.), *Prejudice, discrimination, and racism* (pp. 315–332). Orlando, FL: Academic Press.

Gaertner, S. L., Dovidio, J. F., Anastasio, P. A., Bachman, B. A., & Rust, M. C. (1993). The common ingroup identity model: Recategorization and the reduction of intergroup bias. In W. Stroebe & M. Hewstone (Eds.), *European review of social psychology* (Vol. 4, pp. 1–26). New York: John Wiley & Sons.

Gaertner, S. L., Dovidio, J. F., & Bachman, B. A. (1996). Revisiting the Contact Hypothesis:

The induction of a common ingroup identity. *International Journal of Intercultural Relations, 20*(3 & 4), 271–290.

Gaertner, S. L., Dovidio, J. F., Banker, B., Houlette, M., Johnson, K., & McGlynn, E. (2000). Reducing intergroup conflict: From superordinate goals to decategorization, recategorization, and mutual differentiation. *Group Dynamics, 4,* 98–114.

Gaertner, S. L., Dovidio, J. F., Banker, B. S., Rust, M. C., & Nier, J. A., & Ward, C. M. (1997). Does pro-Whiteness necessarily mean anti-Blackness? In M. Fine, L. Powell, L. Weis, & M. Wong (Eds.), *Off White* (pp. 167–178). New York: Routledge.

Gaertner, S. L., Dovidio, J. F., Mann, J. A., & Anastasio, P. A. (1988). *Are there benefits of recategorization when original group boundaries are restored?* Unpublished data, Department of Psychology, University of Delaware, Newark, DE.

Gaertner, S. L., Dovidio, J. F., Nier, J., Banker, B., Ward, C., Houlette, M., & Loux, S. (2000). The Common Ingroup Identity Model for reducing intergroup bias: Progress and challenges. In R. Brown & D. Capozza (Eds.), *Social identity processes: Trends in theory and research* (pp. 138–148). London, UK: Sage.

Gaertner, S. L., Dovidio, J. F., Nier, J. A., Ward, C. M., & Banker, B. S. (1999). Across cultural divides: The value of a superordinate identity. In D. Prentice & D. Miller (Eds.), *Cultural divides: Understanding and overcoming group conflict* (pp. 173–212). New York: Russell Sage Foundation.

Gaertner, S. L., Dovidio, J. F., & Rust, M. C. (1997). *The trade-off hypothesis: Group representations and generalization of increased positive attitudes toward outgroup members present during intergroup contact and the generalization this change to outgroup members generally.* Unpublished data, Department of Psychology, University of Delaware, Newark, DE.

Gaertner, S. L., Dovidio, J. F., Rust, M. C., Nier, J., Banker, B., Ward, C. M., Mottola, G. R., & Houlette, M. (1999). Reducing intergroup bias: Elements of intergroup cooperation. *Journal of Personality and Social Psychology, 76,* 388–402.

Gaertner, S. L., Mann, J. A., Dovidio, J. F., Murrell, A. J., & Pomare, M. (1990). How does cooperation reduce intergroup bias? *Journal of Personality and Social Psychology, 59,* 692–704.

Gaertner, S. L., Mann, J. A., Murrell, A. J., & Dovidio, J. F. (1989). Reduction of intergroup bias: The benefits of recategorization. *Journal of Personality and Social Psychology, 57,* 239–249.

Gaertner, S. L., & McLaughlin, J. P. (1983). Racial stereotypes: Associations and ascriptions of positive and negative characteristics. *Social Psychology Quarterly, 46,* 23–30.

Gaertner, S. L., Rust, M. C., & Dovidio, J. F. (1997). *The value of a superordinate identity for reducing intergroup bias.* Unpublished manuscript, Department of Psychology, University of Delaware. Newark, DE.

Gaertner, S. L., Rust, M. C., Dovidio, J. F., Bachman, B. A., & Anastasio, P. A. (1994). The Contact Hypothesis: The role of a common ingroup identity on reducing intergroup bias. *Small Groups Research, 25*(2), 224–249.

Gaertner, S. L., Rust, M. C., Dovidio, J. F., Bachman, B. A., & Anastasio, P. A. (1996). The Contact Hypothesis: The role of a common ingroup identity on reducing intergroup bias among majority and minority group members. In J. L. Nye & A. M. Brower (Eds.), *What's social about social cognition?* (pp. 230–360). Newbury Park, CA: Sage.

Gonzalez, R., & Brown, R. J. (1999, October). *Maintaining the salience of subgroup and superordinate group identities during intergroup contact.* Paper presented at the annual meeting of the Society of Experimental Social Psychology, St. Louis, MO.

Gouldner, A. (1960). The norm of reciprocity: A preliminary statement. *American Sociological Review, 25,* 161–178.

Green, C. W., Adams, A. M., & Turner, C. W. (1988). Development and validation of the School Interracial Climate Scale. *American Journal of Community Psychology, 16,* 241–259.

Greenland, K., & Brown, R. J. (1999). Categorization and intergroup anxiety in contact between British and Japanese nationals. *European Journal of Social Psychology, 29*, 503–521.

Greenwald, A. G., & Banaji, M. R. (1995). Implicit social cognition: Attitudes, self-esteem, and stereotypes. *Psychological Review, 102*, 4–27.

Hamberger, J., & Hewstone, M. (1997). Inter-ethnic contact as a predictor of blatant and subtle prejudice: Tests of a model in four West European nations. *British Journal of Social Psychology, 36*, 173–190.

Hamilton, D. L., & Sherman, S. J. (1996). Perceiving persons and groups. *Psychological Review, 103*, 336–355.

Hamilton, D. L., & Trolier, T. K. (1986). Stereotypes and stereotyping: An overview of the cognitive approach. In J. F. Dovidio & S. L. Gaertner (Eds.), *Prejudice, discrimination, and racism* (pp. 127–163). Orlando, FL: Academic Press.

Harrington, H., & Miller, N. (1995). Do group motives differ from individual motives? Considerations regarding process distinctiveness. In M. A. Hogg & D. Abrams (Ed.), *Group motivation: Social psychological perspectives* (pp. 149–172). London, UK: Harvester Wheatsheaf.

Haunschild, P. R., Moreland, R. L., & Murrell, A. J. (1994). Sources of resistance to mergers between groups. *Journal of Applied Social Psychology, 24*, 1150–1178.

Hense, R., Penner, L., & Nelson, D. (1995). Implicit memory for age stereotypes. *Social Cognition, 13*, 399–415.

Hewstone, M. (1990). The "ultimate attribution error"? A review of the literature on intergroup attributions. *European Journal of Social Psychology, 20*, 311–335.

Hewstone, M. (1996). Contact and categorization: Social psychological interventions to change intergroup relations. In C. N. Macrae, C. Stangor, & M. Hewstone (Eds.), *Stereotypes and stereotyping* (pp. 323–368). New York: Guilford.

Hewstone, M., & Brown, R. J. (1986). Contact is not enough: An intergroup perspective on the "Contact Hypothesis." In M. Hewstone & R. J. Brown (Eds.), *Contact and conflict in intergroup encounters* (pp. 1–44). Oxford, UK: Basil Blackwell.

Higgins, E. T., & Bargh, J. A. (1987). Social cognition and social perception. *Annual Review of Psychology, 38*, 369–425.

Hochschild, J. L. (1995). *Facing up to the American dream: Race, class, and the soul of the nation.* Princeton, NJ: Princeton University Press.

Hogg, M. A., & Abrams, D. (1988). *Social identification: A social psychology of intergroup relations and group processes.* London, UK: Routledge.

Holtz, R. (1989, May). *New and old group members and the locus of intergroup bias: Evidence for in-group favoritism and out-group derogation.* Paper presented at the annual meeting of the Midwestern Psychological Association, Chicago, IL.

Hornsey, M. J., & Hogg, M. A. (2000). Sub-group relations: Two experiments comparing Subgroup Differentiation and Common Ingroup Identity Models of prejudice reduction. *Personality and Social Psychology Bulletin, 28*, 242–256.

Hornstein, H. A. (1976). *Cruelty and kindness: A new look at aggression and altruism.* Englewood Cliffs, NJ: Prentice Hall.

Hornstein, H. A., Masor, H. N., Sole, K., & Heilman, M. (1971). Effects of sentiment and completion of a helping act on observer helping: A case for socially-mediated Ziergarnik effects. *Journal of Personality and Social Psychology, 17*, 107–112.

Howard, J. M., & Rothbart, M. (1980). Social categorization for in-group and out-group behavior. *Journal of Personality and Social Psychology, 38*, 301–310.

Huo, Y. J., Smith, H. J., Tyler, T. R., & Lind, A. E. (1996). Superordinate identification, subgroup identification, and justice concerns: Is separatism the problem? Is assimilation the answer? *Psychological Science, 7*, 40–45.

Isen, A. M. (1970). Success, failure, attention, and reaction to others: The warm glow of success. *Journal of Personality and Social Psychology, 15*, 294–301.

Isen, A. M. (1987). Positive affect, cognitive processes, and social behavior. In L. Berkowitz (Ed.), *Advances in experimental social psychology* (Vol. 20, pp. 203–253). Orlando, FL: Academic Press.

Isen, A. M. (1993). Positive affect and decision making. In M. Lewis & J. M. Haviland (Eds.), *Handbook of emotion* (pp. 261–277). New York: Guilford.

Isen, A. M., & Daubman, K. A. (1984). The influence of affect on categorization. *Journal of Personality and Social Psychology, 47*, 1206–1217.

Isen, A. M., Daubman, K. A., & Nowicki, G. P. (1987). Positive affect facilitates creative problem solving. *Journal of Personality and Social Psychology, 52*, 1122–1131.

Isen, A. M., & Geva, N. (1987). The influence of positive affect on acceptable level of risk: The person with a large canoe has a large worry. *Organizational Behavior and Human Decision Processes, 39*, 145–154.

Isen, A. M., Johnson, M. M. S., Mertz, E., & Robinson, G. F. (1985). The influence of positive affect on the unusualness of word associations. *Journal of Personality and Social Psychology, 48*, 1413–1426.

Isen, A. M., & Levin, P. F. (1972). Effect of feeling good on helping: Cookies and kindness. *Journal of Personality and Social Psychology, 21*, 384–388.

Isen, A. M., Niedenthal, P. M., & Cantor, N. (1992). An influence of positive affect on social categorization. *Motivation and Emotion, 16*, 65–78.

Isen, A. M., Nygren, T. E., & Ashby, F. G. (1988). The influence of positive affect on the subjective utility of gains and losses: It is just not worth the risk. *Journal of Personality and Social Psychology, 55*, 710–717.

Isen, A. M., & Patrick, R. (1983). The effect of positive feelings on risk-taking: When the chips are down. *Organizational Behavior and Human Performance, 31*, 194–202.

Islam, M. R., & Hewstone, M. (1993). Dimensions of contact as predictors of intergroup anxiety, perceived outgroup variability and outgroup attitude: An integrative model. *Personality and Social Psychology Bulletin, 19*, 700–710.

James, S. D., & Johnson, D. W. (1987). Social interdependence, psychological adjustment, and marital satisfaction in second marriages. *Journal of Social Psychology, 128*, 287–303.

Jemison, D. B., & Sitkin, S. B. (1986). Corporate acquisitions: A process perspective. *Academy of Management Review, 11*, 145–163.

Johnson, D. W. (1991). *Active learning: Cooperation in the college classroom.* Edina, MN: Interaction Book Co.

Johnson, D. W. & Johnson, F. P. (1975). *Joining together: Group theory and group skills.* Englewood Cliffs, NJ: Prentice-Hall.

Johnson, D. W., Johnson, F. P., & Maruyama, G. (1983). Interdependence and interpersonal attraction among heterogeneous and homogeneous individuals: A theoretical formulation and a meta-analysis of the research. *Review of Educational Research, 52*, 5–54.

Johnston, L., & Hewstone, M. (1992). Cognitive models of stereotype change III: Subtyping and perceived typicality of disconfirming group members. *Journal of Experimental Social Psychology, 28*, 360–386.

Judd, C. M., & Kenny, D. A. (1981). Process analysis: Estimating mediation in evaluation research. *Review of Educational Research, 55*, 5–54.

Kafati, G. (1999). *Assessing the intergroup climate at Colgate University.* Unpublished manuscript, Department of Psychology, Colgate University, Hamilton, NY.

Karpinski, A., & Von Hippel, W. (1996). The role of the linguistic intergroup bias in expectancy maintenance. *Social Cognition, 14*, 141–163.

Katz, I., & Hass, R. G. (1988). Racial ambivalence and value conflict: Correlational and priming studies of dual cognitive structures. *Journal of Personality and Social Psychology, 55*, 893–905.

Katz, I., Wackenhut, J., & Hass, R. G. (1986). Racial ambivalence, value duality, and behavior. In J. F. Dovidio & S. L. Gaertner (Eds.), *Prejudice, discrimination, and racism* (pp. 35–59). Orlando, FL: Academic Press.

Kawakami, K., Dion, K., & Dovidio, J. F. (1998). Racial prejudice and stereotype activation. *Personality and Social Psychology Bulletin, 24*, 407–416.

Kawakami, K., Dion, K., & Dovidio, J. F. (in press). Implicit stereotyping and prejudice and the primed Stroop task. *Swiss Journal of Psychology.*

Kelman, H. C. (1997). Group processes in the resolution of international conflicts: Experiences from the Israeli-Palestinian case. *American Psychologist, 52*, 212–220.

Kelman, H. C. (1999). The interdependence of Israeli and Palestinian national identities: The role of the other in existential conflicts. *Journal of Social Issues, 55*(3), 581–600.

Kihlstrom, J. F., Cantor, N., Albright, J. S., Chew, B. R., Klein, S. B., & Niedenthal, P. M. (1988). Information processing and the study of the self. In L. Berkowitz (Ed.), *Advances in experimental social psychology* (Vol. 21, pp. 145–180). Orlando, FL: Academic Press.

Kleinpenning, G., & Hagendoorn, L. (1993). Forms of racism and the cumulative dimension of ethnic attitudes. *Social Psychology Quarterly, 56*, 21–36.

Kovel, J. (1970). *White racism: A psychohistory.* New York: Pantheon.

Kramer, R. M., & Brewer, M. B. (1984). Effects of group identity on resource utilization in a simulated commons dilemma. *Journal of Personality and Social Psychology, 46*, 1044–1057.

Krieger, L. H. (1995). The content of our categories: A cognitive bias approach to discrimination and equal employment opportunity. *Stanford Law Review, 47*, 1161–1248.

Krieger, L. H. (1998). Civil rights perestroika: Intergroup relations after affirmative action. *California Law Review, 86*, 1251–1333.

LaFromboise, T., Coleman, H. L. K., & Gerton, J. (1993). Psychological impact of biculturalism: Evidence and theory. *Psychological Bulletin, 114*, 395–412.

Lane, J. D., & Wegner, D. M (1995). The cognitive consequences of secrecy. *Journal of Personality and Social Psychology, 69*, 237–253.

Leippe, M. R., & Eisenstadt, D. (1994). Generalization of dissonance reduction: Decreasing prejudice through induced compliance. *Journal of Personality and Social Psychology, 67*, 395–413.

Lepore, L., & Brown, R. (1997). Category and stereotype activation: Is prejudice inevitable? *Journal of Personality and Social Psychology, 72*, 275–287.

Levine, J. M., & Moreland, R. L. (1994). Group socialization: Theory and research. In W. Stroebe & M. Hewstone (Eds.), *European review of social psychology* (Vol. 5, pp. 305–336). Chichester, England: Wiley.

LeVine, R. A., & Campbell, D. T. (1972). *Ethnocentrism: Theories of conflict, ethnic attitudes and group behavior.* New York: Wiley.

Lott, A. J., & Lott, B. E. (1965). Group cohesiveness as interpersonal attraction: A review of relationships with antecedent and consequent variables. *Psychological Bulletin, 64*, 259–309.

Lott, A. J., & Lott, B. E. (1974). The role of reward in the formation of positive interpersonal attitudes. In T. Huston (Ed.), *Foundations of interpersonal attraction* (pp. 171–189). New York: Academic Press.

M & A Almanac (1996). *Mergers and Acquisitions, 30*, 37.

Maass, A., & Arcuri, L. (1996) Language and stereotyping. In N. Macrae, C. Stangor, & M. Hewstone (Eds.), *Stereotypes and stereotyping* (pp. 193–226). New York: Guilford.

Maass, A., Ceccarelli, R., & Rudin, S. (1996). Linguistic intergroup bias: Evidence for in-group-protective motivation. *Journal of Personality and Social Psychology, 71*, 512–526.

Maass, A., Salvi, D., Arcuri, L., & Semin, G. R. (1989). Language use in intergroup contexts: The linguistic intergroup bias. *Journal of Personality and Social Psychology, 57*, 981–993.

MacDonald, T. K., & Zanna, M. P. (1998). Cross-dimensional ambivalence toward social groups: Can ambivalence affect intentions to hire feminists? *Personality and Social Psychology Bulletin, 24,* 427–441.

Mackie, D. M., Hamilton, D. L., Schroth, H. A., Carlisle, C. J., Gersho, B. F., Meneses, L. M., Nedler, B. F., & Reichel, L. D. (1989). The effects of induced mood on expectancy-based illusory correlations. *Journal of Experimental Social Psychology, 25,* 524–544.

Mackie, D. M., & Worth, L. T. (1989). Processing deficits and the mediation of positive affect in persuasion. *Journal of Personality and Social Psychology, 57,* 27–40.

Macrae, C., Bodenhausen, G., & Milne, A. (1995). The dissection of selection in person perception: Inhibitory processes in social stereotyping. *Journal of Personality and Social Psychology, 69,* 397–407.

Macrae, C. N., Milne, A. B., & Bodenhausen, G. V. (1994). Stereotypes as energy-saving devices: A peek inside the cognitive toolbox. *Journal of Personality and Social Psychology, 66,* 37–47.

Macrae, C. N., Stangor, C., & Milne, A. (1994). Activating social stereotypes: A functional analysis. *Journal of Experimental Social Psychology, 30,* 370–389.

Mael, F., & Ashforth, B. E. (1992). Alumni and their alma mater: A partial test of the reformulated model of organizational identification. *Journal of Organizational Behavior, 13,* 103–123.

Marcus-Newhall, A., Miller, N., Holtz, R., & Brewer, M. B. (1993). Cross-cutting category membership with role assignment: A means of reducing intergroup bias. *British Journal of Social Psychology, 32,* 125–146.

Marks, M. L., & Mirvis, P. (1985, Summer). Merger syndrome: Stress and uncertainty. *Mergers and Acquisitions,* 50–55.

McConahay, J. B. (1986). Modern racism, ambivalence, and the modern racism scale. In J. F. Dovidio & S. L. Gaertner (Eds.), *Prejudice, discrimination, and racism* (pp. 91–125). Orlando, FL: Academic Press.

Meyer, D. E., & Schvaneveldt, R. W. (1971). Facilitation in recognizing pairs of words: Evidence of dependence between retrieval operations. *Journal of Experimental Psychology, 90,* 227–234.

Migdal, M. J., Hewstone, M., & Mullen, B. (1998). The effects of crossed categorization on intergroup evaluations: A meta-analysis. *British Journal of Social Psychology, 37,* 303–324.

Miller, N., & Brewer, M. B. (1984). (Eds.). *Groups in contact: The psychology of desegregation.* Orlando, FL: Academic Press.

Miller, N., & Brewer, M. B. (1986). Categorization effects on ingroup and outgroup perception. In J. F. Dovidio & S. L. Gaertner (Eds.), *Prejudice, discrimination, and racism* (pp. 209–230). Orlando, FL: Academic Press.

Miller, N., Brewer, M. B., & Edwards, K. (1985). Cooperative interaction in desegregated settings: A laboratory analog. *Journal of Social Issues, 41*(3), 63–75.

Miller, N., & Davidson-Podgorny, G. (1987). Theoretical models of intergroup relations and the use of cooperative teams as an intervention for desegregated settings. In, C. Hendrick (Ed.), *Review of personality and social psychology, Vol. 9: Group processes and intergroup relations* (pp. 41–67). Beverly Hills, CA: Sage.

Miller, N., & Harrington, H. J. (1995). Social categorization and intergroup acceptance: Principles for the design and development of cooperative learning teams. In R. Hertz-Lazarowitz & N. Miller (Eds.), *Interaction in cooperative groups: The theoretical anatomy of group learning* (pp. 203–227). New York: Cambridge University Press.

Monteith, M., Sherman, J., & Devine, P. (1998). Suppression as a stereotype control strategy. *Personality and Social Psychology Review, 1,* 63–82.

Moreland, R. L., & Levine, J. M. (1982). Socialization in small groups: Temporal changes in individual-group relations. In L. Berkowitz (Ed.), *Advances in experimental social psychology* (Vol. 15, pp. 137–192). New York: Academic Press.

Moreland, R. L., & McMinn, J. G. (1999). Gone but not forgotten: Loyalty and betrayal among ex-members of small groups. *Personality and Social Psychology Bulletin, 25,* 1476–1486.

Mottola, G. (1996). *The effects of relative group status on expectations of merger success.* Unpublished Ph.D. Dissertation, Department of Psychology, University of Delaware, Newark, DE.

Mottola, G. R., Bachman, B. A., Gaertner, S. L., & Dovidio, J. F. (1997). How groups merge: The effects of merger integration patterns on anticipated commitment to the merged organization. *Journal of Applied Social Psychology, 27,* 1335–1358.

Mullen, B., Brown, R. J., & Smith, C. (1992). Ingroup bias as a function of salience, relevance, and status: An integration. *European Journal of Social Psychology, 22,* 103–122.

Mullen, B., & Copper, C. (1994). The relation between group cohesiveness and performance: An integration. *Psychological Bulletin, 115,* 210–227.

Mullen, B., & Hu, L. T. (1989). Perceptions of ingroup and outgroup variability: A meta-analytic integration. *Basic and Applied Social Psychology, 10,* 233–252.

Mummendey, A., & Otten, S. (in press). Aversive discrimination. In R. J. Brown & S. L. Gaertner (Eds), *Blackwell handbook of social psychology: Intergroup processes.* Oxford, UK: Blackwell.

Mummendey, A., & Schreiber, H. J. (1983). Better or just different? Positive social identity by discrimination against or differentiation from outgroups. *European Journal of Social Psychology, 13,* 389–397.

Mummendey, A. & Wenzel, M. (1999). Social discrimination in intergroup relations: Reactions to intergroup difference. *Personality and Social Psychological Review, 3,* 158–174.

Murray, N., Sujan, H., Hirt, E. R., & Sujan, M. (1990). The influence of mood on categorization: A cognitive flexibility interpretation. *Journal of Personality and Social Psychology, 59,* 411–425.

Murrell, A. J., Dietz-Uhler, B. L., Dovidio, J. F., Gaertner, S. L., & Drout, C. (1994). Aversive racism and resistance to affirmative action: Perceptions of justice are not necessarily color blind. *Basic and Applied Social Psychology, 15,* 71–86.

Neuberg, S. L., & Fiske, S. T. (1987). Motivational influences on impression formation: Outcome dependency, accuracy-driven attention, and individuating processes. *Journal of Personality and Social Psychology, 53,* 431–444.

Niemann, Y. F., & Dovidio, J. F. (1998). Relationship of solo status, academic rank, and perceived distinctiveness to job satisfaction of racial/ethnic minorities. *Journal of Applied Psychology, 83,* 55–71.

Nier, J. A., Gaertner, S. L., Dovidio, J. F., Banker, B. S. & Ward, C. M. (1999). *Changing interracial evaluations, affective reactions, and behavior: The effects of a common group identity.* Unpublished manuscript, Department of Psychology, Connecticut College, New London CT.

Nye, J. L., & Brower, A. M. (Eds.) (1996). *What's social about social cognition.* Newbury Park, CA: Sage.

Oakes, P. J. (1987). The salience of social categories. In J. C. Turner, M. A. Hogg, P. J. Oakes, S. D. Reicher, & M. S. Wetherell (Eds.), *Rediscovering the social group: A self-categorization theory* (pp. 117–141). Oxford, UK: Blackwell.

Oakes, P. (in press). The root of all evil in intergroup relations? Unearthing the categorization process. In R. J. Brown & S. L. Gaertner (Eds), *Blackwell handbook of social psychology: Intergroup processes.* Oxford, UK: Blackwell.

Oakes, P. J., & Turner, J. C. (1990). Is limited information the cause of social stereotyping? In W. Stroebe & M. Hewstone (Eds.), *European review of social psychology* (Vol. 1, pp. 111–135). Chichester, England: Wiley.

Ogbu, J. U., & Matute-Bianchi, M. A. (1986). Understanding sociocultural factors: Knowledge, identity, and social adjustment. In California State Department of Education,

Bilingual Education Office, *Beyond language: Social and cultural factors in schooling* (pp. 73–142). Sacramento, CA: California State University—Los Angeles, Evaluation, Dissemination and Assessment Center.

Operario, D., & Fiske, S. T. (in press). Stereotypes: Content, structures, processes, and context. In R. J. Brown & S. L. Gaertner (Eds.), *Blackwell handbook of social psychology: Intergroup processes*. Oxford, UK: Blackwell.

Opotow, S. (1990). Moral exclusion and injustice: An introduction. *Journal of Social Issues, 46*(1), 1–20.

Osgood, C. E. (1962). *An alternative to war or surrender*. Urbana, IL: University of Illinois Press.

Otten, S., & Wentura, D. (1999). About the impact of automaticity in the minimal intergroup paradigm: Evidence from affective priming tasks. *European Journal of Social Psychology, 29*, 1049–1072.

Park, B., & Rothbart, M. (1982). Perception of out-group homogeneity and levels of social categorization: Memory for the subordinate attributes of in-group and out-group members. *Journal of Personality and Social Psychology, 42*, 1051–1068.

Pasquali, E. A. (1985). The impact of acculturation on the eating habits of elderly immigrants: A Cuban example. *Journal of Nutrition for the Elderly, 5*, 27–36.

Perdue, C. W., Dovidio, J. F., Gurtman, M. B., & Tyler, R. B. (1990). "Us" and "Them": Social categorization and the process of intergroup bias. *Journal of Personality and Social Psychology, 59*, 475–486.

Perdue, C., & Gurtman, M. (1990). Evidence for the automaticity of ageism. *Journal of Experimental Social Psychology, 28*, 199–216.

Pettigrew, T. F. (1979). The Ultimate Attribution Error: Extending Allport's cognitive analysis of prejudice. *Personality and Social Psychology Bulletin, 55*, 461–476.

Pettigrew, T. F. (1997). Generalized intergroup contact effects on prejudice. *Personality and Social Psychology Bulletin, 23*, 173–185.

Pettigrew, T. F. (1998a). Intergroup Contact Theory. *Annual Review of Psychology, 49*, 65–85.

Pettigrew, T. R. (1999b). Applying social psychology to international social issues. *Journal of Social Issues, 54*(4), 663–675.

Pettigrew, T. F., & Meertens, R. W. (1995). Subtle and blatant prejudice in Western Europe. *European Journal of Social Psychology, 25*, 57–76.

Piliavin, J. A., Dovidio, J. F., Gaertner, S. L., & Clark, R. D., III. (1981). *Emergency intervention*. New York: Academic Press.

Rabbie, J. M. (1982). The effects of intergroup competition and cooperation on intragroup and intergroup relationships. In V. J. Derlega & J. Grzelak (Eds.), *Cooperation and helping behavior: Theories and research* (pp. 128–151). New York: Academic Press.

Rabbie, J. M., & Horwitz, M. (1969). Arousal of ingroup-outgroup bias by a chance win or loss. *Journal of Personality and Social Psychology, 13*, 269–277.

Rodriguez-Scheel, J. (1980). *An investigation of the components of social identity for a Detroit sample*. Unpublished manuscript, Psychology Department, Occidental College, Los Angeles, CA.

Rogers, R. W., & Prentice-Dunn, S. (1981). Deindividuation and anger-mediated interracial aggression: Unmasking regressive racism. *Journal of Personality and Social Psychology, 41*, 63–73.

Rouhana, N. N., & Kelman, H. C. (1994). Promoting joint thinking in international conflicts: An Israeli-Palestinian continuing workshop. *Journal of Social Issues, 50*(1), 157–178.

Rosch, E. (1975). Cognitive representaetions of semantic categories. *Journal of Experimental Psychology: General, 104*, 192–233.

Rosenbaum, M. E., & Holtz, R. (1985, August). *The minimal intergroup discrimination effect: Out-group derogation, not in-group favoritsm*. Paper presented at the 93rd annual meeting of the American Psychological Association, Los Angeles, CA.

Rothbart, M. (1996). Category-exemplar dynamics and stereotype change. *International Journal of Intercultural Relations, 20,* 305–321.

Rothbart, M. (in press). Categorization processes and the modification of outgroup stereotypes. In R. J. Brown & S. L. Gaertner (Eds.), *Blackwell handbook of social psychology: Intergroup processes.* Oxford, UK: Blackwell.

Rothbart, M., & John, O. P. (1985). Social categorization and behavioral episodes: A cognitive analysis of the effects of intergroup contact. *Journal of Social Issues, 41*(3), 81–104.

Rust, M. C. (1995). *Effects of mood on categorization.* Unpublished Masters Thesis, Department of Psychology, University of Delaware, Newark, DE.

Rust, M. C. (1997). *Social identity and social categorization.* Unpublished Ph.D. Dissertation, Department of Psychology, University of Delaware, Newark, DE.

Ryan, C. S., Park, B., & Judd, C. M. (1996). Assessing stereotype accuracy: Implications for understanding the stereotyping process. In N. Macrae, C. Stangor, & M. Hewstone (Eds.), *Stereotypes and stereotyping* (pp. 121–157). New York: Guilford.

Sachdev, I., & Bourhis, R. Y. (1991). Power and status differentials in minority and majority group relations. *European Journal of Social Psychology, 21,* 1–24.

Sauer, L. E., & Fine, M. A. (1988). Parent-child relationships in stepparent families. *Journal of Family Psychology, 1,* 434–451.

Scarberry, N. C., Ratcliff, C., D., Lord, C. G., Lanicek, D. L., & Desforges, D. M. (1997). Effects of individuating information on the generalization part of Allport's Contact Hypothesis. *Personality and Social Psychology Bulletin, 23,* 1291–1299.

Schofield, J. W. (1986). Causes and consequences of the colorblind perspective. In J. F. Dovidio & S. L. Gaertner (Eds.), *Prejudice, discrimination and racism* (pp. 231–253). Orlando, FL: Academic Press.

Schofield, J. W., & Eurich-Fulcer, R. (in press). When and how school desegregation improves intergroup relations. In R. J. Brown & S. L. Gaertner (Eds.), *Blackwell handbook of social psychology: Intergroup processes.* Oxford, UK: Blackwell.

Schopler, J., & Insko, C. A. (1992). The discontinuity effect in interpersonal and intergroup relations: Generality and mediation. In W. Stroebe & M. Hewstone (Eds.), *European review of social psychology* (Vol. 3, pp. 121–151). Chichester, UK: Wiley.

Schroeder, D. A., Penner, L. A., Dovidio, J. F., & Piliavin, J. A. (1995). *Psychology of helping and altruism: Problems and puzzles.* New York: McGraw-Hill.

Schwarz, N., Bless, H., & Bohner, G. (1991). Mood and persuasion: Affective states influence the processing of persuasive communications. In M. P. Zanna (Ed.), *Advances in experimental social psychology* (Vol. 24, pp. 161–199). Orlando, FL: Academic Press.

Schweiger, D. M., & Walsh, J. P. (1990). Mergers and acquisitions: An interdisciplinary view. *Research in Personnel and Human Resources Management, 8,* 41–107.

Sears, D. O. (1988). Symbolic racism. In P. A. Katz & D. A. Taylor (Eds.), *Eliminating racism: Profiles in controversy* (pp. 53–84). New York: Plenum Press.

Sears, D. O., van Laar, C., Carillo, M., & Kosterman, R. (1997). Is it really racism? The origin of White Americans' opposition to race-targeted policies. *Public Opinion Quarterly, 61,* 16–53.

Semin, G. R., & Fiedler, K. (1988). The cognitive functions of linguistic categories in describing persons: Social cognition and language. *Journal of Personality and Social Psychology, 54,* 558–568.

Semin, G. R., & Fiedler, K. (1992). The inferential properties of interpersonal verbs. In G. R. Semin & K. Fiedler (Eds.), *Language, interaction, and social cognition* (pp. 58–78). Newbury Park, CA: Sage.

Settles, B. H. (1993). The illusion of stability in family life: The reality of change and mobility. *Marriage and Family Review, 19,* 5–29.

Shaffer, D. R., Pegalis, L. J., & Bazzini, D. G. (1996). When boy meets girl (revisited): Gender, gender-role orientation, and prospect of future interaction on self-disclosure among same- and opposite-sex acquaintances. *Personality and Social Psychology Bulletin, 22*, 495–506.

Sherif, M. (1966). *In common predicament*. Boston: Houghton Mifflin Co.

Sherif, M., & Sherif, C. W. (1969). *Social psychology*. New York: Harper & Row.

Sherif, M., Harvey, O. J., White, B. J., Hood, W. R., & Sherif, C. (1954). *Experimental study of positive and negative intergroup attitudes between experimentally produced groups. Robbers Cave experiment*. Norman, OK: University of Oklahoma.

Sherif, M., Harvey, O. J., White, B. J., Hood, W. R., & Sherif, C. W. (1961). *Intergroup conflict and cooperation: The Robbers Cave experiment*. Norman, OK: University of Oklahoma Book Exchange.

Sherif, M., Harvey, O. J., White, B. J., Hood, W. R., & Sherif, C. W. (1988). *The Robbers Cave experiment: Intergroup conflict and cooperation*. Hanover, NH: University Press of New England.

Simon, B., Aufderheide, B., & Kampmeier, C. (in press). The social psychology of minority-majority relations. In R. J. Brown & S. L. Gaertner (Eds.), *Blackwell handbook of social psychology: Intergroup processes*. Oxford, UK: Blackwell.

Skinner, M., & Stephenson, G. M. (1981). The effects of intergroup comparisons on the polarization of opinions. *Current Psychological Research, 1*, 49–61.

Slavin, R. E. (1985) Cooperative learning: Applying contact theory to desegregated schools. *Journal of Social Issues, 41*(3), 45–62.

Smith, E. R., & Henry, S. (1996). An ingroup becomes part of the self: Response time evidence. *Personality and Social Psychology Bulletin, 22*, 635–642.

Smith, H. J., & Tyler, T. R. (1996). Justice and power: When will justice concerns encourage the advantaged to support policies which redistribute economic resources and the disadvantaged to willingly obey the law? *European Journal of Social Psychology, 26*, 171–200.

Snider, K., & Dovidio, J. F. (1996). *A survey of the racial climate at Indiana State University*, Institutional Research and Testing, Indiana State University, Terra Haute, IN.

Sole, K., Marton, J., & Hornstein, H. A. (1975). Opinion similarity and helping: Three field experiments investigating the bases of promotive tension. *Journal of Experimental Social Psychology, 11*, 1–13.

Spears, R., & Haslam, S. A. (1997). Stereotyping and the burden of cognitive load. In R. Spears, P. J. Oakes, N. Ellemers, & S. A. Haslam (Eds.), *The social psychology of stereotyping and group life* (pp. 171–207). Oxford, UK: Blackwell.

Spears, R., & Manstead, A. S. R. (1989). The social context of stereotyping and differentiation. *European Journal of Social Psychology, 19*, 101–121.

Staats, A. W. (1968). *Language, learning, and cognition*. New York: Holt, Rinehart & Winston.

Staats, A. W., & Staats, C. K. (1958). Attitudes established by conditioning. *Journal of Abnormal and Social Psychology, 57*, 74–80.

Stangor, C., & Sechrist, G. B. (1998). Conceptualizing the determinants of academic choice and task performance across social groups. In J. K. Swim & C. Stangor (Eds.), *Prejudice: The target's perspective* (pp. 105–124). San Diego, CA: Academic Press.

Stangor, C., Sullivan, L. A., & Ford, T. E. (1991). Affective and cognitive determinants of prejudice. *Social Cognition, 9*, 359–380.

Steele, C. M. (1997). A threat in the air: How stereotypes shape intellectual identity and performance. *American Psychologist, 52*, 613–629.

Stephan, W. G. (1987). The contact hypothesis in intergroup relations. In C. Hendrick (Ed.), *Review of personality and social psychology, Vol. 9: Group processes and intergroup relations* (pp. 13–40). Beverly Hills, CA: Sage.

Stephan, W. G. (1999). *Reducing prejudice in schools*. New York: Teachers College Press.

Stephan, W. G., & Stephan, C. W. (1984). The role of ignorance in intergroup relations. In N. Miller & M. B. Brewer (Eds.), *Groups in contact: The psychology of desegregation* (pp. 229–257). Orlando, FL: Academic Press.

Stephan, W. G., & Stephan, C. W. (1985). Intergroup anxiety. *Journal of Social Issues, 41*(3), 157–175.

Stephan, W. G., & Stephan, C. W. (1996). *Intergroup relations.* Boulder, CO: Westview Press.

Stroessner, S. J., Hamilton, D. L., & Mackie, D. M. (1992). Affect and stereotyping: The effect of induced mood on distinctiveness-based illusory correlations. *Journal of Personality and Social Psychology, 62,* 564–576.

Struch, N., & Schwartz, S. H. (1989). Intergroup aggression: Its predictors and distinctness from ingroup bias. *Journal of Personality and Social Psychology, 56,* 364–373.

Sumner, W. G. (1906). *Folkways.* New York: Ginn.

Tajfel, H. (1969). Cognitive aspects of prejudice. *Journal of Social Issues, 25*(4), 79–97.

Tajfel, H., Billig, M. G., Bundy, R. F., & Flament, C. (1971). Social categorisation and intergroup behavior. *European Journal of Social Psychology, 1,* 149–177.

Tajfel, H., & Turner, J. C. (1979). An integrative theory of intergroup conflict. In W. G. Austin & S. Worchel (Eds.), *The social psychology of intergroup relations* (pp. 33–47). Monterey, CA: Brooks/Cole.

Taylor, S. E., Fiske, S. T., Etcoff, N. L., & Ruderman, A. J. (1978). Categorical bases of person memory and stereotyping. *Journal of Personality and Social Psychology, 36,* 778–793.

Turner, J. C. (1975). Social comparison and social identity: Some prospects for intergroup behavior. *European Journal of Social Psychology, 5,* 5–34.

Turner, J. C. (1981). The experimental social psychology of intergroup behavior. In J. C. Turner & H. Giles (Eds.), *Intergroup behavior* (pp. 66–101). Chicago: University of Chicago Press.

Turner, J. C. (1985). Social categorization and the self-concept: A social cognitive theory of group behavior. In E. J. Lawler (Ed.), *Advances in group processes* (Vol. 2, pp. 77–122). Greenwich, CT: JAI Press.

Turner, J. C., Hogg, M. A., Oakes, P. J., Reicher, S. D., & Wetherell, M. S. (1987). *Rediscovering the social group: A self-categorization theory.* Oxford, UK: Blackwell.

Turner, J. C., & Reynolds, K. J. (in press). The social identity perspective in intergroup relations: Theories, themes and controversies. In R. J. Brown & S. L. Gaertner (Eds.), *Blackwell handbook of social psychology: Intergroup processes.* Oxford, UK: Blackwell.

Tversky, A., & Gati, I. (1978). Studies of similarity. In E. Rosch & B. B. Lloyd (Eds.), *Cognition and categorization* (pp. 79–98). Hillsdale, NJ: Erlbaum.

Tyler, T. R. (in press). Social justice. In R. J. Brown & S. L. Gaertner (Eds.), *Blackwell handbook of social psychology: Intergroup processes.* Oxford, UK: Blackwell.

Tyler, T. R., & Lind, E. A. (1992). A relational model of authority in groups. In M. Zanna (Ed.), *Advances in experimental social psychology* (Vol. 25, pp. 115–191). San Diego, CA: Academic Press.

Tyler, T., Lind, E. A., Ohbuchi, K., Sugawara, I., & Huo, Y. J. (1998). Conflict with outsiders: Disputing within and across cultural boundaries. *Personality and Social Psychology Bulletin, 24,* 137–146.

Urada, D. I., & Miller, N. (2000). The impact of positive mood and category importance on crossed categorization effects. *Journal of Personality and Social Psychology, 78,* 417–433.

Urban, L. M., & Miller, N. (1998). A theoretical analysis of crossed categorization effects: A meta-analysis. *Journal of Personality and Social Psychology, 74,* 894–908.

van den Bos, K., Wilke, H. A. M., Lind, E. A., & Vermunt, R. (1998). Evaluating outcomes by means of the fair process effect: Evidence for different processes in fairness and satisfaction judgments. *Journal of Personality and Social Psychology, 74,* 1493–1503.

van Knippenberg, A. (1984). Intergroup differences in group perceptions. In H. Tajfel (Ed.), *The social dimension: European developments in social psychology* (Vol. 2, pp. 560–578). Cambridge, UK: Cambridge University Press.

van Oudenhoven, J. P., Groenewoud. J. T., & Hewstone, M. (1996). Cooperation, ethnic salience and generalization of interethnic attitudes. *European Journal of Social Psychology, 26,* 649–661.

van Oudenhoven, J. P., Prins, K. S., & Buunk, B. (1998). Attitudes of minority and majority members towards adaptation of immigrants. *European Journal of Social Psychology, 28,* 995–1013.

Vanbeselaere, N. (1987). The effects of dichotomous and crossed social categorization upon intergroup discrimination. *European Journal of Social Psychology, 17,* 143–156.

Vanman, E. J., Paul, B. Y., Ito, T. A., & Miller, N. (1997). The modern face of prejudice and structural features that moderate the effect of cooperation on affect. *Journal of Personality and Social Psychology, 74,* 941–959.

Veitch, R., & Griffitt, W. (1976). Good news—bad news: Affective and interpersonal effects. *Journal of Social Psychology, 6,* 69–75.

Velten, E. (1968). A laboratory task for induction of mood states. *Behavioral Research and Therapy, 6,* 473–482.

Verkuyten, M., & Hagendoorn, L. (1998). Prejudice and self-categorization: The variable role of authoritarianism and in-group stereotypes. *Personality and Social Psychology Bulletin, 24,* 99–110.

Vivian, J., Hewstone, M., & Brown, R. J. (1997). Intergroup contact: Theoretical and empirical developments. In R. Ben-Ari & Y. Rich (Eds.), *Enhancing education in heterogeneous schools: Theory and application* (pp. 13–46). Ramat-Gan, Israel: Bar-Illan University Press.

Watson, G. (1947). *Action for unity.* New York: Harper.

Wegner, D. M. (1994). Ironic processes of mental control. *Psychological Review, 101,* 34–52.

Weigel, R. H., Wiser, P. I., & Cook, S. W. (1975). The impact of cooperative learning experiences on cross-ethnic relations and attitudes. *Journal of Social Issues, 31,* 219–244.

Weitz, S. (1972). Attitude, voice, and behavior: A repressed affect model of interracial interaction. *Journal of Personality and Social Psychology, 24,* 14–21.

Wenzel, M., & Mummendey, A. (1996). Positive-negative asymmetry of social discrimination: A normative analysis of differential evaluations of in-group and out-group on positive and negative attributes. *British Journal of Social Psychology, 35,* 493–507.

Wilder, D. A. (1978). Reducing intergroup discrimination through individuation of the outgroup. *Journal of Personality and Social Psychology, 36,* 1361–1374.

Wilder, D. A. (1981). Perceiving persons as a group: Categorization and intergroup relations. In D. L. Hamilton (Ed.), *Cognitive processes in stereotyping and intergroup behavior* (pp. 213–257). Hillsdale, NJ: Erlbaum.

Wilder, D. A. (1984). Predictions of belief homogeneity and similarity following social categorization. *British Journal of Social Psychology, 23,* 323–333.

Wilder, D. A. (1986). Social categorization: Implications for creation and reduction of intergroup bias. In L. Berkowitz (Ed.), *Advances in experimental social psychology* (Vol. 19, pp. 291–355). Orlando, FL: Academic Press.

Wilder, D. A., & Simon, A. F. (in press). Affect as a cause of intergroup bias. In R. J. Brown & S. L. Gaertner (Eds.), *Blackwell handbook of social psychology: Intergroup processes.* Oxford, UK: Blackwell.

Williams, R. M., Jr. (1947). *The reduction of intergroup tensions.* New York: Social Science Research Council.

Wills, T. A. (1981). Downward comparison principles in social psychology. *Psychological Bulletin, 90,* 245–271.

Woodmansee, J. J., & Cook, S. W. (1967). Dimensions of verbal racial attitudes: Their identification and measurement. *Journal of Personality and Social Psychology, 7,* 240–250.

Worchel, S. (1979). Cooperation and the reduction of intergroup conflict: Some determining factors. In W. Austin & S. Worchel (Eds.), *The social psychology of intergroup relations* (pp. 262–273). Monterey, CA: Brooks/Cole.

Worchel, S. (1986). The role of cooperation in reducing intergroup conflict. In S. Worchel. & W. Austin (Eds.), *The psychology of intergroup relations* (pp. 288–304). Chicago: Nelson-Hall.

Worchel, S., Andreoli, V. A., & Folger, R. (1977). Intergroup cooperation and intergroup attraction: The effect of previous interaction and outcome of combined effort. *Journal of Experimental Social Psychology, 13,* 131–140.

Worchel, S., Axsom, D., Ferris, F., Samaha, C., & Schweitzer, S. (1978). Determinants of the effect of intergroup cooperation on intergroup attraction. *Journal of Conflict Resolution, 22,* 393–410.

Worchel, S, Wong, F.Y., & Scheltema, K. E. (1989). Improving intergroup relations: Comparative effects of anticipated cooperation and helping on attraction for an aid-giver. *Social Psychology Quarterly 52,* 213–219.

Worth, L. T., & Mackie, D. M. (1987). Cognitive mediation of positive affect on persuasion. *Social Cognition, 5,* 76–94.

Wright, S. C. (in press). Strategic collective action: Social psychology and social change. In R. J. Brown & S. L. Gaertner (Eds.), *Blackwell handbook of social psychology: Intergroup processes.* Oxford, UK: Blackwell.

Wright, S. C., Aron, A., McLaughlin-Volpe, T., & Ropp, S. A. (1997). The extended contact effect: Knowledge of cross-group friendships and prejudice. *Journal of Personality and Social Psychology, 73,* 73–90.

AUTHOR INDEX

Abelson, R. P., 84, 85
Abrams, D., 35, 56
Adams, A. M., 71
Adorno, T. W., 2, 14, 21
Allen, J., 135
Allen, M., 134
Allport, G. W., 2, 8, 15, 34, 35, 43, 48, 49, 69, 71, 72, 83, 86, 92, 93, 146, 157, 176, 179, 180
Altman, I., 134
Amir, Y., 71
Anastasio, P. A., 7,8,88,144,151
Anderson, J. Z., 93
Andreoli, V. A., 117
Archer, R. L., 138
Arcuri, L., 39, 65
Aron, A., 46, 134
Aron, E. N., 134
Aronson, E., 72
Ashby, F. G., 119
Ashforth, B. E., 140
Ashmore, R. D., 15
Aufderheide, B., 167
Axsom, D., 60

Bachman, B. A., 7, 13, 61, 87, 88, 96, 151
Banaji, M. R., 82, 107, 181
Banker, B. S., 13, 63, 94, 95, 171
Bargh, J. A., 109, 180, 181
Baron, R. M., 74
Batson, C. D., 46, 133
Bazzini, D. G., 134
Beach, K. R., 14
Bennett, C., 140
Berg, J. H., 138
Berger, J., 87
Berger, S. H., 93
Berkowitz, L., 22

Berry, J. W., 67, 163, 167
Bettencourt, B. A., 44, 169, 173
Billig, M., 36, 38
Blair, I., 13, 107, 181
Blake, R. R., 88
Blanchard, F. A., 71
Blaney, N., 72
Bless, H., 119, 126, 129
Bobo, L., 37
Bodenhausen, G. V., 18, 34, 103, 107, 115, 118, 119, 181
Bohner, G., 119
Bourhis, R. Y., 86, 87, 92
Bowditch, J. L., 61
Bray, J. H., 93
Brewer, M. B., 7, 8, 14, 16, 19, 35, 37, 40–45, 56, 57, 71, 72, 73, 77, 92, 110, 129, 134, 138, 142, 144, 146, 152, 159, 162, 173
Brigham, J. C., 15
Bromley, S., 16
Brown, A. C., 93
Brown, R. J., 9, 36, 40, 41, 42, 44, 45, 50, 62, 71, 73, 77, 80, 81, 97–100, 107, 133, 146, 147, 149, 150, 167, 168, 170
Bundy, R. F., 38
Buono, A. F., 61
Burnam, M. A., 166
Buunk, B., 163
Byrne, D., 117

Cadinu, M. R., 42
Campbell, D. T., 34, 37, 54, 60
Cantor, N., 114
Carillo, M., 3
Carter, D. J., 140
Ceccarelli, R., 39, 65
Chaikin, A. L., 134

SUBJECT INDEX